Iowa Baseball Greats

ALSO BY DON DOXSIE

*Iron Man McGinnity:
A Baseball Biography* (McFarland, 2009)

Iowa Baseball Greats
*Sixteen Major Leaguers
Who Were in the Game for Life*

Don Doxsie

McFarland & Company, Inc., Publishers
Jefferson, North Carolina

ISBN 978-0-7864-9894-9 (softcover : acid free paper) ∞
ISBN 978-1-4766-2292-7 (ebook)

LIBRARY OF CONGRESS CATALOGUING DATA ARE AVAILABLE

BRITISH LIBRARY CATALOGUING DATA ARE AVAILABLE

© 2015 Don Doxsie. All rights reserved

No part of this book may be reproduced or transmitted in any form or by any means, electronic or mechanical, including photocopying or recording, or by any information storage and retrieval system, without permission in writing from the publisher.

Front cover illustration by Kerry Crow (Thinkstock)

Printed in the United States of America

*McFarland & Company, Inc., Publishers
Box 611, Jefferson, North Carolina 28640
www.mcfarlandpub.com*

To Gale,
one of the best things
I found in Iowa

Table of Contents

Acknowledgments — ix
Preface — 1
Introduction — 5

1. Utility: Cal McVey — 7
2. Designated Hitter: Cap Anson — 16
3. Outfield: Fred Clarke — 28
4. Outfield: George Stone — 40
5. Pitcher: Jack Coombs — 48
6. Catcher: Hank Severeid — 60
7. Shortstop: Dave Bancroft — 71
8. Pitcher: Red Faber — 81
9. Outfield: Bing Miller — 92
10. Pitcher: Dazzy Vance — 100
11. Pitcher: Earl Whitehill — 110
12. First Base: Hal Trosky — 119
13. Pitcher: Bob Feller — 129
14. Second Base: Gene Baker — 141
15. Pitcher: Mike Boddicker — 152
16. Third Base: Casey Blake — 162

17. The Best of the Rest: Position Players   171
18. The Best of the Rest: Pitchers   188

Appendix: Iowa Records (Prior to 2015)   209
Chapter Notes   211
Selected Bibliography   221
Index   225

Acknowledgments

Obviously, a project of this size cannot be completed without the generous assistance of a great many people and organizations.

I am indebted to Iowa baseball historian John Liepa, Kate Feil of the Story County Historical Society in Story City, Shona Frese and Jim Van Scoyoc of the Iowa Baseball Museum of Norway and Anne Kauder and Lee Simon of the Tri-County Historical Society Museum in Cascade for their help in researching specific players and in obtaining photographs.

I also would like to thank employees at the Duke University archives, Duke's Rubenstein Library, the Baseball Hall of Fame, the Bob Feller Museum in Van Meter, Iowa, the Chicago History Museum and public libraries in Davenport, Des Moines, Cedar Rapids, Clinton, Dubuque and Chicago.

Several of the players profiled in this book have had full-length books written about them, and although great pains were taken not to simply duplicate the efforts of such gifted biographers as Brian Cooper, John Skipper, Ronald Waldo, John Tierney, Howard Rosenberg and David Fleitz, their works occasionally provided valuable direction and background information. I also benefited greatly from the Society for American Baseball Research Biography Project, baseball-reference.com and SABR's other far-reaching resources. Bill Johnson's SABR bios of Iowa-born players were especially helpful.

Through the years, I had the chance to personally interview four of the men profiled in the book. Mike Boddicker, Casey Blake, the late Bob Feller and the late Gene Baker all provided invaluable insights into their own personal experiences and an interview with the great Ernie Banks many years ago also provided insightful details about Baker's career.

Jeremy Feador of the Cleveland Indians, Daisuke Sugiura of the Los Angeles Dodgers, Chris Martrich of the Baltimore Orioles and the *Quad-*

Acknowledgments

City Times all were of tremendous help in contributing photos for the book. Jan Touney, executive editor of the *Times*, made some valuable observations that helped further refine the book in its final stages. And, of course, I have to thank my family for their support, especially my wife Gale, who was totally understanding of her husband's need to stay up until the wee hours of the morning immersing himself in baseball history.

Preface

The roots of this project can probably be traced to a June day in 1973.

Summer jobs were hard to come by that year so a college sophomore with little else to do with his spare time attempted on a whim to chase a far-off dream. He went to a Pittsburgh Pirates tryout camp in Morris, Illinois.

Forget the fact that all of his previous baseball experience had come on the sandlots of Chicago's western suburbs. He hadn't even played Little League baseball. But he was determined to impress this stern-faced, barrel-chested chief scout who was running the camp. When it came time for the lanky kid to step up and show what he could do as a pitcher, he whipped several pitches that were clocked in the low 80s. Some of them were even strikes although more of them sent the catcher diving in the dirt or sailed over his head.

"OK," said a different scout, who was supervising the pitching drills. "Let me see your breaking pitch."

The kid ducked his head, hesitated, thought for a moment, then wound up and fired another fastball with greater vigor than those that came before. This one was 10 feet over the catcher's head and chipped a sizeable chunk of bark off an oak tree about 30 feet behind him.

The chief scout, the one with the stoic exterior, happened to be wandering nearby at the moment. He turned to the kid with questioning eyes and the kid knew exactly what he wanted to know.

"I don't have one," he said. "No breaking pitch."

A fatherly grin came across the scout's face and he didn't really need to say anything for me to know that the Pirates weren't going to be interested.

That was the day it was clearly confirmed for me that my future lay in writing about baseball, not playing it.

But it wasn't the last time I would cross paths with Gene Baker. Twenty years later, when the former player and manager and longtime Pirates scout was voted into the Quad-City Sports Hall of Fame in his hometown of Davenport, Iowa, I was the newspaper reporter who showed up on his doorstep to interview and write about him.

I learned about his life before he became a scout, how he felt he had been kept from playing for his high school team because of the color of his skin, how he had languished in the minors longer than was necessary before the Chicago Cubs summoned the courage to bring a couple of black players to the major leagues, how he had mentored a young teammate named Ernie Banks, how he became the first black manager in the minor leagues and how he then became the second black coach in the majors.

I profiled him for *Quad-City Times* readers then, knowing that I someday needed to find a way to relate his story in greater detail to a wider audience.

Through the years I also crossed paths with other men profiled in this book.

In 1983, as a sportswriter with the *Cedar Rapids Gazette*, I was dispatched to the World Series in Baltimore to write about a hometown boy named Mike Boddicker in his finest hour.

A few years after that, I was one of a handful of media types given a chance to see what they could do against the pitching of Bob Feller, who, although pushing 70, still threw a decent fastball and a devious curve, and changed speeds well enough to have a bunch of reporters flailing in vain at his offerings.

I eventually learned more about some of the other major league players who had their roots in the state of Iowa. I learned about Hank Severeid's dogged focus on the fundamentals of the game, Fred Clarke's competitive fire, Dave Bancroft's moxie, Earl Whitehill's temper, Dazzy Vance's whimsy, Jack Coombs' persistence, Hal Trosky's courage, Cap Anson's determination and Casey Blake's dedication to those around him.

If there's a common thread to the 16 native Iowans profiled in this book, it's their total, enduring devotion to the game they all loved.

Four of them—Bancroft, Clarke, Anson and Coombs—became major league managers. Severeid and Baker managed in the minors, then served as major league scouts for more than two decades. Bing Miller, Red Faber and Whitehill were coaches in the majors. Trosky did some scouting. George Stone owned a minor league team. Coombs became one of the most respected college head coaches in the country. Both Coombs and

Severeid wrote instructional books about baseball. And Feller served as one of the greatest activists and ambassadors the game has ever known.

All their stories are here, all unique, all compelling.

But perhaps none more so than the wonderful old gentleman I first met on a ball field at Morris High School back in 1973.

Introduction

Going into the 2015 season, a total of 216 men born in the state of Iowa had played major league baseball.

For a state that comprises less than one percent of the American population and which is more often associated with sports such as wrestling and football, Iowa has made an indelible mark on the game.

Not all of those 216 have been All-Stars or World Series heroes. Some saw action in just one game. However, among the natives of the state who played the game at its highest level are one of the brightest stars of the first decade of professional baseball, the biggest star of the 19th century and one of the most dominating pitchers ever.

The only major league catcher ever to catch no-hitters on back-to-back days was an Iowan. The only pitcher ever to lead the National League in strikeouts seven years in a row was an Iowan. The pitcher who enjoyed the best second half ever by any pitcher was born in the state.

A player born in Iowa drove in 162 runs in one season. Another won the 1906 American League batting title. Another struck out 17 men in a game as a 17-year-old prodigy. Another became the first black manager for a minor league team in organized baseball.

Six native Iowans have been elected to the Baseball Hall of Fame as players, and had the breaks happened differently, it's not hard to imagine that Jack Coombs, Hal Trosky, Hank Severeid and Bing Miller might have joined Bob Feller, Red Faber, Cap Anson, Dazzy Vance, Fred Clarke and Dave Bancroft in being enshrined in Cooperstown.

All of those men were obvious choices when it came time to select the few elite players to be profiled in this book.

Not every choice was so obvious. This was purely a subjective process. An effort was made to select at least one player at every position and there were a few difficult choices.

Because the state has produced two extraordinary first basemen—Anson and Trosky—both men were chosen to be included. Anson is listed as the designated hitter in my lineup even though he retired as a player 76 years before the advent of the DH.

The toughest decision was at second base, where a pair of modern-era Sioux City natives—Bobby Knoop and Dick Green—were worthy candidates. Both had longer major league playing careers than Gene Baker, but the extenuating circumstances of Baker's experience and his perseverance in overcoming racial obstacles was too much to overlook. He got the nod over Knoop and Green, who are included in a closing chapter recognizing other exceptional players from the state.

There also were difficult choices among the pitchers. Hurlers such as Stan Bahnsen, Joe Hoerner, Bob Locker and Mace Brown easily could have been selected but I narrowed the list to just six.

One player is listed as a utility man despite the fact that the term didn't even exist during the era in which he played. Cal McVey played every position at one time or another during an 11-year 19th century career in which he helped develop the template for others to follow.

He is a fitting place to start since he was the first native Iowan ever to play the game as a professional.

Utility

Cal McVey

"He is very conscientious and a hard worker ... a good fielder, but his strength is with the ash in his hands."—*Cincinnati Daily Times*[1]

We can only imagine what sort of aspirations Cal McVey must have had as a kid growing up on a farm near Montrose, Iowa.

Perhaps he thought about going into farming with his family. Perhaps he contemplated a career as a piano tuner, another profession that was taken up by his father. At a very early age, he demonstrated the God-given athletic ability to be a boxer or even an acrobat.

A ballplayer? There was no such profession in existence at the time.

McVey ultimately helped create the profession. He was a member of the first professional baseball team ever assembled—the 1869 Cincinnati Red Stockings. He became the youngest player on the team and was the only team member born west of the Mississippi River.

McVey was among the elite players in the first decade of professional baseball, a .346 career hitter who played every position on the field at one time or another. That included 34 games as a pitcher. He also played 186 games at first base, 182 as a catcher, 110 in the outfield, 84 at third base, five at second and five at shortstop.

It's difficult to compare the statistics of that time to later eras of the sport. The rules were different, the seasons were shorter, the equipment was much more primitive. Batters could demand to have the pitcher throw the ball in a certain spot, usually underhanded. The fielders did not wear gloves.

Nevertheless, .346 was an exceptional average in any era. John Liepa, a modern-day historian who dresses in an authentic Red Stockings uniform to give presentations about McVey, feels he should be in the Baseball Hall of Fame.

McVey was born in 1849 near Montrose, a small village in the southeast corner of Iowa, just north of Keokuk. His parents, William and Caroline McVey, had come from Indiana, as many others did, to find a new life farming in a new territory that was not opened for settlement until 1833 and did not become a state until three years before Cal's birth.

Montrose is just across the Mississippi from Nauvoo, Illinois, which only a few years earlier had been home to the founders of the Church of Jesus Christ of Latter Day Saints, also known as the Mormons. After leader Joseph Smith was killed in 1844, a majority of the Mormons followed a new leader, Brigham Young, to what is now Utah. By 1849, Nauvoo had been taken over by a French group called the Icarians, who built a utopian socialist commune there.[2]

Just a few miles away, the McVeys struggled to find prosperity in farming. They finally moved back to Indianapolis in 1860 and William McVey found work as a piano tuner and tax collector.

That is where his son found baseball. At five feet, nine inches, and 170 pounds, Cal was fairly average in size but his athleticism was obvious. Some felt he could have had a career in boxing and he also displayed gymnastic ability. In ensuing years, when the baseball teams for which he played were victorious, it was not uncommon for him to celebrate by doing handsprings or cartwheels as he left the field.[3]

Baseball in some form or another had been played for centuries and in the middle stages of the 19th century it became especially prevalent in large cities along the east coast. The American Civil War, which

Cal McVey (John Liepa collection).

lasted from 1861 through 1865, was the tipping point in its development.

A game that had mostly been played in small pockets here and there with varying sets of rules became very popular among the soldiers in camps and during leisure times between battles. When the soldiers went home following the war, they took baseball and a somewhat standardized set of rules with them, and it spread throughout the country.

Amateur and club teams popped up all over the landscape and inevitably the competitive drive to be the best led teams to pay players. At first, it was a covert practice. Teams would slip a few dollars to a top player under the table to play for their club. But in 1869, a man named Aaron B. Champion made a bold recommendation. As president of the Red Stockings' board of directors, he proposed that the team begin openly paying salaries to players with the funding coming from a group of Cincinnati businessmen.[4]

McVey had begun playing baseball at the age of 11. As a teenager, he found work as a piano maker and tuner, and he attended North Western Christian University in Indianapolis. He landed a spot on the university nine when he was 16 and also played for several town teams, including a team called the Westerns in 1867 and another called the Actives in 1868. While playing second base for the Westerns in a game in 1867, he played against the famous Nationals team of Washington, D.C., getting a hit the first time up and leaving a lasting impression on spectators despite the fact that Indianapolis lost the game 106–21.[5] He may have also played at some point against the Red Stockings.

Acting on Champion's proposal, Red Stockings captain Harry Wright and other team officials began assembling the most powerful team possible for 1869. Possibly because of that 1867 game against the Nationals, McVey was recruited by team secretary Colonel Johnny Joyce and given the job of playing right field for Cincinnati.

Only one of the Red Stockings, first baseman Charlie Gould, was actually from Cincinnati. The rest of them were men from different walks of life brought together mostly from places on the east coast. Harry Wright was a jeweler and his brother, George, was an engraver. Both of them came from the Bronx and had developed their reputations playing for the Knickerbockers team of New York City. Second baseman Charles Sweasy and left-fielder Andy Leonard were hat-makers from Newark. Pitcher Asa Brainard and third baseman Fred Waterman were insurance brokers. Catcher Doug Allison was a marble-cutter.[6]

Most of the players were to be paid $800 for what amounted to seven

The 1869 Cincinnati Red Stockings, including Cal McVey (back row, far left), went 57–0.

months of work, but George Wright made $1,400, Harry Wright $1,200, Brainard $1,100 and Waterman $1,000.[7] For a young man such as McVey, $800 must have seemed like a windfall. Consider that an unskilled laborer earned about 15 cents an hour in that era. Toiling 60 hours a week—the norm at that time—he would earn less than $500 for a full year.[8]

The Red Stockings were a true all-star team and were almost never challenged, and they quickly became local and national celebrities.

They began by rolling up huge scores against teams from the Midwest, starting with a 24–15 victory over a team of top players from Cincinnati, then toured the east coast, winning 23 straight games there over the course of little more than a month. Following a 24–8 victory over the Washington Nationals on June 25, a game played in front of 8,000 fans, the Red Stockings were invited to the White House to meet president Ulysses S. Grant, who told them, "I believe you warmed the Washington boys somewhat yesterday."[9]

The Red Stockings frequently won by 50 or 60 runs. They won one game 103–8. Few teams came close to them. On the eastern tour, the only really competitive game was a 4–2 win over the New York City Mutuals.

Later in the summer, they had another tough game against a team from Troy, New York, called the Haymakers. The Red Stockings had beaten

Troy in June by a 37–3 score but this time the two teams were tied 17–17 in the fifth inning when the Haymakers catcher claimed to have caught a foul tip hit by McVey. The umpire ruled otherwise. The Haymakers disputed the call, eventually walked off the field in anger and the Red Stockings were awarded the win on a forfeit.

Any time the Red Stockings returned from one of their road trips, it was a gala occasion. On July 1, they were welcomed home from their eastern trek with a big parade and were presented with a mammoth bat that was 27 feet long and weighed 1,600 pounds.[10]

"There would be brass bands, torches and fireworks, then a big banquet for the players," McVey recalled in later years. "Once we were met at the railroad station by a horse-drawn bus shaped like a baseball bat—all gilded and draped with flags."[11]

In September, the Red Stockings took a tour westward, traveling by stage coach from St. Louis to Omaha and by train from there to San Francisco. They played only three games on the west coast and won by a combined score of 289–22.

They finished the year with a record of 57–0 although some historians list their mark as 65–0, counting eight games that were billed as "exhibitions." They scored nearly 2,400 runs, once getting 40 in one inning. Perhaps the most staggering statistic: In all those games, while scoring all those runs, Red Stockings players struck out only eight times.

Although McVey was the final player to be added to the team, he emerged as one of its stars and was almost certainly its best hitter. In an August 16 game in Cincinnati, he collected seven hits and drove in seven runs.

The Red Stockings managed to keep all their players intact for 1870 and they continued to rampage through the opposition on another east coast tour before finally losing on June 14, 1870, to the Atlantics in Brooklyn, snapping an 81-game streak. Attendance for that game has been estimated as high as 15,000, an indication of just how popular the game was becoming. The score was tied at 5–5 after nine innings and while Harry Wright and Brooklyn manager Bob Ferguson were content to call it a draw, Aaron Champion insisted that the teams play extra innings, something that was not always done in that era.[12]

Cincinnati scored two runs to take a 7–5 lead in the top of the 11th. The first Atlantics player reached base on an error in the bottom of the inning and the next batter, Joe Start, hit the ball over McVey's head and into the crowd seated on a small hillside in right field. The spectators parted somewhat as the ball landed among them but as McVey reached for the ball, one fan leaped on his back. There were no ground rules or anything forbidding fan interference in that era. Another fan flung the ball back onto the field. Start was held to a triple, but he scored the tying run on a double by Ferguson. The next batter, George Hall, hit a ground ball to short. Ferguson jumped over the grounder, distracting shortstop George Wright, who mishandled the ball. By the time it was retrieved, Ferguson had scored the winning run and the Red Stockings' streak was over.[13]

They finished 1870 with a 68–6 record, but the team was coming apart for a variety of reasons.

There was dissension among the players. The Wright brothers, Charlie Gould and McVey generally abstained from alcoholic beverages but the other players on the team had become notorious for their drinking binges and parties.[14]

Probably a bigger factor was the fact that despite their wild success, the Red Stockings were not a profitable venture. While Champion's idea led to nationwide fame, fortune did not follow. The team made a net profit of $1.39 in its first year. It later was forced to double its ticket prices and it still was not making ends meet. Champion finally resigned and the board of directors voted to return the team to amateur status.[15]

But the Red Stockings had made an indelible mark on the American sports landscape. An entire league of professionals—the National Association—was now being formed and the Cincinnati players were quickly scooped up by those teams.

McVey, whose occupation in the 1870 Indianapolis census was listed as "baseballist,"[16] quickly found a new home further east. Harry Wright became captain of the newly-formed Boston Red Stockings team and he took the three other tee-totaling Cincinnati players—brother George, Charlie Gould and McVey—with him.

McVey played two seasons in Boston, being used primarily as a catcher. He was second in the league in hitting with a .431 average in 1871 and batted .321 in 1872.

In 1873, he was on the move again, going to play for and manage the National Association team in Baltimore, which was sometimes known as the Canaries and sometimes as the Lord Baltimores. He played every position there except pitcher, batting .380 and managing the team to a 23–14 record.

He then went back to Boston and over the next two years, playing mostly in the outfield and at first base, helped the Red Stockings win their third and fourth consecutive pennants. In late July of the 1874 season, the team went on an overseas tour to England and Ireland, where it played cricket as well as baseball against teams there. On June 10, 1875, the team played an exhibition game in Iowa against the Keokuk Westerns although newspaper reports at the time made no mention of it being any sort of homecoming for McVey.

The Red Stockings, bolstered by such other stars as Albert Spalding, Deacon White and Ross Barnes, rolled up a 71–8 record in league play in 1875. In truth, the imbalance of power in the National Association probably contributed to its demise.

In 1876, it gave way to a new coalition that still exists today—the National League.

The Chicago franchise in the new league was assembling a powerhouse team and it recruited what came to be known as the "Big Four" from Boston—McVey, Spalding, White and Barnes. The quartet won yet another pennant in 1876 with McVey batting .345 and going 6–0 as a pitcher. He had perhaps his hottest stretch ever as a hitter in the middle of that summer. He put together a 30-game hitting streak and in one span of four games late in July had 18 hits. On both July 22 and July 25 he had six hits in a game.

The team, known as the White Stockings, fell to fifth place in 1877 despite a .368 average by McVey. It was the only time in his entire career that McVey played on a team with a losing record.

McVey moved on to Cincinnati in 1878. He played mostly third base there, but also served as the manager. The Reds had finished last in the first two years of the NL, but McVey steered them to a 37–23 record and a second-place finish in his first season, and also became something of an innovator. He was the first to realize that there was an advantage to using left-handed batters against right-handed pitchers and vice versa.[17] He began manipulating his lineup accordingly and in a way, gave birth to the modern-day concept of platooning.

McVey batted just .306 in 1878 and fell off to .297 in 1879 when the Reds went 43–37. He also still did some more pitching although with less success than in previous seasons. On June 13, 1879, pitcher Will White was injured prior to the game so McVey took the mound himself. He allowed 28 hits in a 19–6 loss to Providence.

The Cincinnati team was disbanded late in the 1879 season with all the players being released and losing a month's pay. McVey, who by that time was earning $3,000 a season, was understandably upset. He went on a barnstorming trip to California after the season and liked the look of the place.[18] He also had visited there with the Red Stockings in 1869. This time he stayed, never returning to the eastern or Midwestern part of the country to live.

His parents also moved to California and moved in with Cal and his wife Abbey, who he had married in 1874.

McVey was involved in west coast baseball for many years afterward. He played for a variety of teams in the San Francisco area in several different leagues over the next six or seven years. In the late 1880s, he played for the Hamilton team in San Diego and became a popular figure with teams and players wherever he played.

An 1885 story in *Sporting Life* about the baseball scene in San Francisco reported, "Cal McVey's saloon out at Central Park is the rendezvous of the baseball players. Cal is a most genial Boniface, and we take pleasure in chronicling his success."[19]

When not playing baseball, McVey dabbled in several different professions. In 1880, one source listed him as a real estate agent. By 1893, he had moved from San Diego back to the northern part of the state and was working as a conductor, according to an 1895 *Sporting Life* story.[20] Another 1895 source mentioned that he was working for a "wine concern" in Fresno. It noted that he was in good health, weighed close to 200 pounds and was "keeping himself in condition by frequent wrestling and scrapping. He is the official referee of the Fresno Athletic Club."[21]

In 1900, he was working as a policeman in San Francisco, where he also owned a cigar store.[22] He apparently also did some scouting. It was reported in some places that the Chicago Cubs signed future Hall of Famer Frank Chance on the recommendation of McVey, who saw him play in Fresno.[23]

The famous San Francisco earthquake of April 1906 changed his life, as it did with so many others in that city. McVey's home and cigar store were completely destroyed and his wife Abbey was seriously injured in the quake.[24]

His baseball friends stepped up to help him. A fund was developed to help McVey, who was living in a shack in San Francisco, with Cap Anson serving as treasurer. Spalding was the first to donate. The Cubs, then managed by Chance, were given a banquet by the Chicago Board of Trade following their record-setting 1906 season and there was about $100 left over in the budget for the event. It was decided to give it to the McVey fund.[25]

In 1910, McVey worked as a night watchman in the camp of heavyweight boxing champion Jack Johnson.[26] He later got involved with a mining venture in Nevada, but suffered a 30-foot fall into a mine in 1913, disabling him to some extent for the remainder of his life.[27]

In 1915, the advisory board of the Base Ball Players Fraternity voted to award McVey a pension. Even though he had played long before the players ever organized themselves into a union, the feeling was that his early contributions to the game and his hardship situation merited special consideration. Fraternity president Dave Fultz issued a lengthy statement: "Our Board of Directors, at the Fall meeting, voted unanimously to leave the matter of helping McVey in the hands of the Advisory Board for Investigation ... and the Advisory Board has voted a monthly allowance which, while not large, will furnish McVey with the necessities of life."[28]

McVey continued to work after that, however, serving as a watchman in a lumberyard for many years.

He had a final moment of glory in 1919, when he traveled back to Cincinnati for festivities celebrating the 50th anniversary of the Red Stockings. He and George Wright and Oak Taylor, the only other two surviving players from the team, rode in a parade prior to the World Series between the Reds and White Sox.[29]

McVey died in California at the age of 76 on August 20, 1926.

Designated Hitter
Cap Anson

> "The game was dying. Cap Anson is the man who really changed that ... not all by himself, but more than anyone else."—Historian and statistician Bill James[1]

More than 100 years after he played and managed his final game, Cap Anson's place in baseball history still is a topic of scrutiny and discussion.

A man with definite and undeniable racist leanings, Anson had a hand in drawing the color line that kept African American players out of the major leagues for many decades. How large a role he played in that movement is subject to debate.

One thing about Anson is beyond dispute: He was baseball's biggest and brightest star of the 19th century, a major figure in popularizing the sport in its infancy, a leader in elevating it to its place as the national pastime.

When he died in 1922, the starting time of some major league games was adjusted to accommodate his funeral. His honorary pallbearers included the commissioner of baseball and the presidents of both the National and American Leagues. He had been universally referred to for years as "the grand old man of baseball." Grantland Rice of the *New York Herald Tribune* called him "baseball's greatest figure, the most noted of the supermen who helped to start and build the nation's greatest sport."[2]

Anson was the first man to collect 3,000 hits. More than 117 years after his retirement as an active player, he was seventh on baseball's all-time list in that statistic, eighth in runs scored and third in runs batted in behind Hank Aaron and Babe Ruth, two men who each clubbed more than 700 home runs. Anson hit 97.

Considering he played in an era in which he sometimes fashioned his own bats out of yellow poplar, those numbers are nothing short of staggering.

Anson also managed in the majors for 21 years and compiled a winning percentage of .578, eighth best among those with more than 1,000 career victories.

It all began modestly enough in 1852 when Anson was the first white child born in Marshall County, Iowa.

His father, Henry Anson, clearly had a serious case of wanderlust. As a young man, he drifted around the middle of the country with his wife Jennette, trying to find a place he liked enough to put down roots. Henry was born near Rochester, New York, lived in Ohio as a child and dragged his family through different towns in Michigan and Illinois in his quest to find the perfect spot. In 1851, he left Jennette and two young sons, Sturgis and Melville, in Illinois while he wandered westward across the Mississippi River looking for a place to live. He finally happened upon an area that was inhabited mostly by members of the Sioux and Potawatomi tribes and pronounced it "the prettiest place in Iowa."[3] He built a cabin there, started a town that he eventually decided to name Marshalltown and brought his young family there.

Cap Anson.

A year later, Jennette gave birth to another son. As with Sturgis, they decided to name this boy after towns in which they had lived in Michigan so he they called him Adrian Constantine Anson. The more commonly used nicknames—"Cap" and "Pop"—would come much later.

Melville Anson died sometime in the late 1850s[4] and Jennette died in 1860, but Henry continued to be the most prominent citizen of the new town. He built a lumber mill and served the community in a variety of ways, as surveyor, land agent, justice of the peace, county supervisor. There were even reports that he may have been the town's dentist. Today an elementary school, a street and a park in Marshalltown all are named for

Henry Anson and a statue of him was erected in front of the county courthouse in 2003. A plaque at 112 W. Main Street marks the spot of the original Anson cabin.

However, Henry's youngest son was to become famous far beyond the bounds of the small community. And he did it by playing baseball.

The Marshalltown Baseball Club came into existence in 1866 and a year later the Anson family became a prominent part of the team. Initially, Henry and Sturgis played for the main team while young Adrian was on the second team but even then, although he was barely in his teens, he seemingly became obsessed with the game.

Henry Anson wanted his sons to receive an education so he sent both of them off to a boarding school at Notre Dame in Indiana when Adrian was only 14. Notre Dame historians credit the Anson brothers with introducing the university to the fledgling sport of baseball.[5]

After two years there, Adrian enrolled at the University of Iowa but he didn't even last a full semester there. He soon came home to Marshalltown and became the starting third baseman for one of the most formidable town teams in Iowa. Henry played second base while Sturgis was the center-fielder.

The Marshalltown nine handled almost all of the local competition with ease but in September of 1870 the Forest City team of Rockford, Illinois, stopped off for a pair of games. Forest City was led by pitcher Albert Spalding, who would later found a sporting goods company that still bears his name, and it was among the elite amateur teams in the entire country. It made short work of Marshalltown, sweeping a doubleheader by scores of 17–3 and 34–5. Spalding told reporters in later years that there was a great deal of betting on the games and that Henry Anson lost his best cow in a wager.[6]

Despite the lopsidedness of the games, Spalding and his mates must have been impressed by the competition they faced because they invited all three Ansons to join Forest City. Henry and Sturgis declined, but Adrian jumped at the opportunity. When Forest City became part of the new National Association of Professional Base Ball Players in 1871, Adrian Anson was given a salary of $66.66 a month to play for the team.[7]

Forest City only went 4–21 in that first season, but Anson batted .325 and was signed to a contract to play for the Philadelphia Athletics, the best team in the league. He spent the next four years with Philadelphia and quickly developed into one of the best hitters around, batting .415 in 1872.

In 1874, the Athletics and the Boston Red Stockings took a three-week tour of England in which they played both the relatively new American sport of baseball and the old English sport of cricket. In one particularly memorable contest, they defeated the Marylebone Cricket Club at its own game by a score of 107–105.[8]

The trip brought Anson back together with Spalding, who was the star pitcher for Boston, and the two men rekindled a relationship that would pave the way for Anson to become a national icon. Two years later, in 1876, Spalding became the player-manager of the Chicago team in the newly-formed National League. Owner William Hulbert gave Spalding a free hand to acquire whatever players he felt he needed to compete and one of those he signed was the young Iowan who had developed into a great hitter for the Philadelphia club.

Anson spent the next 22 years playing for the team then known as the Chicago White Stockings. In ensuing years, they would sometimes be known as the Colts and the franchise remains in existence today as the Chicago Cubs.

After playing every position on the field at one time or another for Philadelphia, Anson settled in as primarily a first baseman in Chicago. He was large, somewhat clumsy and not very swift afoot, and Anson never became a great fielder at first base or anywhere else.

But for the next two decades he was almost unmatched as a hitter. He batted over .300 in 19 of his 22 years in Chicago with a career average of .331.

He was at least six feet tall, possibly as tall as six feet, two inches, and his playing weight has been listed anywhere between 200 and 227 pounds. He had very large hands and forearms and an exceptional eye. He stood tall and erect at the plate with his feet very close together and he stood far back from the plate. In fact, there is no record of him ever being hit by a pitch in his 27-year career.

He also used perhaps the longest, heaviest bat of anyone in history. One of his contemporaries, Sam Crane, was exaggerating somewhat when he described it as "heavy as a telegraph pole,"[9] but at least one of the surviving bats from Anson's collection weighs 60 ounces,[10] nearly double the size of those used in the modern era. Anson took a slow, easy swing without much of a stride. He was fully under control, never off-balance and he was very selective about the pitches at which he swung. Legend has it that he never swung at a first pitch.

The rules of the game were much different when Anson first turned pro. Pitchers threw underhand and stood only 45 feet from the plate. The distance increased to 55 feet in 1881 and to the present distance of 60 feet, six inches in 1893, and the pitchers eventually began throwing overhand, but no matter how the ball was thrown or from what distance, very few pitches got past Adrian Anson. In 1878, he struck out only once in 60 games and in 9,101 career at-bats, he fanned just 294 times.

Despite the fact that the ball used in that era did not have a cork center and was difficult to hit for distance, Anson was noted for his ability to rip wicked line drives past infielders, some of whom did not embrace the use of gloves until the 1890s.

Anson won the National League batting title in 1879, 1881, 1887 and 1888. Although runs batted in were not kept as a statistic in that era, latter-day statisticians have combed through records and determined that he also led the league in RBI eight times, reaching a high of 147 in 1886.

Home runs were not prevalent and were not considered a major part of the game in that era, but Anson was fully capable of hitting for power, too. He slugged 21 homers in 1884, benefitting greatly from some very short fences—180 feet down the left-field line, 300 to straightaway center—and a change in the ground rules at Chicago's Lakefront Park. Before that, balls hit over the fence in the little wooden stadium counted as doubles but that year the rules were changed to make them home runs.[11] Anson had one stretch in August in which he clubbed the ball over the fence in five consecutive at-bats. It's something that never has done by any other player.

Anson had been studying and analyzing the game since his teenage years and in 1879, at the age of 27, he became the player-manager of the White Stockings. The team went 41–21 in his first season and in 1880 the White Stockings went 67–17, winning the first of three consecutive National League pennants.

He was a commanding figure on the field and in the dugout. The combination of his imposing size, booming voice, explosive temper, penchant for bench-jockeying and an overbearing demeanor allowed him to intimidate umpires and opponents. There is evidence to suggest that even some of his own players weren't too crazy about him. He wasn't blessed with either tact or charisma.

But he got results.

Anson rode his players hard and was likely to fine them for almost anything he felt was detrimental to their performance on the field—smoking, drinking, being overweight, missing curfew.[12] At the time of Anson's death, it was reported that he never smoked or drank alcohol in his entire life although some sources indicate he probably did both in the earliest stages of his career.

He believed in a simple diet, especially before games, almost always consuming a bowl of bread and milk before taking the field.[13]

He also was among the first to recognize a correlation between physical fitness and performance on the field. He encouraged his players to skip rope, punch heavy bags, play handball and swing Indian clubs, and in 1886 he came up with an idea that had a far-reaching impact. He gathered his team in Hot Springs, Arkansas, two months before the season began, telling reporters back in Chicago that he intended to "boil out the alcoholic microbes" of his players.[14] When the White Stockings went on to register a 90–34 record that year, Anson's concept of holding "spring training" began to be copied by other teams.

Anson also developed a reputation for integrity and high moral standards. He had been married to a Philadelphia girl named Virginia "Jennie" Fiegel around the time he joined the White Stockings in 1876 and he did not tolerate promiscuity among his players. *Chicago Tribune* sporting editor E.S. Sheridan once wrote that Anson was "deaf to the particular type of flattery and female attention that flirts about the heels of him who gains notoriety."[15]

Sheridan also noted that "Anson brought to professional baseball four great qualities of professional character that have helped to make the profession what it is. He had integrity, sobriety, personal purity and dignity—the last named quality almost to the point of arrogance."[16]

One other thing made Anson a superior manager: He despised losing ... in any activity. In an 1884 clubhouse poker game, Anson had four jacks and he kept bidding the pot higher and higher until it reached $95. He was flabbergasted when third baseman Ed Williamson produced four kings. Anson refused to pay up and the two men began throwing fists at one another before being separated.[17]

Sadly, Anson's reputation as a player and manager have been stained through the years by increased speculation that he had a major role in perpetuating the gentleman's agreement that kept baseball from embracing players of color until 1947 when the Brooklyn Dodgers employed Jackie Robinson.

It all stems from an August 10, 1883, exhibition game between the White Stockings and the Toledo Blue Stockings of the Northwestern League. Toledo had a black catcher named Moses Fleetwood Walker and the start of the game was delayed for more than an hour as Anson refused to let his team take the field against a team with a black player. He finally realized that he would lose the gate receipts if the game was not played so he went ahead and allowed the contest to take place.[18]

The two teams were scheduled to play again the following season and this time Anson got it in writing that the game would be played only if Walker did not participate.

In 1887, several teams in the International league signed black players before the league formally voted to reject all future contracts with African American players.[19] It is believed to be the first official ban of black players by any league in organized baseball although teams that already had players of color were allowed to keep using them.

Anson's White Stockings were scheduled to play an exhibition against the Newark Little Giants of the International League, who had an exceptional black pitcher named George Stovey. Anson again refused to play if Stovey pitched and this time there was no backing down. Stovey developed some sort of phantom injury and the game went on.[20]

Anson was hardly alone in his racist leanings. It was rampant throughout baseball at that time, but because of his prominence as both a player and manager, his refusal to play carried more weight and undoubtedly influenced others to take the same stance.

Sol White, in his 1907 book entitled *History of Colored Base Ball*, wrote that Anson's "repugnant feeling, shown at every opportunity, toward colored ball players, was a source of comment throughout every league in the country, and his opposition, with his great popularity and power in base ball circles, hastened the exclusion of the black man from white leagues."[21]

Major league baseball never had a written policy, as the International League did, but it would be 60 years before a team dared to put a black player on the field.

There has been speculation that Anson's racist feelings stemmed from his childhood in Marshalltown when he and his family lived among and perhaps had friction with native Americans who preceded them as residents of the area. Anson never really addressed the topic. The roots of his leanings, as well as their actual impact on the sport, are open to conjecture.

In the late 1880s, there began to be speculation about how much longer Anson would continue to play the game. He said at that time that he would play at least three more seasons but when he retired, he would likely go into the bat-making business with Spalding.[22]

It was around that time that he took part in another overseas tour organized by Spalding, who hoped to spread baseball around the globe and thereby increase business for his sporting goods company. The tour featured a series of games between the White Stockings and an all-star team. It began in October in Chicago and spread westward with a series of games in the U.S. The original plan was for the tour to then go to Hawaii and Australia on the ocean liner *Alameda* but on the way to Hawaii, Spalding convinced the participants to make it into a full-fledged world tour.[23]

After playing 11 games in Australia in late December and early January, the tour continued on to Egypt, Ceylon, Italy, France, England, Scotland and Ireland before landing back in the U.S. in early April. It ended up including 56 games in 13 countries and was regarded by Anson as the high point of his career. When he published his autobiography a decade later, nearly half the book was devoted to the world tour.

Professional baseball reached a crossroads of sorts in 1890. Members of the Brotherhood of Professional Ball Players, disgruntled at the way they were treated and compensated by owners, quit the National League in large numbers and formed their own association—the Players League. Anson was one of the few who refused to become part of the revolt. He called the defectors "traitors"[24] and was at the forefront of a campaign to discredit the new league.

The Players League collapsed after one season and most of the players came back to the National League in 1891 although many of them continued to resent and harbor a grudge against Anson for his stance against their rebellion. Anson's White Stockings held first place for much of the 1891 season but were swiftly overtaken in September when the Boston Beaneaters reeled off 18 consecutive wins to take the pennant. There were rumblings that some players threw games against Boston simply to keep Chicago from finishing first.[25]

Under Anson's stern guidance, the White Stockings finished lower than third place only once from 1880 through 1891, but then Spalding stepped down as the team president and was replaced by Jim Hart, who didn't get along as well with Anson. At about that time, the fortunes of both the team and the player took a downward turn. Anson batted .272 in 1892, the lowest figure of his career, and the White Stockings finished in eighth place.

He rebounded to bat .388 in 1894 and was over .330 in the two seasons after that, but the White Stockings took a backseat to teams such as the raucous Baltimore Orioles in the National League. When the 45-year-old Anson hit just .285 and Chicago went 49–73, finishing ninth in the 12-team NL, in 1897 the end was in sight. Speculation that he would not be retained began as soon as the season ended although the formal announcement did not come until the end of January.

It was not a popular move with the fans. The *Chicago Daily News* told its readers that the team would regret its decision every time it needed a clutch hit in a key situation with the game on the line: "How they will miss the ringing crack of bat and ball that turned the tide in countless desperate games—yes, it will be a long time before they will cease regretting Anson. And they will never forget him.... There never was, and there never will be, but one Anson, and his passing leaves a gap that can never be filled."[26]

Tom Burns, one of the few White Stockings players who joined Anson in fighting the Players League, was named to replace him as manager. There were reports that the Orioles, a rowdy, freewheeling band that was the antithesis of what Anson espoused, were interested in signing him to play first base.[27] That never came about.

Anson was hired to manage the New York Giants, but that lasted only 22 games. He and owner Andrew Freedman were almost constantly at odds and with the team floundering along with a 9–13 record, Freedman fired him.

Anson spent the next 20 years trying to find a comfortable niche in life after baseball. He seemingly never did. Grantland Rice wrote in 1922 that while Anson was dabbling in all sorts of other pursuits, "his spirit was still in uniform upon the field."[28]

Some of the character traits that had made him a successful manager were his undoing in the business world. Anson was difficult to get along with, overly demanding, blunt, stubborn, austere. His personality—or lack thereof—seemed to poison most of his post-baseball endeavors.

"He was wholly devoid of political sense, even of social tact," John B. Sheridan wrote in *The Sporting News* many years later. "Had he been in the least bit politically minded he could have been mayor of Chicago, governor of or even senator from Illinois. Had he business sense or tact he could have reaped a fortune. But Anson was blunt as a trip hammer. He always spoke as he thought or rather without thinking at all."[29]

He started out trying to perform on vaudeville. In fact, he began doing that in 1895, before his playing days ended, when he acted with fellow player Arlie Latham in a play called *The Runaway Colt* that was written just for him.

He opened a bowling and billiards hall in downtown Chicago, which prospered for awhile then failed. He served as vice president of the American Bowl-

Adrian Constantine "Cap" Anson in the years following his playing career (John Liepa collection).

ing Congress. He served a two-year term as Chicago's city clerk, then lost a bid to be elected Cook County sheriff.

He owned 13 percent of the Cubs when he retired but was forced to sell out in 1905. He used much of that money to fund a semi-pro team called the Anson Colts, even going so far as to have a small ballpark complete with steel bleachers built for the team on the south side of the city. In order to bolster gate receipts, Anson even suited up and played a little first base in 1908. He could no longer run or field but he could still swing the bat. He even played several games against the Chicago Leland Giants, an all-black team.

He ended up losing thousands on the Colts and filed for bankruptcy in 1910.[30]

He even was forced to get rid of the collection of bats he had assembled through the years. Jack Corbett, who played for the Anson Colts, said that when Anson quit playing he had more than 400 bats in his cellar. He kept them all oiled and dusted nearly every day, but when his financial problems arose he began selling them off.[31]

Through it all, Anson remained an amazing physical specimen and was active in a variety of sports.

"He was an all-around sportsman, a great bowler, a fine billiardist, a competent golfer and a great man at them all," Charles Comiskey said. "He excelled at more branches of sport than any man I ever knew in baseball."[32]

Anson did not take up golf until the age of 55 but he shot an 18-hole score of 100 in the Western Golf Association championships when he was almost 70.[33]

He and two companions were playing a round of golf at Chicago's Jackson Park in January 1912 when they spotted two boys trying to walk across the frozen surface of the park's lagoon. When the boys broke through the ice, the 59-year-old Anson dove into the freezing waters and rescued them.[34]

He later took another shot at vaudeville, often performing with his daughters Dorothy and Adele in skits written by Ring Lardner and George M. Cohan.[35] Early in 1922, he was hired to run Dixmoor Golf Club in south suburban Homewood.

Anson made one more lasting contribution to the game during his final vaudeville years. While performing in Baltimore, a young songwriter named Jack Norworth approached him with the idea of using a tune he had co-written with Albert Von Tilzer. Anson put the song in his act and it became so popular, he began using it for both his entrance and his exit.

"Take Me Out to the Ballgame" is now essentially baseball's national anthem.[36]

Through his financial struggles, Anson's intense pride kept him from accepting help from friends. World-famous evangelist Billy Sunday had been a fledgling ballplayer in Iowa who was signed by Anson on the recommendation of many people back in the state, including one of his aunts. Sunday played for Anson for five years before finding his true calling and often introduced Anson in ensuing years as "the man to whom I owe more than to anyone else for my start in life."[37] In 1909, Sunday told Chicago newspapers that he wanted to give a free lecture combined with musical entertainment as a fundraiser for his old friend. Anson told him that wouldn't be necessary.

Spalding, with whom Anson had a falling out, tried to organize a testimonial to raise money for Anson but he ordered Spalding not to do so. National League president John Tener, who had played for Anson with the White Stockings, tried to arrange some sort of pension for him. Anson refused that, too, saying such gestures would "stultify" his manhood.[38]

There also were some rough times in his personal life in that period. Henry Anson died back in Iowa in 1905, brother Sturgis passed away in 1911 and in 1916, Anson's beloved wife Jennie died of cancer. They had met during his first year playing in Philadelphia when he was 20 and she was only 13, and they were married four years later. They had seven children together—three sons (Adrian H., Adrian C. and Henry) who died in infancy and four daughters (Grace, Adele, Dorothy and Virginia) who lived to adulthood.

After Jennie died, Anson lived with one of his daughters. In April 1922, he underwent abdominal surgery and was still recuperating in the hospital when he suffered a cerebral hemorrhage. On April 14, just a few days before his 70th birthday, he died.

Prior to his funeral, seemingly half of Chicago came to pay its respects. The *Chicago Daily News* noted that "all day long they came, some in limousines, some on street cars, others on foot. Mingling with carefully dressed men of wealth were unshaved, unkempt persons in rags. Sidewalk traffic was blocked and hundreds were unable to get into the chapel for the services."[39]

The tributes flowed in from around the world, from baseball officials, players, managers, politicians, people whose lives had been touched by him.

St. Louis Star reporter Billy Murphy described Anson as "honest, honorable, clean, he could not understand tricky people. He believed that this is the best day the world has ever seen and that tomorrow would be better."[40]

Charles Comiskey called him "the greatest batter that ever walked up to hit a baseball thrown by a pitcher.... He was a fine, big honorable man on and off the baseball field."[41]

Baseball commissioner Judge Kennesaw Mountain Landis delivered the eulogy at the funeral, telling those in attendance, "He was always straight and fair and square in all things."[42]

In death, Anson was unable to refuse assistance. The National League paid his hospital bill, paid for the funeral and picked up the tab for a massive marker in Chicago's Oakwoods Cemetery. It shows two crossed bats, a wreath and a ball along with the words "He Played the Game."[43]

Seventeen years later, Anson was voted into the Baseball Hall of Fame by a special committee at the same time as his old friend, Spalding. The first few words of the inscription on Anson's plaque are as blunt and direct as the man himself: "Greatest hitter and greatest National League player-manager of 19th century."[44]

Outfield
Fred Clarke

"With the possible exception of Cobb and John McGraw, baseball never knew a sturdier competitor."—Sportswriter Fred Lieb[1]

As a youngster growing up in 1880s Iowa, Fred Clarke seemingly was a boy without direction.

He ran away from home several times and had a variety of small jobs during his teenage years. He delivered groceries for the C.C. Loomis company, worked in Des Moines' Foster Theater, worked as a bellboy and elevator operator in the nearby Savery Hotel and even delivered newspapers for the *Des Moines Register*. One day, he got into a fight with a fellow newspaper carrier and accidentally broke a window. The Register's stern-faced circulation manager, Ed Barrow, made him pay 35 cents to have the window repaired.[2]

However, the relationship between Clarke and Barrow ultimately led to something more productive. Barrow also was involved in the management of local semipro baseball teams and he recruited Clarke to become a member of one of those teams. It led to the vocation that would give shape and purpose to Clarke's life.

By the age of 22, Clarke was playing in the major leagues. At 24, he became the first "boy wonder" major league player-manager.

He compiled a career batting average of .312 in 21 years as a major league player and had a winning percentage of .576 in 19 years as a manager, developing a reputation as an exceptional hitter, an intrepid base runner, a ferocious competitor and an inspirational leader who eventually landed in baseball's Hall of Fame.

Barrow, only four years older than Clarke, also ended up in Cooperstown. He served as general manager and president of the New York Yankees for nearly a quarter century, overseeing the development of the most storied franchise in the game.

But perhaps his first big contribution to the game was the direction and discipline he gave to Fred Clarke.

Clarke was born in 1872 in Winterset, Iowa, about 35 miles southwest of Des Moines, one of the youngest in a large brood of kids born to William and Lucy

Fred Clarke.

Clarke. William, who worked as a blacksmith and a farmer, piled his family into a covered wagon when Fred was only two and moved them to Cowley County, Kansas.[3]

Apparently he didn't find what he was looking for there because about five years later he moved the family back to Iowa and settled in Des Moines.

Young Fred tried just about everything to earn a few bucks and he even thought about taking a stab at acting. The Foster Theater was doing a play that called for some boys to portray African natives so Clarke blackened his face and hands and showed up to audition. Then he learned that the role called for him to appear wearing only a "breech cloth." He didn't get the part.[4]

But he did finally find his niche at the age of 17 as the starting second baseman for the Des Moines Mascots, a semipro team that Barrow had organized. After two years with the Mascots and another team called the Des Moines Stars, he was lured away to join a semipro team in Carroll, Iowa, which promised to pay him $40 a month.[5] Clarke went to Carroll against the wishes of his parents, who felt he was wasting his time playing a boys game.

His performance in Carroll led to a minor league contract in 1892 to play for the Hastings team in the Nebraska State League. In later years, Clarke told an interviewer that he secured his spot in Hastings by placing an ad in the *Sporting News*.[6]

Clarke was a proficient hitter right away in the minors, but it took hours of extra practice for him to adjust to playing the outfield. He never did become great at going back on the ball, but he was exceptional at handling balls hit in front of him. As a result, he played deeper than almost any other left-fielder in the major leagues when he finally reached the big time.[7]

Those were tough times in minor league baseball. The Nebraska State League went out of business later in that 1892 season and Clarke caught on in 1893 with St. Joseph's of the Western Association. He batted .346 in 20 games before that league also went under. His next stop was Montgomery in the Southern Association, where he came under the tutelage of veteran manager John McCloskey and continued to hit well. But a yellow fever epidemic in the Deep South caused that team to suspend operations.[8]

Frustrated by his run of bad luck, Clarke decided to quit baseball and attempted to acquire a piece of farm land in Indian Territory, which later became the state of Oklahoma. He was not successful in doing so and McCloskey convinced him to come back to baseball with Savannah of the Southern Association in 1894. Clarke batted .311 and stole 21 bases in 54 games and this time, when the Savannah club went out of business in late June, he landed on his feet. McCloskey sold his rights to the Louisville Colonels of the National League.

Clarke had been promised $100 upon his arrival at Louisville. He asked manager Billy Barney for the money before taking the field for the first time. Barney assured him he would give him a check following the game. Clarke insisted on getting the money upfront and in cash. Barney delivered and Clarke played his first game with five $20 bills clipped to the inside of his jersey with a safety pin.[9]

All uncertainty about Clarke's future disappeared in that game when he collected four singles and a triple against Philadelphia. The next week he got a taste of what major league baseball was like in that era. In the fifth inning of a game against Brooklyn he was knocked down in a collision with Brooklyn catcher Con Daily and as he climbed to his feet, Daily punched him in the mouth.[10]

In Louisville, Clarke embarked on a long relationship with Barney Dreyfuss, who was then the treasurer and a stockholder of the Colonels. When Clarke first joined the team, he became one of the boys. In the major leagues at that time, postgame drinking and carousing was as much a part of a players' lifestyle as hitting and pitching, and the 21-year-old Clarke became part of that.

Dreyfuss, a German immigrant who had fallen in love with the American pastime, pulled Clarke aside and challenged him to be different, telling him, "You will live in the major leagues a few years only if you continue to dim your batting eye and weaken your physical self by carousing around."[11]

Clarke batted a respectable .274 in 76 games in the remainder of that 1894 season but in 1895, apparently heeding Dreyfuss' advice, he emerged as one of the genuine stars of the National League. He strung together a 35-game hitting streak that extended from late July to the end of August and finished the season at .347. Two years later, he batted a career-high .390, good for second in the NL batting race behind Brooklyn's Wee Willie Keeler.

In mid–June of that season, the 24-year-old Clarke was named the manager of the Colonels, raising his salary from $2,400 a year to $2,900.

One of Clarke's first acquisitions as manager came courtesy of his old friend, Barrow, who was now in charge of the Paterson, New Jersey, team in the Atlantic League. Barrow sold him a big-beaked, bow-legged utility man from the Pennsylvania coal fields by the name of Honus Wagner.[12] Five years later, Clarke made the shrewd decision to move Wagner to shortstop on a permanent basis. The player known as the Flying Dutchman became the greatest player ever to play the position.

The Colonels finished 1897 with a winning percentage of just .393 but they improved to .464 in 1898 and .493 in 1899. In spite of that, the franchise was struggling. Attendance was so bad near the end of 1899 that Dreyfuss opted to play the final 14 scheduled home games on the road.

Prior to 1900, it was common for syndicates to own all or part of multiple teams in the NL, which led to some imbalances in power. In 1899, the group of men who owned both the St. Louis and Cleveland teams piled all their good players onto the St. Louis club. The result was that the stripped-down Cleveland Spiders went 20–134 and had six losing streaks of 11 or more games.

The NL opted to eliminate multiple ownership and condense from 12 teams to eight in 1900 and it was inevitable that Louisville (along with Cleveland) would be among the discontinued teams.

Dreyfuss had bought out all his partners in the Louisville franchise but he also had a 50-percent ownership share of the Pittsburgh Pirates, and he negotiated a deal to transfer most of the best players on the Louisville roster over to Pittsburgh. In one dynamic maneuver in early December, Clarke, Wagner, hard-hitting third baseman Tommy Leach, catcher Chief Zimmer, pitchers Rube Waddell and Deacon Phillippe and six other players all became Pittsburgh Pirates.

Dreyfuss ultimately became the primary owner of the Pirates and he knew exactly who he wanted to manage his team. Clarke became the field general of a Pittsburgh team on the brink of arguably the most sustained era of success in the history of the franchise.

The Pirates went 79–60 and finished second to Brooklyn by just 4½ games in 1900, then won three consecutive pennants under the management of their still-young left-fielder.

Clarke was a fiery competitor who was not adverse to being openly combative on the playing field and his players followed his lead. While he and New York Giants manager John McGraw became bitter rivals, they were not terribly different in their approach to constructing and guiding their teams. Both wanted players who were smart and assertive. Errors of aggression were tolerated. Mental lapses were not. Neither was adverse to openly berating a player in order to get across his point.

But unlike McGraw, Clarke was not as tolerant of erratic off-field behavior, believing that it damaged team chemistry. That led him to trade the fun-seeking Waddell in 1901 even though Clarke many years later admitted he was among the best pitchers he ever saw. High morale, he felt, was vital to on-field success. He often said that to be successful, a manager not only had to know baseball and have the resources necessary to bring in talent but he had to be able to mold players "into a big, happy whole, both on and off the field."[13]

It was an effective formula. Clarke was destined to guide the Pirates into the first division 14 consecutive years and have 13 straight seasons with a winning percentage above .550.

While Clarke was providing strong leadership as a manager, he also was in the midst of a remarkable run of consistency as a player. He stole 10 or more bases 18 years in a row and had nine or more triples 16 years in a row.

A daring and adventuresome base runner, he seldom settled for a double if he thought there was the slightest chance he could get to third base. As a result, he had two seasons in which he had more triples than doubles and he ranks seventh on baseball's all-time list with 220 three-base hits.

He was primarily a table-setter who batted near the top of the batting order. His career high in runs batted in was only 82, but he had 13 seasons in which he scored more than 80 runs.

He also didn't back down from anyone. Clarke often recalled the first time he faced the Chicago White Stockings, whose player manager was fellow Iowan Cap Anson. Clarke slammed a base hit and was rounding first heading for second when Anson, playing first base, tripped him. Clarke had to scramble back to first to avoid being tagged out.

"I didn't say a word," Clarke recalled in an interview with the *Des*

Moines Register, "but the next time I deliberately hit an infield out and as I got to first I landed on his shoe with my spikes and ripped the shoe open. He was a rough man with a good punch, but I knew he could never catch me. Anson was slow and had to hit for his reputation. He let me alone after that."[14]

Clarke had one of his best seasons in 1903, when he batted .351 and led the league in slugging percentage despite an array of physical ailments. There were reports early in the season that he had suffered a nervous breakdown, prompting Wagner to briefly fill in as manager.[15] On the Fourth of July, he dove for a fly ball in the outfield and separated his shoulder, sidelining him for more than a month.

The Pirates still managed to clinch their third straight pennant on September 18 and this time they became part of a new baseball tradition—the World Series.

The National League had been at war with the American League since the AL came into existence in 1901, but the two leagues had begun to reach a certain level of accord. Dreyfuss and Boston Americans owner Henry Killea decided to capitalize on the existence of two major leagues by arranging a series between their teams after both clubs won their respective leagues in 1903.

McGraw and the Giants declined to continue the practice when they won the National League pennant in 1904 but beginning in 1905, it became an annual tradition.

Unfortunately, Clarke's Pirates were not at full strength when they went up against Boston in that very first best-of-nine World Series. Wagner was nursing injuries to his thumb and right leg, and ended up committing six errors in the series. Pitcher Sam Leever, who won 25 games in the regular season, aggravated a shoulder injury by going trap-shooting. Another starting pitcher, Ed Doheny, disappeared for a few days, never did pitch in the series and was subsequently committed to an insane asylum.[16]

Pittsburgh still made a good showing, thanks largely to the heroics and durability of Phillippe, who threw five complete games and earned victories in three of the first four games. But Boston, led by its own pitching duo of Cy Young and Bill Dinneen, won the last four games. Dinneen hurled a four-hit shutout in Game 8 to take the title.

As with the modern-day World Series, the players each were given a share of the money with the winning team receiving a larger amount. But Dreyfuss decided to give his players his share of the gate receipts, resulting in the Pirates actually pocketing more money than the Americans.[17]

In the decade that followed, the National League became an almost continuous three-way tussle between the Pirates, Giants and Chicago Cubs. From 1903 through 1912, those three teams occupied the top three spots in the NL standings every year except for a fourth-place finish by the Pirates in 1904 and one by the Giants in 1907. In the amazing and controversial 1908 pennant race, the Cubs went 99–55 while the Giants and Pirates each were 98–56.

The rivalry between the Pirates and Giants was especially contentious, occasionally resulting in violence. Prior to a game in June of 1903, a few New York players enticed Clarke into the Giants offices at the Polo Grounds, where burly catcher Frank Bowerman assaulted him with his fists. Clarke came away with a black eye. Bowerman was fined $100.[18]

Clarke and McGraw got into a fight on the field in 1905 and the following day McGraw hurled insults and accusations at Dreyfuss during a game, resulting in another fracas. The New York manager ended up being suspended for 15 days as a result of that incident.

The rivalry between the Pirates and Cubs wasn't quite as heated, perhaps because Clarke's brother-in-law, Chick Fraser, pitched for Chicago for a few of those years. Clarke's youngest brother, Josh, also spent parts of five seasons in the major leagues, starting in the outfield for the Cleveland Indians in 1908.

The Giants won the NL pennant in 1904 and 1905 and the Cubs, led by their own Hall of Fame player-manager, Frank Chance, finished on top in 1906, 1907 and 1908.

Finally, after three second-place finishes in four years, the Pirates broke through to win another pennant in 1909. They won a franchise-record 110 games to out-distance the Cubs, who won 104. The Pirates removed all doubt about their superiority by reeling off 16 straight victories in September, clinching the pennant in the first game of a double-header on September 27. The following day, Clarke was honored in pregame ceremonies and presented with a watch and $600 in gold.[19]

Clarke batted only .287 that season but in an era dominated by pitching, that was the eighth best average in the league. He also led the league with 80 walks. Wagner won the batting title with a .339 average and true to the aggressive nature of Clarke-led teams, every Pittsburgh starter stole at least nine bases, led by Wagner's 35 and Clarke's 31.

The Pirates faced Ty Cobb and the Detroit Tigers in the World Series and Clarke began the best-of-seven set with a surprise. He had three pitchers who won 19 of more games during the season, but in the series opener he opted to start rookie Babe Adams, who had won only 12 although his earned run average was a scintillating 1.11.

3. Outfield: Fred Clarke

Fred Clarke (in suit) chats with Pittsburgh players Honus Wagner, Mike Donlin and Marty O'Toole in 1912.

Using an assortment of slow, tantalizing curve balls, Adams confirmed Clarke's faith in him as the Pirates defeated the Tigers 4–1 with Clarke hitting a home run. Adams pitched another complete game in Game 5 and Clarke, who had only 67 regular-season homers in his career, belted another one out of the park to give Pittsburgh a 3–2 lead in the series. After the Tigers eked out a 5–4 win in Game 6, Clarke went with Adams again in Game 7 in Detroit and the rookie threw a six-hit shutout to clinch the world championship.

Clarke's offensive production began to decline in the years that followed. He batted a career-low .263 in 1910 although he still was helping the team win in other ways. On August 23 of that year, he tied a major league record that still stands by throwing out four baserunners from left field in one game.

He bounced back to bat .324 in 1911, but decided he could be a more effective manager if he ceased to be an everyday player. He did not play in a single game in 1912, played only two games in the outfield and took only 13 at-bats in 1913, and made just two pinch-hitting appearances in 1914.

The Pirates' days as an NL contender were gone, too, and in 1914 their record dropped below .500 for the first time since 1899. Wagner, after winning eight NL batting titles, was now 40 and batted just .252. Leach, one of Clarke's stalwarts for so many years, was traded to the Cubs in the middle of the 1912 season. Right-fielder Chief Wilson, who clubbed a major-league record 36 triples in 1912, was dealt to the Cardinals.

Things got worse in 1915 as the Pirates went just 73–81. Clarke had been toying with the idea of retiring as the manager since the 1909 championship. A few papers even reported that he had retired in December 1909 only to have him renew his contract just a day or two later.[20] But with the team now descending into mediocrity, the time was right. On September 8, 1915, Clarke resigned.

The Pirates held a Fred Clarke Day on September 23 and in addition to being showered with gifts, Clarke took the field as a player one last time. He played four innings and lashed a clean single in two at-bats.

Dreyfuss admitted in a post-season banquet honoring Clarke that he wasn't sure how he was going to replace his longtime manager. "Fred and I have been associated together so long that we seem to have become a part of each other, and it will hardly seem like a Pirate team next season without him in charge," he added.[21]

Clarke said his only desire at that point was "to go to my farm in Winfield, Kansas, for the remainder of my days." Among the farewell gifts he received was a box of silver and 50 apple trees to plant on his ranch in Kansas.[22]

He had taken a portion of his first year's salary in the major leagues and made a down payment on 160 acres of land in southern Kansas, not far from where he had lived for five years as a kid. He had gradually expanded his property through the years and he and his wife Annette, who he married in 1898, lived there in the off-season with their two daughters. Now he planned to spend all his time there growing wheat and raising cattle on what came to be known as Little Pirate Ranch.

Over the years, it grew to about 22,000 acres and in 1916, the year after Clarke retired from baseball, a deep vein of oil was discovered on the land. Almost instantly, he became a millionaire.[23]

He spent the next several years doing all the things he loved—hunting, fishing, horseback riding—while also working the farm. He even won the Kansas state trapshooting championship one year.

Clarke, in conjunction with some of his new oil friends, attempted to buy the Pirates during those years but Dreyfuss wasn't ready to get out of the business.[24] Clarke had very little else to do with baseball, but it seemed

3. Outfield: Fred Clarke

inevitable that he would eventually drift back to the game. When his old catcher, George Gibson, became manager of the Pirates, Clarke accepted an invitation to help out as a coach in spring training in 1921 and 1922.

Dreyfuss had rebuilt the Pirates around an energetic outfielder named Kiki Cuyler, a deft third baseman named Pie Traynor and versatile shortstop Glenn Wright, but he couldn't quite match McGraw's Giants, who won the NL pennant in 1921, 1922 and 1923. Dreyfuss despised McGraw, who ridiculed his German accent, and he finally prevailed upon Clarke to help put the Pirates over the top.

When Pittsburgh fell behind the Giants again early in the 1925 season, Clarke came on board as team vice president and assistant manager under Bill McKechnie. He also was allowed to purchase stock in the team as part of his compensation. Dreyfuss wanted Clarke to sit on the bench alongside McKechnie and hopefully instill the same competitive fire that his earlier Pirates teams possessed.

It worked. The Pirates surged into first place within a few weeks after Clarke joined them and went on to win the pennant by 8½ games. Clarke was given much of the credit for the championship. Dan Daniel wrote in *Baseball Magazine* that he was "the spiritual advisor and the father confessor of the players and the strategical aid of McKechnie."[25]

After falling behind the Washington Senators three games to one in the World Series, the Pirates won three straight games to also take the world championship.

Despite his apparent role in their success, the Pittsburgh players voted to give Clarke only about a one-fifth share of the World Series winnings. There was speculation that it was because they knew he already was independently wealthy and didn't really need the money. There also were rumblings that the players didn't like having Clarke on the bench, that they felt he sometimes gave orders that conflicted with what McKechnie wanted.

When the Pirates were not as successful in 1926, some of that resentment bubbled to the surface. Three veteran players lobbied to have Clarke removed from the bench in August. One of them was Babe Adams, whose heroics had helped win the 1909 World Series, and he was joined by Carson Bigbee and Max Carey, who also had come up to the majors during Clarke's tenure as manager. When the other players voted to have Clarke stay on the bench, Adams, Bigbee and Carey were released.

The whole story later came out in the *Pittsburgh Press* and although Clarke defended himself in what came to be known as the ABC incident (Adams-Bigbee-Carey), he had no desire to become further embroiled in controversy. He resigned his position with the team and sold back all of his Pirates stock. He never again was connected in any formal way with the Pittsburgh organization.

He and Chick Fraser did attend the first two games of the 1927 World Series between the Yankees and the Pirates at Dreyfuss' invitation. He was there among the mourners when Dreyfuss passed away in 1932. And he remained an avid Pirates fan for the rest of his life.

He also held leadership positions with the National Baseball Congress through the years, holding the title of director of the National Association of Leagues in 1951.

In 1945, he earned the biggest honor of all when he was elected to the baseball Hall of Fame by the veterans committee.

He spent most of his remaining years with the leisurely pursuits he loved. He went all over the country to fish. He and Annette had their boat capsize in a storm while fishing on a lake in northern Minnesota in 1947 and they were in the bone-chilling water for three hours before being rescued. Annette took a few days to recover, but Clarke emerged unscathed, telling friends there was nothing wrong with him that a couple of highballs couldn't cure. He was back out on the same lake with rod and reel in hand the following day.[26]

Des Moines Register columnist Sec Taylor wrote that he once ran into Clarke in Florida and learned that he had just caught a 36-pound kingfish and a 60-pound sailfish. Taylor also noted that Clarke "hunted pheasants in South Dakota, quail in Oklahoma and Texas, ducks in Kansas and Oklahoma, and deer in Colorado."[27]

Only a few weeks after the Minnesota fishing mishap, Clarke had another near miss during a quail hunting trip. A friend's shotgun misfired but the stray pellets deflected harmlessly off the bill of Clarke's cap.[28]

In 1956, at the age of 83, he broke his hip and was not as active after that although he still drank two bourbon highballs almost every day—that's all his doctor would allow—and kept a close eye on the Pirates as they built toward another championship. He never got to see it, however. Two months before they knocked off the Yankees in the 1960 World Series, Clarke died of pneumonia in Winfield at the age of 87.

He'll go down in the history of the game as one of the few men who had Hall of Fame caliber credentials as both a player and a manager. Not as well known was Clarke's role as an innovator. He invented baseball's first flip-down sunglasses in 1912 and also held patents on several other baseball-related items, including sliding pads, equipment bags and a pulley system used to pull a tarpaulin on and off the field. At his suggestion, the Pirates became the first team to use a large tarp to cover the entire infield to protect it from weather. It's a practice that other teams soon emulated.[29]

Most of all, though, he was remembered by old-timers as a feisty, relentless competitor who refused to back down from anyone at any time.

His widow, Annette, recalled that it was left to her to compile the stacks of scrapbooks that detailed his achievements.

"He was too busy managing and getting himself thrown out of ballgames," she said. "He was the fightingest manager out there."[30]

Outfield
George Stone

"Cobb is a great hitter, and so is Lajoie, and there are others, but Stone has a little on them all."—*Washington Times*[1]

George Stone seemingly had two primary ambitions in his life—to become a highly successful businessman and a great violinist. He achieved both.

Baseball? It was OK. It could be fun at times and it was a good way to make money to fund the business and banking career that Stone always felt was his future.

"I don't intend to play baseball many more years," Stone said during one of his infrequent interviews following the 1906 season. "While I should probably be good for several years to come and draw a pretty fairly good salary, I realize that each year I continue in baseball sets me just that much further back in a business career. I am still a young man and believe that it should be the ambition of every young man to get in business for himself. Baseball is not a business, except to the club owners, and you could hardly call it a profession."[2]

It was a strange comment from a man who had just won the American League batting title, beating out such enduring luminaries as Ty Cobb and Napoleon Lajoie for the honor. In fact, in the first 28 years that the American League existed, the batting championship was won by a future Hall of Fame member 27 times.

The lone exception was in 1906 when a quiet, demure, somewhat offbeat but fleet-footed St. Louis Browns outfielder from Eastern Iowa got the best of everyone.

4. Outfield: George Stone

Stone, whose nickname was "Silent," batted .301 over the course of a relatively short major league career and in only his second full season, he hit .358. Lajoie, who won the AL batting title four straight years from 1901 through 1904, finished at .355. Cobb, who won the title in 12 of the next 13 years, checked in at .320.

Stone, who was five feet, nine inches, and 175 pounds, had very broad shoulders and employed an unorthodox left-handed batting stance that was frequently questioned and occasionally ridiculed. He used an extremely heavy bat and bent over into an exaggerated crouch, held his hands about six inches apart, leaned the bat flat against his left shoulder and stood completely motionless as the pitch approached. Billy Evans wrote that anyone who didn't know

George Stone (courtesy *Quad-City Times*).

Stone might assume he was "humpbacked. Stone stands close to the plate and in reality half of his body is extending over it when he crouches."[3]

Stone felt that his crouch gave him an advantage because the ball was almost at eye-level as it approached the plate. He also felt it put him in position to chop at the ball with a very short, compact swing instead of using a long, looping swing like many other hitters.[4] When infielders crept in too close to defend against Stone's bunts and chops, he was fully capable to rifling line drives past them and he used the entire field, hitting the ball to left and center as much as he did to right.

"He controls the ball better in bunting now, and with his speed that makes him a far more dangerous man than he would otherwise be," *The Sporting News* reported after the 1906 season. "With the infield pulled in, he drives the ball so hard than an infielder's chances of stopping it are small. With the infield out, he is liable to bunt and beat the ball out."[5]

"When he meets the ball, he hits it hard and on a line," the *Washington Star* added. "Most of his safeties are sharp line drives. His ability to wait until the ball is upon him before offering at it is in a great measure responsible for his success."[6]

Stone was just as effective against left-handed pitchers as he was right-handers. He still led the American League in strikeouts during his best season, but his chopping swing also got him moving toward first base as he swung, resulting in a high number of infield hits.

"This helps his batting average considerably as he beats out many a slow infield hit which for a slower man would mean a putout," Hall of Fame pitcher Addie Joss said of Stone. After Stone went 9 for 15 against him one season, Joss added, "Stone apparently has no weakness at bat."[7]

Besides being a highly effective table-setter at the top of the St. Louis batting order, Stone was an anomaly in an era of boisterous, boastful, beer-brawling ballplayers. He always was in bed by 10 o'clock each night and never was the slightest source of worry for any of his managers.[8]

"Stone seldom, if ever, takes a drink and he is absolutely sober and clean in his way of living," the *Globe-Democrat* reported in 1906. "He is well-educated, uses excellent language both in conversation and writing, and would be considered well in comparison with the average teacher in a school or college. He never talks loud and is one of the most inconspicuous men on the team outside of the fact that he is a man way above the average in physical development and has a head and face that indicate a man of business or one following a profession rather than a ball player. Stone's taste runs to reading and his hobby is violin playing. In fact, he would rather be a great violinist with a limited income than he would a great ballplayer with a handsome salary."[9]

He was equally stoic and understated on the playing field.

James Crusinberry of the *St. Louis Post-Dispatch* described him as "one of those plugging players who always gives the team the best he has. He never sulks. Because he is so modest and quiet, the fans are sometimes a bit disappointed, thinking he lacks enthusiasm. But George controls himself in victory and in defeat.... He's always the same. He never gets excited."[10]

Stone was born in Lost Nation, Iowa, in northwest Clinton County in 1876 to Sam and Hannah Stone, who had emigrated from England just eight years earlier.[11] The family eventually moved to Sac County in western Iowa and ultimately settled near Coleridge, Nebraska.

Stone began working as a clerk in a general store in Coleridge as a teenager and through the years played baseball in his spare time for a variety of town teams in such nearby communities as Laurel, Hartington, Bloomfield and Pierce.

There are numerous stories explaining how he was first discovered by professional scouts, all of them involving a game in which he collected five hits, including three home runs.

According to one story, the three-homer game came while he was playing for a team in Onawa, Iowa, and an old Western League pitcher named Dick Buckley witnessed it and spread the word about Stone's potential.

Another version has it occurring against Onawa, which had a pitcher who was being scouted by the Omaha team in the Western League. The scout went back to Omaha and told owner William "Pa" Rourke that he was trying to sign the wrong player. He should get this Stone guy instead.[12]

Yet another version of the tale has Stone getting three home runs, a double and a single against a pitcher named Alloway who already was employed by the Omaha team. Alloway went back and told the team it would be wise to recruit Stone.[13]

However it happened, the 25-year-old Stone signed to play for the Omaha Omahogs in 1902 for $75 a month.[14] He split that season between Omaha and Peoria, batting .346, and after another successful season in which he also played for Peoria and Omaha, he was sold to Boston of the American League for $2,000.

Less than two years removed from his clerking job in Coleridge, Stone found himself in a major league uniform in the spring of 1903. But Boston manager Jimmy Collins didn't think much of Stone's weird stance and after he struck out twice as a pinch-hitter early in the season, he was dispatched to Milwaukee of the American Association.

He prospered there, batting .298 in 100 games in the rest of that season. In 1904, again with Milwaukee, he had one of the most amazing seasons in the history of minor league baseball, batting .406 with 254 total hits, seven home runs, 19 triples and 36 doubles. In one series against the Toledo Mud Hens, he reached base 17 straight times, on 15 hits and two walks.

In August, Boston included Stone in a three-way trade that would have sent him to the Washington Senators but the deal fell through when the third team, the Philadelphia Athletics, backed out of the bargain. The Americans then tried to bring Stone up to the major leagues. Most players would have leaped at the opportunity but Stone, apparently peeved that the Americans didn't give him much of a chance in 1903 and then tried to trade him in 1904, simply refused to report. He stayed and finished the season in Milwaukee.[15]

In December, Boston traded him to the St. Louis Browns for veteran outfielder Jesse Burkett and an undisclosed amount of cash, and Stone was set to finally get his major league opportunity at the age of 28. He didn't sound terribly enthused about it, though, telling the *Sporting Life*, "I dislike the idea of playing with a tailender, but will go if I get the money."[16]

Browns manager Jimmy McAleer at first had the same thoughts about Stone's batting stance as Jimmy Collins, calling it "clumsy,"[17] but he also saw what sort of results Stone got. Stone became the Browns' starting left-

George Stone batted .301 during a relatively brief major league career.

fielder, playing in every game in 1905 and batting .296 while leading the American League in total hits (187) and at-bats (632).

That season stamped him as a hot commodity and one of the game's coming stars. In February of 1906, White Sox owner Charles Comiskey was looking to bolster his team's offense and was reportedly offering four players—19-game winner Frank Smith, infielders Gus Dundon and George Rohe and outfielder Danny Green—plus $1,000 cash in exchange for Stone.[18] The Browns rejected the offer. Owner Robert Hedges told the *Sporting Life* that such an offer was "absurd" and that Stone would remain with the Browns for many years to come.

"Chicago isn't the only club that wants Stone," Hedges added. "New York has been dickering for him since last fall and had I turned him over to Clark Griffith, I could have named the terms. You know what I could have received for G., all right, as Griff told me he would rather have him than any ball player in America.... Stone will be a member of the 1906 Browns."[19]

Stone's landmark season followed. He not only won the batting title but also led the AL in total bases, slugging percentage and on-base percentage. He was second in hits and triples, third in home runs, fifth in runs scored and sixth in stolen bases. There was no Most Valuable Player award then, but if there had been, Stone would have been the clearcut choice despite the fact that St. Louis finished fifth in the standings.

"I wouldn't trade him for any player in the business," McAleer reiterated after the season.[20]

The *Sporting News*, in reporting that Stone had won the batting title, noted that "it would not be surprising to see him bat around the .400 mark next season."[21]

The *St. Louis Globe-Democrat* described Stone as "a good hitter, a very fair fielder, unusually fast on his feet, handicapped only by an ordinary throwing arm."[22]

For all his offensive prowess, Stone apparently had deficiencies in the field. Hall of Fame second baseman Eddie Collins often told a story about hitting a ball to left field that Stone lost in the sun. It ended up hitting him in the head and bouncing over the fence, caroming off a sign that said, "Hit this and win $10." Even then, Stone had strong business instincts. Collins said he came to him the next day and asked for a cut of the $10.[23]

Stone's business impulses also came out following his spectacular 1906 season. He became one of the first major-league players ever to hold out, skipping all of spring training in 1907 and saying he would not sign for less than $5,000. The Browns were only offering $3,500. In a telephone conversation with a reporter, he said, "They will either have to come up with that amount or I will stay in Coleridge and sell cigars. I have a good business here, and don't have to play ball for a living."[24]

Rumors began to circulate that the Browns might actually trade him this time. Hedges tried to calm the fears of the St. Louis fans by publicly announcing that there were no plans to deal Stone. He told reporters he thought there were only two other outfielders in the league who could match Stone—Cobb and his Detroit teammate, Sam Crawford. Hedges further added that he thought Crawford was the best player and that he didn't think Cobb would have a long career.[25]

As spring training came to a close, Hedges finally relented and met Stone's demands.

Stone momentarily made Hedges look like a prophet as he batted .320 in 1907, third best in the AL behind Cobb and Crawford. He also narrowly averted a possible disaster late in the season. On September 19, he and three teammates—Jack Powell, Jack O'Connor and Bill McGill—were in a car on the way to a game in Cleveland when they were broadsided by a streetcar. The side of their vehicle was bashed in, an axle was broken and McGill nearly was pinned beneath the car. Powell and O'Connor were described in slightly exaggerated news reports as being "near death" and were taken away on stretchers. Stone jumped from the vehicle and landed on his feet, unharmed. He played in the game that day.[26]

Stone's numbers began to decline in his fourth season with the Browns. He batted a more pedestrian .281 in 1908 and .287 in 1909 although he still stole 20 or more bases and was among the top 10 in the league in runs scored for the fourth straight year in 1908.

There were some reports that he suffered from malaria in that season[27] and Stone ran into more health issues the following year. On May 10, 1909, he severely sprained his ankle sliding into first base while trying to beat out a dribbler against the White Sox. He missed almost half the season and when he came back in 1910, his speed was diminished. Without the steady stream of leg hits, his average dropped to .256 and his play suffered in other ways, too.

"Stone's none-too-strong left arm troubled him all year, and any time a ball was hit into his territory the opposing baserunners advanced almost at will," the *Globe-Democrat* reported. "As a result, the sensation of the American League of 1906 was a near joke in 1910."[28]

In December, the *Sporting Life* reported "Nobody seems to want George Stone. The Browns are dead willing to sell or trade him, but no one is making any offers for the man who once led the American League with the willow."[29]

The Browns finally released him and none of the other teams in the league picked him up for the waiver price of $1,500.

In 1911, Stone found himself back with the Milwaukee Brewers in the American Association, where he batted a solid .282 in 114 games. Seven games into the 1912 season, the Brewers released him and he caught on with Portland of the Pacific Coast League. He played in only five games there and was done. It was time to get on with that business career.

Stone's only connection with baseball in the ensuing years was as an owner. He purchased a controlling interest in the Lincoln team in the Western League in 1916[30] and moved to Lincoln for a short time, but didn't stay in the baseball business for long.

He spent most of the rest of his life as a banker in Coleridge, serving at one time as the president of the Cedar County Bankers Association.[31] He had married his hometown sweetheart, Pearl Moore, after the 1906 season, and she gave birth to their only child in 1913. Vean Stone grew up to be a respected eye surgeon in California.

George and Pearl returned to Eastern Iowa in later years to oversee land holdings and to open a bowling alley, moving into a large, Victorian house at 561 S. 5th Street in Clinton. That is where Stone died early in 1945.

When the Browns moved to Baltimore and became the Orioles in 1952, the franchise named an all-time Browns team. Despite the fact that he played only seven major league seasons, one of the outfielders was George Stone.

Pitcher
Jack Coombs

"No better pitcher ever walked out onto a mound."—Hall of Famer Frank "Home Run" Baker[1]

Connie Mack served as the manager of the Philadelphia Athletics for 50 years, earning a reputation for his insight and knowledge of the game of baseball, but the man everyone reverently referred to as Mr. Mack wasn't quite perfect.

In 1908, he decided one of the best pitchers he ever had was an outfielder.

Jack Coombs, born in Iowa and raised in Maine, had gone 16–19 as a pitcher in his first two years with the Athletics and he was nursing a sore arm. So Mack played him in the outfield for 47 games at the outset of that 1908 season.

It seems ludicrous now because two years later Coombs enjoyed arguably the finest second half of a season of any pitcher in the history of the major leagues. All Coombs did during the months of July, August and September of 1910 was pitch 250 innings, throw 12 shutouts, claim 18 victories in 19 starts and string together 53 consecutive scoreless innings. He topped that off with three complete-game victories in the World Series, dispelling once and for all the notion that he was best suited to playing the outfield.

Coombs' playing career eventually was shortened by a lengthy bout with typhoid fever. But he never stopped loving, learning and teaching baseball as a major league manager and coach, as the author of one of the most thorough how-to books ever written about the game and finally as

5. Pitcher: Jack Coombs

the beloved and highly-respected head coach at Duke University.

John Wesley Combs was born in 1882 in the small town of LeGrand, Iowa, just east of Marshalltown. He was the oldest child of Frank and Ellen Snow Coombs, a Quaker couple who had traveled from their home in Maine to procure a piece of land in Iowa through the Homestead Act. Things apparently did not work out in Iowa because Frank Coombs, a blacksmith by trade, ultimately took his family back to Maine. John—most family members called him by that name through his entire life—was only four years old when his parents moved back east and bought a farm near Kennebunk, a coastal town in southern Maine.[2]

Jack Coombs.

Coombs grew up to be a tremendous all-around athlete, first at Freeport High School, then at Colburn Classical Institute and finally at Colby College in Waterville, Maine. Slightly more than six feet tall and weighing 185 pounds, he was a multi-sport star at Colby—a running back and tackle on the football team, a sprinter on the track team and captain of the basketball team. In baseball, his favorite sport, he played pretty much every position at one time or another. There were even rumblings that he might have tried his hand at tennis.

Coombs also starred for a handful of semi-pro baseball teams throughout New England in the summer months and his pitching skills eventually caught the eye of Tom McGillicuddy, Connie Mack's brother, who lived in Worcester, Massachusetts. He had several people tell him about Coombs and may have seen him pitch against Holy Cross, and he told his brother he should sign the kid.[3]

Coombs had every intention of graduating from Colby in 1906, then continuing on to do graduate work at MIT and becoming an accomplished chemist. Connie Mack had another thought. He convinced Coombs that he could make good money playing baseball to help pay for his MIT tuition. He signed a contract stipulating that he be allowed to finished his college career and graduate, then join the Athletics in the middle of the 1906 season. He would be paid $2,400 a season,[4] probably much more than he could expect to earn as a chemist.

Coombs, destined to forever be known as Colby Jack, finished his college career in glorious fashion, shutting out the University of Maine 1–0 and hitting a home run for the only run, then blanking Bowdoin College 6–0 to win the Maine state championship.

Within days after graduation, he joined the Athletics, becoming one of the first college players to join a major league club. It was an eye-opening experience for a 23-year-old fresh from taking chemistry exams and attending Delta Upsilon fraternity functions, and Coombs, who became an accomplished storyteller, relished telling the tale of his first day in the big leagues.

"I was out there tossing a few to a rookie catcher and in a few minutes, a big elephant with arms like a gorilla's came lumbering up," Coombs said. "He had a big wad of tobacco in his jaw and when he spit it was a like a shower bath if you were to the windward. Well, I thought I'd give the big scoundrel a show and I drew back and let my fast ball fly. The big gorilla waved one of the catchers over and he drew back and let a fast one fly. Well, sir, when I tried to see that ball go in there, I was amazed. Why, it threw out steam. But, I thought, maybe I can show him up with my curve. I threw it and, if I do say it myself, it had a right good hop on it. Then he let his go and, by the gollies, I've never seen anything like it in my life. It curved in and out and sideways. With that exhibition of how they pitched them in the majors, I was all ready to go pack up and go back to Dad's farm at Kennebunk."[5]

Then he found out the big man next to him was the incomparable Rube Waddell, one of the most naturally gifted pitchers ever to play the game.

It didn't take long for Coombs to show that he also belonged in the majors. He threw a seven-hit shutout against Washington in his major league debut on July 5 and within two months made an even larger splash.

On September 1, he matched up with the Boston Americans and fellow rookie Joe Harris in a memorable duel. Both men pitched 24 innings. Coombs allowed 15 hits but he struck out 18 batters (then a major league record) and finally won the battle, 4–1.

The modest Coombs always gave credit in later years to the guidance he received from catcher Mike Powers and from Connie Mack in that game. It also didn't hurt that Powers threw out five would-be base-stealers.

"I was nothing but a big overgrown kid and didn't know what it was all about," Coombs said. "I can't take credit for that 24-inning victory. I just threw the ball where I was told. Powers knew all the batters. I had pretty good control that day and threw the ball where Mike and Connie signaled."[6]

According to one report, Coombs was so physically drained by the game that all he could consume for a day or two afterward was "beef tea."[7] But four days later, he was back on the mound again, throwing another complete game in a 3–1 victory over Washington.

He finished his rookie season with a 10–10 record while throwing 173 innings in just half a season. It's small wonder that Coombs first began to experience soreness in his arm in the closing weeks of the season.

He encountered more arm problems in the early stages of the 1907 season. Mack let him go 14 innings in cold, damp conditions on opening day and in a June 27 game, Coombs felt something tear in the arm as he threw a pitch. He sat out nearly two months and still was not quite the same when he returned to action in August. He finished with a 6–9 record but one good thing came out of that season. During a spring training swing through Palestine, Texas, he met an attractive young nurse named Mary Elizabeth Russ. He married her three years later and spent the rest of his life at her side.

Coombs' arm still wasn't quite right in 1908 and when starting outfielders Socks Seybold and Rube Oldring were injured in spring training, Mack decided Coombs was the best man to fill the void. He began playing him in right field on a regular basis. Coombs batted over .300 for awhile and finished the season at .255. He was destined to bat a solid .235 for his career.

He didn't take the mound in a game until the middle of June but he soon was back to being a full-time pitcher, recording a 7–5 record with a 2.00 earned run average.

He was 12–11 with a 2.32 ERA in 1909 as the A's finished 3½ games behind first-place Detroit. "The Colby Carbine"—another of his many nicknames—was beginning to blossom as a pitcher.

Coombs always had been a hard thrower, but he didn't find stardom until he gained control of an overhand curve ball that took a sudden drop as it approached the plate.

"Coombs was one of the greatest pitchers who ever lived, because he mastered the greatest of all twirling assets, the drop ball that does not break from the right-handed batter," veteran catcher and coach Malachi Kittridge once explained. "I don't mean one of those outdrops, but a ball that comes up to the plate squarely in the center and falls from one to two feet without changing its lateral direction."[8]

Mack described it as "a mighty hard ball to hit, and was Jack's best delivery in his later big years."[9]

Coombs struggled a little early in 1910 and Mack briefly dropped him from the starting rotation, but the 27-year-old really hit his stride in the middle of the season. He pitched the first of his 13 shutouts that season on June 22 against the New York Highlanders. He added five more shutouts in July, three in August and four in September. He won 10 games in July alone and on August 4, he and Chicago's Ed Walsh engaged in another amazing marathon duel. For 16 innings, neither of them allowed a run before the game was called on account of darkness, ending in a scoreless tie. Coombs allowed only three hits and struck out 18 in what he often referred to as the best game he ever pitched.

His run of greatness continued on through the pennant race. He did not allow a run from September 5 to September 25, going 53 consecutive innings without an opposing player crossing home plate. He pitched six scoreless innings in relief in the first game of a doubleheader against the White Sox on September 25, then finally lost his scoreless streak in the second inning of the second game.

In one remarkable 16-day period, Coombs threw 10 complete games and finished two other games, earning yet another nickname—"Iron Man." His final record was 31–9 with a 1.30 ERA. Not only did he have 13 shutouts, but he had 12 other games in which he allowed only one run. In 353 innings pitched that season, he did not allow a single home run.

Not surprisingly, Philadelphia won the pennant by 13 games and Coombs carried his Iron Man act into the World Series. Mack used only two pitchers in the series—Coombs and Chief Bender—and the A's won it in five games. Coombs pitched complete game victories in Games 2, 3 and 5—all in a span of six days—although they weren't exactly dominating performances. He allowed 24 hits and issued 14 walks in 27 innings in the series, joining Christy Mathewson as one of only two men ever to win three times in a five-game World Series. Just for good measure, Coombs also batted .385 and drove in three runs in the Series.

In 1911, he won a league-high 28 games and the A's won the pennant again by a wide margin (13½ games), but Coombs' ERA plummeted to 3.53. He led the American League in games started, but he also allowed more runs and hits than any other hurler in the league. It also ended up being his best season as a hitter. He batted .319 and drove in 23 runs, equaling the total he had three years earlier when he was an outfielder, and the two home runs he hit that season both came in extra innings—in the 14th inning against St. Louis on July 17 and in the 11th inning against Detroit on August 29.

The Athletics faced the New York Giants in the World Series and Coombs outdueled Mathewson in a 3–2, 11-inning victory in Game 3, allowing only three hits. He started again in Game 5 but tore a groin muscle when his spikes caught on the mound in the sixth inning. He had a 3–1 lead at the time, but he continued to pitch and eventually allowed the Giants to tie the score. When he grimaced in pain after beating out a bunt in the top of the 10th inning, Mack removed him from the game. The A's went on to lose the contest in the bottom of the 10th, but they clinched their second straight world title when Bender pitched them to victory in Game 6.

The groin seemingly did not heal correctly and Coombs missed a month of action with the same injury early in 1912 although he eventually came back to finish with a 21–10 record.

His physical ailments continued in 1913 and this time it was something much more serious than a groin injury. It nearly cost Coombs his life.

He began feeling sick with a high fever during spring training in Alabama and the ailment originally was thought to be either ptomaine poisoning or pleurisy.[10] He started two games early in the season but was ineffective, giving up six earned runs in 5⅓ innings. Thinking he was suffering from a bad case of the flu, doctors hospitalized him and soon determined that he had typhoid fever, and that the disease had invaded his spine. While newspapers were full of stories about Coombs' illness and it was commonly known within the team that it was typhoid, it was not reported as such until later in the season. Even in later years, Coombs' 1913 affliction frequently was referred to as a back injury. Such was the stigma of typhoid, a disease not unlike salmonella in that it thrives in unsanitary surroundings.

Coombs was said to be near death at one point in May and it's entirely possible that it might have killed someone who was not a finely-tuned professional athlete.

In June, there were reports that Coombs would be moved from the hospital in Atlantic City to his home in Maine to continue his recuperation and that he would be back pitching by the middle of August.[11] He did try to work out with the Athletics in August but that led to a relapse and a return to the hospital.

Typhoid fever was common in that era but having it afflict the spine was rare enough that doctors were not entirely sure how to treat it. They placed Coombs' upper body in a plaster cast at one point and finally subjected him to 17 weeks of bed rest, in which he was laid flat on his back and hooked to a device that hung weights from his neck and feet to stretch his spine. There were some reports in later years that Coombs even devised the contraption himself.[12]

One news report in October painted a dark picture: "As the days went by and Coombs grew gray and hollow-eyed there was doubt in the minds of the doctors whether the man who was making the great, game fight would not lose altogether and never leave his pulley-rigged bed alive."[13]

The same story, however, indicated that his spirits were buoyed by listening to reports of the Athletics winning another World Series. The wife of Ira Thomas, his old catcher, gave him play-by-play over the phone and it helped that Coombs' best friend and mentor, Eddie Plank, played a major role in the championship.[14]

Coombs' weight dropped from his normal 185 pounds to 126 at one point, but he gradually recovered. It was reported in May 1914 that he had finally defeated typhoid and would return to action in July.[15] It actually took a little longer than that. He pitched a few innings in exhibition games against Syracuse in July and against Grand Rapids in early August, and finally returned to active duty in late September. He made just two starts that season, worked only eight innings and gave up four runs.

Philadelphia won the pennant again for the fourth time in five years, but in the World Series it lost to Boston's "Miracle Braves," who had come from last place on the fourth of July to win the National League pennant.

Mack saw the start of a decline and decided it was time to dismantle his powerful team. He began trading and releasing some of his top players and on November 1, he put all three of his stalwart pitchers—Coombs, Bender and Plank—on waivers on the same day.

Bender and Plank ended up in the Federal League, a third major league that had sprouted up to compete with the AL and NL. Coombs landed with the Brooklyn Robins, managed by Wilbert Robinson.

At the age of 32, he still was young enough to make a comeback and despite having missed nearly two full seasons, he had a better ERA in 1915 (2.53) than he had in winning 20-plus games for the A's in 1911 and 1912. Without as strong a supporting cast, he had a more modest 15–10 record.

He put together another solid season for the Robins in 1916, going 13–8 with a 2.66 ERA and Brooklyn won the NL pennant. They lost the World Series to the Boston Red Sox in five games but the one victory came in Game 3 when Coombs claimed a 4–3 win.

He continued to pitch two more seasons for the Robins but all those years of throwing overhand curves had taken their toll on his right elbow. There were some reports that his right arm ended up being shorter than his left because of the strain.[16] The battle with typhoid may have had some residual effect, too.

Coombs had a sub-.500 record and an ERA of close to 4.00 in both 1917 and 1918, and was openly disgruntled with the amount of work he got. He pitched in only 58 games in those two seasons, making just 34 starts. After losing a 1–0 pitcher's duel with the Giants' Pol Perritt late in the season—a game that was completed in an astonishing 57 minutes—Coombs confirmed what had been rumored all season. He was retiring. As the game ended, he walked off the field and flipped his glove to Wilbert Robinson, telling him, "You can have this glove. I won't need it anymore."[17]

He planned to retire to Texas to go into business with his father-in-law, much to the delight of his wife, Mary. But he couldn't stay away from the game. When the Philadelphia Phillies offered to make him their manager just a few months later, Coombs accepted.[18]

He quickly found, however, that the Phillies' ownership didn't share his unrelenting commitment to winning. He "resigned" in mid-season with an 18–44 record although Coombs told reporters he actually had been fired, noting that he had been told "his services were no longer needed."[19] He also served as a coach with Detroit in 1920 and was pressed into duty in a pair of uneventful relief appearances.

He finally found his true calling by going back to the college ranks. Coombs had dabbled in coaching at the college level a few years earlier when he helped the baseball team for Rice Institute in Houston get ready for the 1918 season. Although he is listed in some record books as having been Rice's coach that spring, he left the Owls very early in their season to join the Robins for his final major league campaign.[20] He also helped John E. Anderson coach the Rice football team that fall.

In 1921, he dove into college coaching on a full-time basis, becoming the head baseball coach at Williams College in the northwest corner of Massachusetts. After four years there, he spent another four years as the pitching coach at Princeton from 1925–28.

Down in Durham, North Carolina, Duke University was expanding its campus and also looking to upgrade its athletic programs under the stewardship of president William Preston Few, and it found the right man to guide its baseball program in Jack Coombs.

Coombs ended up staying at Duke for 24 years, compiling a record of 382–171, winning five Southern Conference championships and taking the Blue Devils to the College World Series in his final season. Over that time, he produced 47 major league players, including Pittsburgh Pirates shortstop Dick Groat, a five-time All-Star and the National League MVP in 1960.

Coombs also oversaw the building of a new baseball stadium on campus in 1931, modeled after Shibe Park in Philadelphia. It was remodeled in 1984 and renamed Jack Coombs Field.

Coombs and his wife Mary owned homes in Maine and in her hometown of Palestine, Texas, but at Duke they lived in a dormitory suite at Crowell Quadrangle on the Duke campus and ate most of their meals at the student union.

"I spend my winters in Texas, my summers in Maine and my springs and my autumns at Duke," Coombs said. "What more could I want?"[21]

Coombs became a popular figure on the campus, greeting almost everyone with a cheerful "Hello, kid." Billy Werber, a major league veteran who was Coombs' shortstop from 1928–30, described him as "the most beloved teacher or coach to ever walk the Duke campus."[22] (Obviously, this was long before the arrival of Mike Kzryzewski as the school's basketball coach.)

Jack and Mary, who he almost always referred to as "Miss Mary," never had any children of their own and they embraced the student body as their own.

Duke vice president Dr. Charles E. Jordan said Jack and Mary "belonged to the students and the university community at large and were not just the special property of their baseball boys. He was a great coach but he was even greater as a counselor and a friend of youth throughout the student body."[23]

Dr. Lenox Baker, the team doctor for Duke athletic teams in five decades, added, "He used to walk across the Quad and was a Pied Piper. Coombs would pick up a crowd of students and they'd walk with him. They just wanted to be with him, talk to him and listen to his ideas."[24]

Coombs' players fondly remembered his gentle nature and a crisp but subtle sense of humor. He once issued a catcher's mask, a set of shin guards and a chest protector to an outfielder who had dropped two fly balls in the same game. Larry Karl of the *Durham Herald* noted that Coombs "could always find a laugh even in the darkest moments."[25]

One day as he and Mary were walking across the campus, she slipped on some ice and went down in a heap in spite of Coombs' efforts to catch her. As she laid prone on the sidewalk writhing in pain, the coach bent over her, gave the safe sign like an umpire and said, "Nice slide, Mary."[26]

He almost never raised his voice and never embarrassed a player in front of the rest of the team. Buried deep in the Duke archives is a list of bullet points of Coombs' coaching philosophy, hand-scrawled by the man himself. Near the top is "teach players in gentle and sometimes stern words but never with verbal abuse or ridiculing. Keep negative remarks to ourself."[27]

Another of the hallmarks of Coombs' post-playing career was a compulsion for teaching the game to others. He was a frequent speaker at camps and clinics and put on a series of baseball "schools" across the country, sponsored by the Atlantic Richfield petroleum company and Kellogg's cereal. Coombs reported putting on 87 such clinics during the summer of 1940 and 94 in 1941.[28]

Jack Coombs won 382 games in 24 years as the head baseball coach at Duke (Duke University Archives).

Needless to say, Coombs' own players were extremely well-schooled ... literally. All of them were required to take regular credited classes in baseball that Coombs taught himself. "A coach makes certain that every member of his squad knows the rules governing the game," he once wrote. "Every season he should review the rules carefully and demonstrate every essential point upon the field."[29]

One of his former players, Russ Bergmann, said no Duke player missed one of Coombs' classes if he expected to play for the Blue Devils.[30] Bergmann was one of many who went on to become a coach himself, employing all the things taught to him by the coach who referred to himself as "the old man."

"He was, as far as I'm concerned, the greatest teacher of baseball that has ever lived in this country," said another ex-player, Crash Davis.[31]

Coombs eventually took the manual he assembled for teaching the class and made it into a textbook on the sport. It contains a chapter on each position and meticulously and painstakingly covers every aspect of that position point by point, much like what you would expect from someone who had once been an aspiring scientist.

Famed sportswriter Grantland Rice and Connie Mack both wrote forewords for the book published in 1937 and entitled *Baseball: Individual Play and Team Strategy*. "His book on baseball is by all odds the most complete I have ever seen," Rice wrote. "It is the type of book that baseball has needed for a long time." Mack wrote that the book was the first of its kind ever written, adding that "here we have everything, between the covers of *one* book, about playing the game correctly."[32]

The *Charlotte Observer* reported following the 1941 season that Coombs was getting tired and planned to retire,[33] but he stayed on for 11 more years after that. He may have stayed even longer except that Duke had a mandatory retirement age of 70.

After chalking up a career-high 31 victories and taking his team to the College World Series in 1952, Coombs stepped down. He insisted on keeping his farewell low-key, telling the crowd at his final home game that he loved every minute of his time at Duke. He was presented with a collection of letters from well-wishers and a full set of fishing gear.

"I'll miss the boys," Coombs was quoted as saying, "but I'll catch all the damn catfish in Texas."[34]

He and Mary had accumulated a large amount of real estate in Palestine through the years and they made their permanent home there although he never got teaching out of his blood. He held free baseball clinics in the Texas town for coaches and players every year for the rest of his life.

As with so many players of his era, he also spent a lot of time in the outdoors, fishing for catfish and hunting quail. He had been accidentally shot in the leg by a hunting partner in 1919 and lost a finger on his left hand in 1936 when the shotgun he was carrying malfunctioned. He underwent four surgeries on the hand before it healed properly.[35]

He also spent his later years reaping honors from his long career, including a couple from his alma mater. In 1946, Colby College conferred an honorary masters degree on him and in 1951, the school named its baseball field after him.

On April 15, 1957, Coombs walked a few blocks to downtown Palestine to buy some donuts and as he was walking home, he began to feel ill. At home, he laid down and died of a heart attack at the age of 74.

From both the major leagues and the college ranks, came an outpouring of praise along with expressions of disbelief that Coombs never was considered a strong candidate for the baseball Hall of Fame.

Frank "Home Run" Baker, the third baseman on those old Athletics championship teams, said, "He was not only a great pitcher but a wonderful man. He certainly should be voted into the Hall of Fame."[36]

5. Pitcher: Jack Coombs

The drawback with Coombs as a Hall of Fame candidate obviously was the relative brevity of his playing career. Despite his brilliance of 1910–12, a 2.78 career ERA and a 5–0 record in World Series play, he had only 158 regular-season wins. Typhoid robbed him of two years in his prime in which he likely would have won another 50 games.

Many, however, feel his contributions to the sport as a college coach and teacher should be factored into his Hall of Fame worthiness.

Dick Herbert, sports editor of the *Raleigh News & Observer*, noted that "there are some short memories in baseball. Pitchers of lesser ability who made no contribution to the sport after their playing days made the honor ahead of him. But Old Man Jack can rest with the satisfaction that all of his boys rate him No. 1 of them all."[37]

Catcher
Hank Severeid

"Hank has never drawn the credit due him as a catcher for the reason that he has never catered to the spectacular in baseball. He hasn't had time to be spectacular. He has been too busy catching."—Sportswriter Norman E. Brown[1]

In 15 years in the major leagues, Hank Severeid slugged a grand total of 17 home runs although he did manage to bat a very solid .289. In all likelihood, Severeid would have been embraced as a valuable member of any team even if he had batted .089.

There may not ever have been a more astute and fundamentally sound catcher in the major leagues than Severeid, who emerged from humble beginnings in Story City, Iowa, to catch 1,390 games at the major league level and another 1,190 in the minor leagues. He caught so many games that he was mentioned in a "Ripley's Believe it or Not" column in 1930[2] and he continued to catch for several more years after that.

In all those years, Severeid dropped exactly one pop fly.[3] In one mind-boggling stretch that spanned most of the 1922 season, he threw out 51 of 53 attempted base-stealers.[4] He is the only catcher in history ever to catch no-hitters on back-to-back days.

He was known as the "detective of the diamond" for his on-field acumen. "As an analyst of the hitters, there is not a receiver in baseball who can cope with Severeid," one observer wrote.[5] *San Antonio Light* sportswriter Harold Scherwitz said at the time of Severeid's death in 1968 that the veteran catcher "lived the game on and off the field" and was "unswervingly dedicated to the profession that was his life, studious in a quest for perfection."[6]

6. Catcher: Hank Severeid

Henry Levai Severeid was born in Story City in 1891, the second youngest of nine sons born to Lars and Maria Severeid. Lars, a stone mason, and Maria had immigrated from Norway and as their boys grew, most of them developed an affinity for baseball. A group photo of the 1907 Story City town team shows four Severeid brothers—Hank, Oscar, Chris and Charles.

In the early days, the Story City team played in Marvick's pasture just west of the train station but as the game grew in popularity, a small wooden stadium was built in town.[7]

Hank started out as a batboy for the team at the age of eight in 1899. Older brother Oscar taught him the basics and little Hank began a lifelong quest to learn as much as he could about the game. He started out as the team's "funny man," an archaic term for a player who filled in as needed at any position, but when the team walked over to the rival town of Roland for a game one day in 1905, the regular catcher couldn't make it. At the age of 14, Severeid was pressed into service behind the plate and apparently took to it immediately. Within three years, he was getting paid to do it.

In fact, four Severeid boys at one time earned a living in baseball. Oscar played in the Kansas State League and later became a minor league umpire. Charles and youngest brother Elmer played in the Western League.

Hank also signed to play in the Western League in 1908, playing for the Sioux City Packers, who won the league title under the management of fellow Iowan Ducky Holmes. Severeid batted .224 in 63 games and began a three-year trek through the minor league ranks in his home state.

He spent time in 1909 playing for both the Waterloo Lulus and the Burlington Pathfinders of the Class D Central Association.

Hank Severeid.

Hank Severeid (top row, second from right) was one of four Severeid brothers on the 1907 Story City town team (courtesy Story City Historical Society).

He was nearly flawless behind the plate in both places and batted .302 in 25 games at Burlington to earn a job the following season with the Ottumwa Packers in the same league. He had a breakout season there, hitting .304 in 105 games.

That was enough to convince the Cincinnati Reds to bring him all the way from the Class D minors to the major leagues. The Reds bought his rights for $3,000 and a few weeks before his 20th birthday Severeid became the youngest catcher in the National League.

He didn't see a lot of action with the Reds. He served as an understudy to veteran Larry McLean and played in only 87 games over two seasons. After going 0 for 6 at the plate to open the 1913 season, the Reds sold him to Louisville of the American Association. Severeid told a reporter many years later that he asked to be sent to the minors so that he could get regular playing time and further develop his skills.[8]

He batted .278 in the remainder of that season and really hit his stride at Louisville in 1914, batting .317 with six homers, 10 triples and 24 doubles in 143 games.

That performance caught the eye of the St. Louis Browns and their 33-year-old manager. Thirty years later, Branch Rickey would make a much more significant, far-reaching acquisition when he signed Jackie Robinson to play for the Brooklyn Dodgers, but during the winter of 1914–15 he felt pretty good about hiring Hank Severeid to catch for the Browns.

Severeid made a big impression right away in St. Louis. In the fourth game of the 1915 season, the Browns trailed the White Sox 3–0 entering the final inning. Chicago pitcher Hi Jasper had baffled them all day, but the Browns got something going in the bottom of the ninth. Tillie Walker drove in a run to make it 3–1 and Severeid came to bat with two runners on base. The first three pitches were out of the strike zone and he looked over at Rickey, who gave him the go-ahead to swing at the next pitch if he liked it. The youngster from Story City liked it a lot and clubbed a three-run homer off the scoreboard to win the game.[9]

Owner Robert Hedges had the ball gold-plated and gave it to Severeid, who kept it as a treasured keepsake for the rest of his life.[10]

It began a long association between the catcher and the American League franchise, which exists today as the Baltimore Orioles. Over the next 10 seasons Severeid emerged as one of the elite catchers in baseball, one of the few shining lights for a team that only occasionally contended and never got to the World Series until 1944.

Severeid was an old-school catcher who was adamant that pitchouts were a waste of time, an unnecessary tactic in trying to stop opposing teams from running.[11] Besides, his throwing arm was so deadly accurate he didn't need pitchouts.

He had a gentle, nurturing effect on pitchers and seemed able to coax them over any obstacle or through any jam.

Although only average in size at 6 feet, 175 pounds, Severeid also was among the toughest men around. Harold Scherwitz described him as "calm and dignified" and noted that he didn't get involved in fights on the field, but that doesn't mean he backed down from anyone. If a baserunner came barreling into the plate with spikes high, intent on inflicting injury or jarring the ball loose, Severeid made sure to apply the tag with added force to discourage such tactics in the future.[12]

He had a few encounters with combustible Detroit Tigers player-manager Ty Cobb, who intimidated almost everyone he came into contact with. Cobb once snarled at Severeid that he was going to run on him every time he got on base in a game and he did succeed in stealing three bases that day. But Severeid also gunned him down three times. Cobb often said it was the only time in his life he was thrown out three times in one game.

During a game in 1924, Cobb charged out to the mound with bat in hand and waved it menacingly at Browns rookie pitcher Charlie Root. He supposedly called Root a "fresh bush bastard" and threatened to do him bodily harm. Severeid was there to plant himself between Cobb and the youngster. "You lay one hand on that kid and I'll beat you to death with this mask," he told Cobb. The Georgia Peach quickly went back to the batter's box.[13]

Severeid sustained innumerable broken fingers. It's the one blemish doctors found when he was examined for the draft during World War I. He also ruptured his appendix in November of 1919, was knocked unconscious in a collision at the plate with Babe Ruth in 1916 and once suffered a severed artery when a baserunner spiked him at the plate. He supposedly sat calmly as the wound was stitched up without anesthetic.[14] None of it kept him off the field for very long.

"They signed me to catch and catch I did even with busted fingers," Severeid once told Scherwitz.[15]

At the plate, Severeid swung a bat that weighed 48 ounces, about 50 percent heavier than most bats wielded by modern-day major leaguers, but he made tremendous contact. He struck out once every 27.8 at-bats, setting a record for the Browns/Orioles franchise that isn't likely to ever be broken.

Severeid was a respectable player for the Browns in 1915 and 1916, and he took his performance to a higher level in 1917, catching 143 of the Browns' 154 games and batting .265.

It was early in that season that he achieved his greatest claim to fame when he was on the receiving end of no-hitters on consecutive days. The feat probably would have received greater attention except that the first of the two gems initially was not ruled to be a no-hitter.

On May 5, Browns lefthander Ernie Koob went up against White Sox ace Eddie Cicotte, who had thrown a no-hitter himself a few weeks earlier. Koob threw a 1–0 shutout but Chicago's Buck Weaver originally was credited with a hit on a ground ball he hit to second baseman Ernie Johnson in the first inning. Official scorer J.B. Sheridan was not even in the press box when the play occurred, but his fellow writers told him it should be a hit.[16] Sheridan later was persuaded by the Browns to call it an error and Koob had his no-hitter, even though it took a few weeks of haggling and a ruling by American League president Ban Johnson to make it happen.[17]

The following day, May 6, Browns veteran Bob Groom threw another no-hitter against the White Sox in the second game of a double-header. This time, there was no controversy. In fact, Groom came on in relief at the end of the first game, then worked the entire second game and actually hurled 11 hitless innings that day.

Severeid was behind the plate to coax everything he could out of two pitchers who were hardly Hall of Fame material. Koob won just 23 games in his career and Groom led the American League in losses that season with 19.

Severeid, who never earned more than $8,500 in a single season, felt he was deserving of more money from the Browns and he held out at the start of 1918, threatening to go into the Army if he didn't get what he wanted. He actually sent a letter to Ban Johnson on January 1, 1918, saying he planned to enlist.[18]

About a third of the way through the season, he did it. He could have possibly applied for officers training, but instead became a private in the tank corps and was sent almost directly to the front in France. The armistice ending World War I was signed at almost that exact time, however. Severeid's commanding officer wrote a note to the *Kansas City Times* early in 1919 saying that fellow soldiers didn't even know that Severeid was a major league ballplayer. He was so modest that he never even told them what he did back in the States.[19]

It wasn't long after he returned from the war that Severeid suffered a ruptured appendix that threatened to derail his career. Some newspaper reports even implied that he might be near death,[20] but he came back to bat .248 in 112 games in 1919 and .277 in 1920.

He got married after that season to Adele Bertha Messmer. They were married for 48 years and had three daughters.

Married life seemingly did something to Severeid's hitting skills. Or maybe it was the livelier ball that they began using in the majors. Whatever it was, Severeid began putting up significantly better offensive numbers in the next few years. He batted .324 with only nine strikeouts in 1921 and followed that with seasons of .321, .308 and .308.

At the same time, the Browns actually became a contender. They finished third in 1921 and lost the pennant to the Yankees by just one game in 1922 with a lineup that included seven .300 hitters. "What a club!" Severeid recalled in an interview many years later. "It was worth a pitcher's life to get the call to duty against us."[21]

Severeid also seemingly improved defensively with age. He set what was then a major league record for fielding percentage by a catcher (.993) in 1921, committing only three errors all season with two of them coming on the same play. A ground ball was hit to the infield with the bases loaded and when the ball was thrown home, Severeid failed to step on the plate. He then threw wildly to first base for another error.[22] Other than that one play, he was nearly flawless for the entire season. The following year, he had his amazing stretch in which he threw out 51 of 53 attempted base-stealers.

Famed sportswriter Frederick Lieb wrote that Severeid was the most valuable player on the Browns next to Hall of Fame first baseman George Sisler and possibly star pitcher Urban Shocker. "Hank is a kicker and a fighter, and a darn good catcher," Lieb wrote. "On the whole, Severeid is the best of the ... catchers, taking only the catching end of the game into account. Severeid is in the game every day, crabbing away, but always working hard for his team. He throws exceedingly well, and is a splendid man at putting the ball on a runner."[23]

The Browns dropped back into their accustomed place in the second division in 1923 and it appeared as though Severeid was destined to go through his entire career without playing in a World Series.

He finished sixth in the voting for the American League Most Valuable Player award in 1924, but the Browns began phasing him out in 1925. He played in only 34 games early in the season, batting a torrid .367, and he was traded to Washington in mid-June. The Senators had a stalwart catcher in Muddy Ruel, but Severeid gave them a lift, continued his hot hitting and helped propel the Senators to the pennant.

"Hank is old enough to be slipping but he is by no means on his last legs," sportswriter Norman E. Brown wrote. "He has taken perfect care of himself in his 34 years."[24]

Severeid got into just one game against Pittsburgh in the World Series, starting Game 6 and going 1 for 3.

Washington waived him in July of the following season, but he landed with another top team, the New York Yankees, and again found himself on a pennant-winning club. When starting catcher Pat Collins injured his arm late in the season, Severeid was called upon to start every game of the 1926 World Series against the Cardinals. In the deciding Game 7 at Yankee Stadium, he came to bat with two outs in the sixth inning and doubled in Joe Dugan to cut the St. Louis lead to 3–2. The immortal Grover Cleveland Alexander, then in the twilight of his career, came in and got the last seven outs of the game to preserve the world championship for the Cardinals.

It was the last game Severeid ever played in the major leagues.

He spent much of the winter making public appearances back in Iowa, reliving the World Series for the Des Moines American Legion, the Webster City Elks, the Nevada Community Club and assorted other organizations.

The Yankees released him in January 1927 and in the weeks that followed there was speculation that Severeid would purchase the Lincoln, Nebraska, team in the Western League.[25] He apparently checked out the situation but didn't feel he was finished as a player. He signed instead with the Detroit Tigers, who farmed him out to the Sacramento Senators of the Pacific Coast League.

The PCL at that time was regarded almost on a par with the major leagues and it paid almost as well. Severeid's original Sacramento contract called for him to earn $1,000 a month. He spent five years in the league with the Senators and the Hollywood Stars, and in 1929, splitting time between those two teams, he had the best offensive season of his life. He batted a robust .359 in 142 games and belted more home runs in one season (24) than he had in his entire major league career. He went on to bat .367 and .347 with Hollywood the next two seasons, helping the Stars win the league title in 1930.

It was during his PCL years that Severeid was featured in Ripley's "Believe it or Not" for catching more games in the major and minor leagues combined than any catcher in history. Although many sources listed him as having caught 2,611 games, baseball-reference.com credits him with playing in 2,580 games, all but about 150 of those as a catcher.[26] His record for total games caught between the minors and majors since has been approached by several modern-day catchers and has been surpassed by Ivan Rodriguez and Carlton Fisk.

His PCL years weren't entirely joyous for Severeid. In February of 1930, just after he and his family had departed for the coast for another season, their house along the Skunk River back in Story City was almost completely destroyed by fire.[27]

As one of the most cerebral players of his era, it seemed inevitable that Severeid someday would run a ballclub of his own. It happened in 1932 when the Browns made him player-manager of their farm team at Wichita Falls in the Texas League. The team moved to Longview, Texas, in mid-season and after the season it was absorbed by the San Antonio Missions. Severeid then became the manager of that club.

Baseball interest was sagging in San Antonio at the time and Severeid was determined to change that. In a letter to George White of the *Dallas News*, he said, "San Antonio is through playing the role of door mat for the Texas League. The St. Louis Browns, who will operate the team there this year, intend to bend every effort to give the Alamo City a first-class, hustling nine that will be up in the race and furnish the fans an incentive for a real revival of interest."[28]

He told the *San Antonio Light* the same thing and was true to his word. The Missions won the Texas League pennant and energized their fans. Severeid became an instant hero there. When he did finally retire, he opted to make his home in San Antonio.

In his three years as manager of the Missions, he insisted on discipline and total dedication to the game.

"Severeid had two hard-and-fast rules," Harold Scherwitz wrote. "You showed up at the park in top shape to play your best, and you talked nothing but baseball. He fined some of his stars for not being at their best for the start of a game, and the fines weren't little ones in those days—$100 and up."[29]

He still played occasionally as a catcher for the teams he managed and he still was capable of swinging a potent bat. He hit .341 in 37 games for San Antonio in 1934.

Severeid also was interested in helping tutor younger players. At San Antonio in 1934, he began hosting the Missions Baseball School, an annual camp for boys. He expected about 50 kids to show up at the first one and was a little surprised when 150 turned out.[30]

He took great pride in knowing more about baseball and its intricacies than anyone. Prior to Texas League games, he delighted in presenting the umpires with obscure hypothetical situations and asking them what their ruling would be. They often ended up learning new nuances from the San Antonio manager.[31]

In 1936, Severeid went back to the Midwest as the manager of the Omaha Robin Hoods in the Western League, the league in which he had gotten his pro start. During the team's first visit to play the Des Moines team, more than 300 Story City residents bussed down to the capital city for what was labeled "Hank Severeid Night." But Severeid didn't stay with the troubled Omaha club for very long. The team's ballpark was severely damaged by a windstorm on July 21 and it temporarily moved its games to Lincoln. In the meantime, the ballpark in Omaha burned to the ground and on August 18, the team moved to Rock Island, Illinois. Severeid had stepped down as manager by then.

He went back to Texas as the manager at Galveston in 1937 and at the age of 46, he caught 44 games. On the final day of the season, he caught both ends of a doubleheader.

When he was in his 40s, Severeid insisted that his age on the official roster of the teams he managed always be listed as 39 and he appeared to be even younger than that. Even in the early days of his career, he was devoted to being in top physical condition. When Severeid first joined the Browns in 1915, Branch Rickey had his players do an 18-mile run to and from their clubhouse in spring training. Most of the players only made it for a mile or two. Severeid was the only one who did the full distance.[32]

As he grew older, he managed to stay in shape in a variety of ways. Like many native Iowans, he loved the sport of wrestling and was good friends with such stars of the sport as George Hackenschmidt and Doc Roller, and frequently worked out with wrestlers in the off-season.[33] He also enjoyed getting exercise in the great outdoors as a hunter and trapper during the off-season. He was an expert shot and served as president of the Story City chapter of the Izaak Walton League.[34]

After playing his last game at Galveston, Severeid briefly managed the minor league team in Durham, North Carolina, and served as a coach with Syracuse in the International League. He spent a few years overseeing the Cincinnati Reds' minor league system, starting a school for Reds prospects in Berkeley, California, then served as a scout for the Cubs for one year. He spent the rest of his years in the San Antonio area scouting for the Red Sox organization.

He put his years of baseball expertise into writing in 1941 when he and Charles Chapman, a former Cal-Berkeley professor who Branch Rickey had employed as a scout, co-authored *Play Ball! Advice to Young Ballplayers.*

Early in November of 1968, he was hospitalized in San Antonio with an undisclosed illness and six weeks later he died of a heart attack.

"There doubtless are some men of Severeid's dedicated cut in baseball today," Harold Scherwitz wrote. "But the game has changed and the gallant breed is dying out. Baseball is so much the worse for the loss of such fine men as Hank Severeid."[35]

Because some of his biggest contributions were largely intangible and because he spent most of his time with one of the low-profile franchises in the majors, Severeid has been largely forgotten for the things he did a century ago. Some have suggested that he might be worthy of Hall of Fame consideration even though he received less than one percent of the vote in 1948, the only year he appeared on the ballot. A blog devoted to Hall of Fame elections made a case for Severeid as a viable candidate in 2009. It pointed out that only one catcher who played in his era—Ray Schalk of the White Sox—made the Hall of Fame.[36] Schalk was no better than Severeid defensively and at the plate he batted only .253, 36 points lower than the Browns star.

Chances are, Severeid wouldn't care whether or not he is in the Hall of Fame. His legacy wasn't in some plaque so much as the way he was viewed by his contemporaries.

"As one noses around baseball people he hears only words of praise for Severeid, not only for his playing but also for his character," *Des Moines Register* columnist Sec Taylor wrote in 1932. "He is a straight, clean fellow, respected everywhere, and his long and successful record as a player and a hitter is a monument to the life he has led."[37]

Shortstop
Dave Bancroft

"The best thing about Bancroft is, he can think. He uses his brain. He is more than a great mechanical player."—Hall of Fame shortstop and manager Hughie Jennings[1]

When Dave Bancroft was inducted into baseball's Hall of Fame in 1971, eyebrows were raised and there were grumbles of favoritism. Two old New York Giants comrades, Bill Terry and Frankie Frisch, were on the special veterans committee that elected Bancroft and many figured that must be the only way a player who batted only .279 and hit only 77 home runs in his career could have gained such an honor.

But anyone who played alongside Bancroft during the 16 years he toiled in the National League had no qualms with the selection. Neither did those who played against him.

Although a less-than-prolific offensive force, Bancroft was an early-day Derek Jeter, a shortstop who played his position with so much skill and savvy that it defied definition by mere statistics. The consensus was that he was the best shortstop in baseball in the years following the Honus Wagner era. Hughie Jennings, a tremendous shortstop himself before going on to a lengthy career as a coach and manager, said simply, "Bancroft is one of the greatest shortstops in the history of the game."[2]

Veteran *New York Journal-American* sportswriter Frank Graham wrote that Bancroft was "almost perfect" in terms of his mechanics.[3]

"It is impossible that he ever had an equal at snatching a half-hop or making a cut-off of a throw from the outfield and picking off a careless runner on his way to the next base," Graham added. "In the 1921 World Series, he hamstrung the Yankees with seven cutoffs. At the plate, he was no window breaker but ... he was a tough man up there and got many a double and triple because he could run like a thief."[4]

Bancroft also was a highly intelligent player. When he first was traded to the Giants during his sixth year in the major leagues, he didn't need to be taught their signs. He already had digested and deciphered the signals of every team in the National League.[5]

Umpire Billy Evans, who doubled as a sportswriter, wrote in 1922 that Bancroft "effervesces enthusiasm.... He has brains and uses them.... In the field, Bancroft is a student. He analyzes his batters and plays for them, constantly shifting his position to meet conditions. He starts quickly on the ball, has a good arm and gets the ball away quickly and from any position."[6]

Bancroft was born in Sioux City, Iowa, in 1891, the youngest of three children of Frank and Ella Bancroft. Frank scratched out a living as a truck farmer and news vendor on the Milwaukee Railroad.

Dave Bancroft.

Dave attended Hopkins Grade School and Sioux City High School, and got his start in baseball playing for an amateur team sponsored by the Davis Clothing Company. He was so young he had to get permission from his father in order to become the team's shortstop.[7] Bancroft also picked up two or three dollars a game here and there playing for various town teams in the Sioux City area.

He still had a year of high school left when he signed to play for the Duluth team of the Minnesota-Wisconsin League in 1909. In mid-season, he was sent to the rival Superior (Wisconsin) Blues in the same league. He batted just

.210 in 111 games between the two teams with virtually no power. Of his 77 hits, 71 were singles. He also made his share of mistakes at shortstop, compiling a fielding percentage of only .917.

It was an inauspicious start, but Superior was to become a special place for Bancroft. He spent two more seasons there, becoming a fan favorite and developing into a solid player. He also met his wife, Edna, there and made Superior his off-season home for the rest of his life.

Bancroft was noticeably improved at the plate in his second season at Superior, raising his average to .267. The year after that, he batted .273 with 41 stolen bases and earned a promotion to Portland of the Pacific Coast League for 1912.

The five-foot, nine-inch, 160-pound switch-hitter still was a work in progress at the plate, though. He batted just .212 at Portland, was sent down to the Class B Northwestern League team in the same city for a year, then came back to the Portland PCL team in 1914 and batted .277 while displaying some real pop. Included among his hits were 14 triples and 35 doubles. He was a key component in helping Portland win the league title.

He won something else, too—a new nickname. Every time a pitcher served up a good-looking pitch, Bancroft loved to shout "beauty."[8] Before long, that's what his teammates were calling him. Some teammates also called him "Banny" as the years passed, but more often he was known to fans as Beauty Bancroft.

The Cleveland Indians held the rights to any player they wanted off the Portland roster with the New York Giants having the second choice, but both teams passed up the chance to bring Bancroft to the major leagues. Cleveland drafted second baseman Bill Rodgers and the Giants took third baseman Art Kores because they somehow got the idea that Bancroft might sign with a team in the Federal League, a third major league that popped up in 1914 to compete with the National and American Leagues.

Although the Giants later would employ Bancroft, they made the wrong choice this time. It was Kores who signed with the Federal League while Bancroft signed with the Philadelphia Phillies for the bargain price of $5,000.

The Phillies still were seeking a replacement for fan favorite Mickey Doolin, who had bolted to the Federal League a year earlier, and Bancroft gave them that and more. His biggest contributions were on defense. He immediately became one of the slickest fielders in the NL but he also batted .254, finished among the league leaders in walks and runs scored and amazingly tied for sixth in the league with a career-high seven home runs. He undoubtedly was helped by playing in Philadelphia's cozy Baker

Bowl, where it was only 280 feet down the right-field line and 300 to the power alley. Six of Bancroft's seven homers that season came at home.

The Phillies, a doormat in the years before that and for a long time afterward, stunned the world by winning the NL pennant. They then defeated the Boston Red Sox in the first game of the World Series behind the pitching of Grover Cleveland Alexander, but lost the next four in a row. Bancroft hit .294 in the Series, but only one other Phillies starter batted over .200.

It was the start of 5½-year run in Philadelphia in which Bancroft never hit more than .272 for a full season but earned a reputation as one of the league's toughest and smartest players. The Phillies contended for the pennant again in both 1916 and 17, but finished second both years. They lost out in 1916 largely because Bancroft sprained his ankle late in the season.

He injured his right ankle again sliding into second base on May 4, 1919, in a 4–3 victory over the Giants in the first major league game ever played in New York on a Sunday. He was carried off the field by teammates for what initially was called a sprain, but it later was determined that he had broken a couple of bones in the foot. Reports at the time indicated that he would be sidelined for at least two months and possibly the entire season,[9] but by July 1 Bancroft was back at shortstop for the Phillies.

For years, Giants manager John McGraw watched Bancroft from afar and admired his toughness and moxie. And early in the 1920 season he began maneuvering to get Bancroft on his side.

On May 22 in Chicago, Bancroft ended a string of 28 consecutive games without an error by botching a couple of ground balls and he was abruptly benched by Phillies manager Gavvy Cravath. Bancroft and Cravath had been at odds before—Bancroft had asked to be traded to Cincinnati around the time Cravath was named the team's manager—and now their simmering enmity became an open feud. Cravath sent Russ Wrightstone out to take over at shortstop in the middle of an inning and Bancroft refused to leave. Cravath came onto the field and spoke to him, and Bancroft finally stalked off. In the dugout, he threw his glove at Cravath, threatened him and began to move toward him menacingly before being restrained by teammates.[10]

"Cravath says I laid down on the job—stood around in the shortstop's position with my arms folded," Bancroft said. "I'll tell you it hurts to be called a quitter by the manager of the ball club to which you have given your best efforts for almost six years. I never 'jaked' on a baseball job in my life and Cravath knows it."[11]

7. Shortstop: Dave Bancroft

With Cravath and Bancroft at odds, McGraw saw his chance. He convinced Giants owner Charles Stoneham that they needed to pay a big price to acquire a player they could have had for a relatively small sum in 1915. They offered to give the Phillies their team captain, Art Fletcher, who had been the Giants' starting shortstop for nine years, plus pitching prospect Bill Hubbell and cash. At the time, the Giants denied that any money changed hands in the deal but in subsequent years the amount was reported to be anywhere from $50,000 to $100,000.[12]

Bear in mind that the Yankees had acquired Babe Ruth, one of the greatest home run hitters in history, from the Red Sox for $100,000 just six months earlier. The Giants may have offered the same amount plus an established veteran and another player in exchange for a disgruntled shortstop who hadn't hit a home run since 1917.

Philadelphia owner William Baker, a former New York police commissioner who never was adverse to peddling star players at their peak for large sums of money, could scarcely believe what the Giants were offering. Legend has it that he caught the next train to New York to consummate the deal in person.[13]

Philadelphia sportswriter T.V. Ziekursch was one of many who thought the Giants actually got the best of the deal: "So far as the actual value of the trade is concerned it is horrible from the Phillies' standpoint. There is simply no comparison of the relative value of Bancroft with Fletcher. Bancroft is worth a couple gross of Fletchers. But it does help the Giants."[14]

Ziekursch added: "Even in his palmy days Fletcher never compared with Bancroft in the field. Banny has no peer and few better shortstops ever lived. He was the fastest man on the Phillie team, equally good at getting hits to either side of him, and has the finest throwing arm of any infielder in baseball."[15]

Within three weeks, Bancroft validated the judgment of McGraw. He tied a major league record by collecting six hits in a game (all singles, of course) against his old chums, the Phillies, in an 18–3 win. He went on to bat .299 and finish second in the National League with 102 runs scored that season.

Bancroft became the final lynchpin in one of the most successful eras in Giants history. He was named the team captain the following year for a club that won the NL pennant each of the next three years and claimed two world titles.

In 1921, despite getting a late start of the season after undergoing a tonsillectomy, he batted .318 and reached career highs in stolen bases (17), triples (15), runs scored (121) and runs batted in (67). He hit for the cycle in a game on June 1 although after circling he bases for an inside-the-park home run, he passed out on the bench.[16] The Giants won the pennant by four games over Pittsburgh and beat the despised crosstown Yankees in eight games in what was then a best-of-nine World Series.

Bancroft played in every game in 1922 and batted a career-best .321 while also achieving career highs in hits (209) and doubles (41). Once again, the Giants beat the Yankees in the series, this time with a four-game sweep.

A 1922 story in the *Bridgeport* (Connecticut) *Telegram* called Bancroft the best shortstop in baseball and noted that "the remarkable part about Bancroft is that, at thirty years of age, he still is improving. In Philadelphia, 'Banny' was a great shortstop. In New York he not only is a high grade infielder, but one of the most dangerous batsmen in the game."[17]

In 1923, Bancroft suffered from leg injuries and an extended bout with pneumonia in June, and ended up missing more than 50 games over the course of the season. He still batted .304, though, and the Giants made it an all-New York series for the third straight season. This time, the power-packed Yankees prevailed, however, and McGraw began to look for ways to rebuild and revitalize his team.

McGraw told reporters he was willing to trade anyone on the team except second baseman Frankie Frisch, outfielder Ross Young and promising 20-year-old infielder Travis Jackson, who filled in for Bancroft during his absences in 1923. In mid–November he proved it, sending Bancroft to the Boston Braves as part of a five-player deal. Outfielders Casey Stengel and Bill Cunningham also went to Boston in exchange for pitcher Joe Oeschger and outfielder Billy Southworth, who was the Braves' team captain. The *New York Times* noted that because it involved the captains of both teams, the deal was "the most sensational of recent baseball history."[18]

McGraw admitted that Bancroft was "the best shortstop in baseball without a doubt" but he said he wanted to do a favor for former Giants pitcher Christy Mathewson, who was McGraw's closest friend and who was now the Braves' general manager. "Matty is the only man in baseball who could get Bancroft away from me," he added.[19]

McGraw also said part of his motivation for dealing a player he valued and admired was he wanted to give Bancroft a chance to become a manager himself. Bancroft was to be the player-manager of the Braves, fulfilling what he admitted was one of his ambitions.[20]

Mathewson also was present at the announcement of the trade and clearly was very pleased. McGraw asked him if he wanted to make some sort of statement. "What do you want me to say?" he asked, then pointed to Bancroft sitting nearby. "Here's my statement."[21]

The *Times* predicted big things for the new Braves manager. "Bancroft undoubtedly has the temperament and the brains that a big league manager needs.... He is a fighter but at the same time a keen student of baseball, and he never pushes men farther than they will go.... Bancroft is one of the finest team players in the game, and his presence is certain to steady both the infield and the outfield at Boston."[22]

At the age of 32, Bancroft became the youngest manager in the National League and at the time the only player-manager in the league, taking over a team that had finished in the bottom half of the league in seven of the previous eight seasons. He spent the winter back in Superior resting up for what the hometown paper said Bancroft "expects to be the hardest season in his career."[23]

He handled the dual role with the Braves for the next four seasons with mixed success. He missed almost half the 1924 season with a ruptured appendix, not playing in a game from July 1 to September 10, and the Braves finished last in the National League. But in 1925 they made significant improvements, jumping up to fifth place.

"It was the most talked of team in the two circuits and looms as a threatening one this year," sportswriter Norman E. Brown wrote during spring training in 1926. "Bancroft, after proving himself one of the game's greatest shortstops, is demonstrating his managerial ability. He is one of the keenest men the game boasts."[24]

But he couldn't build on the modest success of 1925. Boston was seventh in each of the next two years. Bancroft still was an effective player. He batted over .300 again in 1925 and '26, but his team was 114 games under .500 in the four seasons he was in charge.

He didn't just take a beating in the won-loss column either. On June 18, 1927, Bancroft walked in the seventh inning of a game against Pittsburgh at Forbes Field and as he was going to first base, catcher Earl Smith fired the ball to first base, whistling it past Bancroft's ear. The Boston manager turned and exchanged a few words with Smith, who the Braves had sold to the Pirates in the middle of the 1924 season, and when Bancroft scored later in the inning, he walked over to umpire Barry McCormick and complained about what Smith had done. Smith, who outweighed Bancroft by at least 20 pounds, responded by throwing down his catcher's mitt and punching Bancroft in the jaw.[25]

Bancroft was carried off the field and needed three stitches to close the cut on his jaw. Smith was fined $500 and suspended for 30 days.

Bancroft also sued Smith for $15,000. When the Pirates made a road trip to Boston later in the season, after he had served his suspension, Smith chose to stay home rather than face the Braves again.

Bancroft asked for and was given his release by the Braves following that 1927 season and he signed with the Brooklyn Robins the same day. It is unclear whether or not the Robins had to compensate Boston in some way. According to some reports, they may have paid the Braves $20,000.[26] Others have speculated that the Braves simply no longer wanted to pay Bancroft a reported $40,000 per season and were delighted to lighten their payroll.

Bancroft spent the next two seasons as the starting shortstop in Brooklyn. His offensive numbers declined but he was still a solid player.

Like many players in the latter stages of their careers, he saw changes in the game and in the players themselves that rubbed him the wrong way, and he voiced his chagrin in a December 1928 interview with Dan Desmond of the *Sioux City Journal*.

"The players aren't what they used to be," he told Desmond. "I can remember when they used to talk baseball morning, noon and night. Now? Well, as soon as a game is over, the topic of conversation ranges all the way from golf to hunting dogs. I guess it's too much of a business now.... Occasionally a club gets a kid who puts his whole heart and soul into winning, but the old spirit just isn't there any more."[27]

While he sounded a bit old school with such comments, Bancroft also was a visionary. In the same interview, he threw out the idea of having a designated hitter who would take the place of the pitcher in the batting order.[28] His suggestion came 45 years before the concept was put to actual use in the American League.

Bancroft also confessed in that interview that he couldn't see himself doing anything outside the sport that had become his life.

"I'll never quit baseball, I guess," he said. "I feel as young as I ever did and I look for 1929 to be a big season for me. When I am through as a player, I'll catch on as a manager somewhere. I get just as much a kick out of the game now as I did when I started."[29]

A year later, he was finished as a player. Brooklyn released him and he went back to the Giants with the title of assistant manager under McGraw.

He told the *Sioux City Journal* in yet another interview while back there visiting his parents, "My greatest pleasure in rejoining the Giants is to be back with a fighting ball club and with John McGraw, one of my dearest friends.... It's going to be tough if I have to sit around and watch the other fellows playing."[30]

He did see action in 10 games early in the 1930 season, collecting just one hit in 17 at-bats. He also managed a team of major league all-stars on a tour of Cuba following the season and openly aspired to be a big-league manager again.

McGraw, approaching the age of 60, was in poor health and sometimes unable to fulfill his managerial duties. Bancroft filled in for him on the bench many times in 1931 and early in 1932. By June of 1932, McGraw had had enough. He announced his retirement.

Bancroft seemed the logical successor but his lack of success as the boss in Boston was a major drawback. Because of that, owner Charles Stoneham lacked confidence in him.

Instead, the job went to Bill Terry, the team's hard-hitting 33-year-old first baseman who had been a rookie in Bancroft's last season with the Giants in 1923. When the season was over, Bancroft walked away from the major leagues forever.

He managed the Minneapolis Millers of the American Association in 1933 and got them to the championship series, but he was not retained. It was the middle of the great depression and the owner of the Millers wanted to save money by having a player-manager.

Bancroft later managed some lower-level minor league teams in his native Sioux City in 1937 and in St. Cloud, Minnesota, in 1946. He also managed the Chicago Colleens and the South Bend Blue Sox in the All-American Girls Professional Baseball League, made famous in the movie *A League of Their Own*.

After that, he went to work for the Interprovincial Pipeline Company as a warehouse manager for a few years, then retired in 1956.

He spent most of the last 15 years of his life enjoying the rich fishing and hunting around his adopted hometown of Superior, often inviting such former major league stars as Pie Traynor, Burleigh Grimes and Freddie Lindstrom to join him.

He died in Superior on October 7, 1972. His dream of being inducted into the Hall of Fame had been fulfilled little more than a year earlier although Bancroft was too ill to attend the ceremonies.

In the years since, the minor controversy surrounding his Hall of Fame election has faded if not disappeared altogether. Noted statistician Bill James wrote in 1995 that Bancroft's election was a "mistake" although he compared him to Yankees shortstop Phil Rizzuto, who also is in the Hall of Fame, and made no mention of the fact that the first third of Bancroft's career fell into the deadball era.[31]

Author and Society for American Baseball Research member David

S. Neft devised his own mathematical formula in 1985 with which to accurately compare shortstops from different eras. Neft's complex formula factors in hitting, fielding and baserunning, and pro-rates the numbers according to the era in which the players performed, distilling everything down to a single number. Such Hall of Famers as Lou Boudreau, Luke Appling, Ernie Banks, Arky Vaughan and Pee Wee Reese did not crack the top 10 on Neft's all-time list.[32]

Not surprisingly, he determined that the No. 1 shortstop of all-time was the incomparable Honus Wagner.

No. 2 was Beauty Bancroft.

8

Pitcher
Red Faber

"A batter cannot guess with Faber. His only chance is to close the eyes and hope the bat meets the ball."—Hall of Fame outfielder Goose Goslin[1]

When major league baseball outlawed the spitball in 1920, it acknowledged the fact that a handful of major league pitchers used the pitch extensively as part of their arsenal and it grandfathered the new rule into existence. It was determined that 17 pitchers would be permitted to continue applying moisture to the ball for the remainder of their careers. Urban Clarence "Red" Faber was among them.

But while many of those hurlers relied almost exclusively on the spitter, it was just one of many weapons in the Faber arsenal. He also had a good, sinking fastball and a slow but effective curve. New York Giants manager John McGraw once said Faber had the best drop curve he ever saw, but Faber often said he felt his fastball was his best pitch.[2] When he mingled in the spitter, it became a diabolical combination.

"Red wouldn't throw more than four or five spitters in some games," said Ray Schalk, the Hall of Fame catcher who was on the receiving end for much of Faber's best work. "In fact, his best pitch was his fastball. He'd just keep the batters guessing."[3]

He did it well enough to win 254 games in a 20-year career despite the fact that he spent his entire career with the Chicago White Sox, who finished in the second division of the American League in 15 of those 20 seasons. Schalk always insisted that Faber would have topped 300 wins if he'd played for a better club.[4]

Faber was a big man at six feet, two inches and 180 pounds, but he didn't overpower hitters. He had seven seasons in which he had fewer strikeouts than walks. Hitters often had no trouble getting the bat on the ball against him. But his blend of spitters, fastballs and curves, and his command over all of them consistently kept hitters from making quality contact.

Faber's control was so sharp that hitters frequently swung at the first or second pitch he delivered. He had one game in 1915 in which he needed only 67 pitches to finish a complete game and he had three innings in his career in which he threw only three pitches.[5] He also was not adverse to pitching inside to intimidate batters. He once forced the cantankerous Ty Cobb to hit the deck on three straight pitches.[6]

Faber was born on the family farm northwest of the town of Cascade, Iowa, in the northeast part of the state. He was the second oldest of four children born to Nicholas and Margaret Faber. Nicholas' father had come from Luxembourg and was one of the earliest settlers of the Cascade area but even though both of Red's parents had been born in the United States, German was the language of choice in both the Faber household and at St. Mary's Catholic School in Cascade. His upbringing was filled with discipline and religion. Nicholas Faber was a stoic, no-nonsense man who was almost fanatical in his devotion to the Roman Catholic church, so much so that some family members admitted many years later to being afraid of him.

When little Red was only five years old, the family moved into town and opened the Hotel Faber, a grand, three-story establishment that remained in the family for more than 50 years and which still stands.

Nicholas and Margaret had other land holdings and were prosperous enough that they were able to send their children to boarding schools around the region. Red attended both Sacred Heart Academy in Prairie du Chien, Wisconsin, and St. Joseph's Academy in Dubuque.

Red Faber.

As a 16-year-old, he sometimes would earn $2 by pitching for a semi-pro team called the Dubuque Tigers on Sunday afternoons, but his baseball skills didn't attract much notice until he began playing at St. Joseph's College (now Loras) in Dubuque. There are no written records indicating that Faber ever was enrolled in the college, but he pitched for the school nonetheless. He struck out 22 batters in a game against St. Ambrose College in Davenport in 1909 and had enough other success pitching for semi-pro teams around the area to attract an offer from the hometown Dubuque Miners of the Three-I League.

He went 7–6 for the Miners in the last two months of the 1909 season and went 18–19 with a sparkling 2.37 earned run average for them in 1910, hurling a perfect game against Davenport in August in which he allowed only one ball to be hit out of the infield.

A story in the *Waterloo Courier* likened the performance to that of Cy Young, who had thrown a perfect game against the Philadelphia Athletics six years earlier.

"Faber's feat, however, was even greater than Young's," the Courier reported. "Young was aided by some sensational fielding in the outfield, numerous fly balls being caught. In the game at Davenport only one ball was hit to the outfield, an easy popup to Taylor in left. Faber was in such wonderful form that the Davenport batters were helpless before him. Few of the chances accepted by the infield were hard."[7]

The story went on to say that "Faber has a collection of the most wonderful curves ever shown in the league.... If he has any fault it is his wildness at times, for his curves break so quickly that it is difficult to control them at all times."[8]

The Pittsburgh Pirates were clearly impressed. The next day they signed Faber to a major league contract.

He opened the following season with Pittsburgh, then managed by fellow Iowan Fred Clarke, but never got into a game and after a few weeks was farmed out to Minneapolis in the American Association. He wasn't there for very long either. After pitching in only five games, he was dispatched to the Pueblo Indians of the Western League. Faber's short stay in Minneapolis was significant for one reason: That's where he learned to throw the spitball.

He had injured his arm, possibly from taking part in a distance-throwing competition in Minneapolis or possibly by simply throwing too many breaking pitches. He even took two weeks off in one stretch, going home to Cascade to rest the arm, but it didn't seem to help. Upon returning to Minneapolis, he started the second game of a July 4 double-header and lasted just two innings before being forced to leave the game.

Hoping to find some other form of off-speed pitch that would put less strain on his arm, he sought help from a veteran teammate. Harry Peaster, who never made it to the major leagues and went just 37–44 in the minors, made his most significant contribution to the game by showing young Faber how to apply moisture to his fingertips and release the ball with virtually no spin, causing it to dip and dive on the whims of air currents.[9]

"I never resorted to the spitter until I was obliged to," Faber recalled many years later. "I nearly ruined my arm throwing curves."[10]

He spent the next few years perfecting the new pitch, learning to launch it from a variety of arm angles for differing effects. Faber sometimes used slippery elm to get his salivary glands flowing but more often he had wads of chewing tobacco and chewing gum in his mouth.

"I used to load up with a mixture," he explained in later years. "On one side of my mouth I'd have a chaw of tobacco and on the other I'd have gum. Never got 'em mixed either."[11]

Before delivering a pitch, he held the ball up to his mouth and concealed it with his glove. The batter never knew for sure whether or not he was applying tobacco juice. More often than not, he didn't. When he did, he would only moisten the tips of his index and middle fingers and then throw the ball with almost as much velocity as his fastball. If he threw it overhand, the ball would take a sharp downward drop. Thrown sidearm, the ball broke just as radically but it moved laterally, drifting away from a right-handed hitter.

Something certainly seemed to change for Faber when he left Minneapolis. In his first game with Pueblo, he struck out 15 and allowed only two hits against Sioux City. Later in the season, he pitched and won both games of a double-header against Omaha. He went 12–8 with a 1.87 ERA in the remainder of that 1911 season, but that didn't stop the Pirates from giving him his release.

Frank Isbell, who owned the Pueblo team, sold the club following the season and became the president of the Des Moines club of the same league. He took Faber with him. The pitcher spent two more years in the Western League with the Des Moines Boosters, going 21–14 in 1912 and 20–17 in 1913. Late in the 1913 season, the White Sox bought Faber's contract for $3,500 with the intention of bringing him to the big leagues in 1914.

It may not have been pure chance that it was the White Sox who signed him. The franchise had plenty of ties to Dubuque. Owner Charles Comiskey had played for a minor league team in Dubuque in 1879 and met his wife, Nan, there. And Pants Rowland, who was to become the White Sox manager in 1915, had grown up in Dubuque after being born just across the border in Wisconsin.

As it turned out, Faber got a chance to see the world before he ever saw any regular-season action in the majors. He was added to the White Sox roster for a post-season series of exhibition games with the New York Giants that included 36 games in smaller cities around the country and then a three-month voyage around the world. He wasn't scheduled to participate in the international portion of the barnstorming tour, but when Giants pitching star Christy Mathewson backed out of the trip, Faber was loaned to the New York club as Matty's replacement.

It was the most ambitious junket ever attempted by any baseball team. The trip departed from Victoria, British Columbia, on November 19 and ended in New York on March 7, meandering through five continents and including games played in Japan, China, Hong Kong, the Philippines, Australia, Egypt, Italy, France and England. The players mingled with royalty, had an audience with Pope Pius X—for the 25-year-old Faber, with his Catholic upbringing, that was the highlight—and played games in the shadows of the Great Pyramids.

Faber somehow took part in the entire trip without ever getting a passport.[12]

When it was all over, Faber finally got his chance to pitch in the major leagues. Despite pitching well overseas, he was used infrequently by the White Sox in the first six weeks of the 1914 season. Once he got his chance in June, he delivered. In a span of less than three weeks, he pitched all 13 innings of a 2–1 loss to the Tigers, shut out the Yankees for his first career win and nearly no-hit the world champion Philadelphia Athletics. He missed about a month because of an arm injury later in the season, but still went 10–9 in his rookie campaign.

He was on his way. In 1915, he led the American League by pitching in 50 games, including 18 relief appearances, and went 24–14. He was second in the league in both wins and strikeouts behind the incomparable Walter Johnson.

Faber was 17–9 during an injury-plagued 1916 season and 16–13 in 1917, but that was a deceptive record. As *Baseball Magazine* pointed out, 39 of the 92 runs Faber allowed during the season were unearned.[13] He helped the White Sox win the American League pennant and they faced McGraw's Giants in the World Series in what was to be Faber's finest moment. He became the only pitcher in major league history to get four pitching decisions in one World Series, including two complete game victories.

The White Sox banged out 14 singles and rallied from an early deficit as Faber notched a 7–2 win in Game 2. The contest also included one of the most embarrassing moments of his career. In the fifth inning, he tried to steal third only to find it already was occupied by teammate Buck Weaver. Faber later explained that as he was running to second base on one of his infrequent hits, he saw Weaver rounding third and assumed that he had scored. He never saw his teammate standing on third before he took off in that direction himself.[14]

Faber took a 5–0 loss in Game 4 as the Giants' Benny Kauff hit two home runs off him. Two days later, in Game 5 in Chicago, Faber came on to pitch the last two innings and got the win when the Sox scored three runs in the seventh inning to tie the score, then scored three more in the eighth inning for an 8–5 victory. That gave them a 3–2 lead with the series shifting back to New York.

Sportswriter James Crusinberry, who also was from Cascade, chronicled the turn of events for the *Chicago Tribune* and wrote, "Although it hasn't been proven, it was said that the screaming at Comiskey Park yesterday at the close of that seventh inning could be plainly heard in Cascade, Ia."[15]

On the train back to New York, manager Pants Rowland and coach Kid Gleason asked Faber if he thought he could go back out to the mound again for Game 6. Faber readily agreed to do it, noting that he'd be less nervous pitching than just sitting and watching.[16]

The Sox opened an early 3–0 lead but the Giants got two runs back on a triple by Buck Herzog in the fifth. Faber stiffened after that, however. The Giants got a man to third base in the seventh with the help of an error and a passed ball, but Faber got Herzog to pop up to short to end the inning. The Sox won 4–2 to clinch the world championship.

Among those in attendance at the game was Dr. W.P. Slattery of Dubuque, who marveled at the aplomb with which Faber dispatched the Giants in an intensely hostile atmosphere, noting that he "walked back to the bench as cool as a cucumber; you would think he was going to fish off the Cascade bridge instead of being in a ball game."[17] As he was riding the train home to Iowa, Dr. Slattery stopped at one point along the way to fire off a telegram to the local paper: "All Iowa is proud of Red Faber."[18]

When Faber himself stepped off the train in Dubuque in the early-morning hours of October 18, he found a large crowd waiting to greet him, including a couple of priests from St. Joseph's College.

In later years, Faber admitted there were some jitters in that final, pivotal Game 6, even if they didn't show them outwardly. "That last game was a crusher," he said. "I didn't feel it at the time but when it was all over and we had come through I was shaking like a leaf."[19]

Famed Chicago sportswriter Hugh S. Fullerton credited Rowland with taking the calculated gamble of going with Faber on two days rest: "He staked Faber in the final game, knowing that if Faber lost the odds would favor the Giants heavily. He did not figure Faber to lose and the tall blonde boy went through with it, pitched a magnificent game of ball and won. He was steady to the finish."[20]

The *Chicago Herald* added: "They should at least name the town pump for him in Cascade."[21]

Faber's winner's share from the World Series triumph came to $3,666. Each player also received a solid gold button about ¾ of an inch in diameter with a small diamond set in the middle and the player's name inscribed on the back.

Faber got off to another great start in 1918, going 4–1 with a 1.23 ERA, but World War I was escalating and it was clear that an unattached 29-year-old was likely to be drafted. He enlisted in the Navy with hopes of being placed in the submarine corps, but never got inside a sub and never saw any action overseas. He was sent to Great Lakes Naval Station near Chicago and spent most of his six-month tour of duty playing baseball.

He was discharged in January and it would seem he should have been able to step right back into the White Sox' starting rotation, but Faber staggered to an 11–9 record in 1919 and his ERA of 3.83 was pretty much double what it had been in his previous full season in 1917. He struggled to overcome a bout with the Spanish flu that took the lives of a half million Americans that year. He later revealed that he lost as much as 30 pounds at one point and he also fought a collection of minor injuries with the result being that he saw very little action late in the season and was not healthy enough to pitch in the World Series after the White Sox again won the AL pennant.

We can only wonder how history might have been altered had Faber been available for the series. Even without him, the Sox were an overwhelming favorite to beat the Cincinnati Reds in the best-of-nine set, but eight White Sox players, including two of the team's top pitchers, became part of a conspiracy to throw the series.

The plot was exposed during the following season and the 1919 Chicago team was forever branded the Black Sox. Faber, like most of the White Sox players not involved in the plot, had very strong suspicions if not first-hand knowledge of what was going on. He reportedly wanted to take the mound in Game 8 of the series when one of the conspirators, Claude "Lefty" Williams, not-so-subtly allowed four runs in the first inning to finish off the fix, but manager Kid Gleason didn't feel Faber was up to it physically.

Faber seldom commented publicly on the fact that he had to stand by helplessly while unscrupulous teammates lost games on purpose, although he once admitted to having mixed feelings about not being able to play in the series, noting, "Nobody likes to sit on the bench and nobody likes to play in crooked games."[22]

He was believed to be one of the primary sources for author Eliot Asinof, who wrote the definitive book on the fix, *Eight Men Out*. He told Asinof that none of the innocent players felt much like discussing the topic when they got together and that he thought the guilty players may have been "too frightened not to comply" with the gamblers.[23]

Although it was difficult to go back onto the field and play with teammates he knew were crooked—the guilty players were not suspended until almost a year later—Faber did some of his best work in the wake of the scandal, stringing together three straight 20-win seasons. He worked more than 300 innings all three years and led the American League in ERA and complete games in both 1921 and 1922.

It may not be a coincidence that the best stretch of Faber's career came in the first three years in which the spitball was outlawed for everyone except he and 16 other pitchers. However, it also marked the end of the so-called deadball era. Baseball began using a much livelier, more tightly sewn ball in 1920, prompting a precipitous jump in home runs and other offensive statistics. It didn't seem to bother Faber at all.

That three-year run is made even more impressive by the fact that he no longer was playing for one of the best teams in baseball. The White Sox finished second in the American League in 1920 before the full details of the Black Sox scandal came to light but with eight of their best players banned from the sport for life, they took a major nosedive afterward. Faber reached a career high in victories in 1921, going 25–15 for a team that was only 62–92. All the team's other pitchers combined were 37–77.

Faber's career began to decline in 1923 at the age of 34 although he continued to pitch for 11 more seasons. He won 14 games in 1923, but then underwent elbow surgery prior to the 1924 season and never quite regained his old form.

He showed only brief glimmers of what he had been before with one of those coming on May 26, 1929, when he faced a Detroit team that included future Hall of Famers Charlie Gehringer and Harry Heilmann.

He fired a one-hit shutout and allowed only two baserunners—on a hit batsman and Gehringer's fourth-inning single.

In those later years, he began using the spitball more and more frequently. Famed sportswriter Westbrook Pegler noted after one 1929 game that "Mr. Faber was soaping the ball with the juice of the elm till it splashed when hit."[24]

He even had a few instances of offensive heroics in later years. Faber, a switch-hitter, was notoriously weak at the plate. He batted only .134 for his career and his only real offensive virtues were a sharp eye and a moderate amount of speed. In 1915, he walked in seven consecutive at-bats and once stole second, third and home in the same inning. For his career, he had almost as many walks (169) as hits (170). But in a 1928 game with the powerful Yankees, he came to bat with two runners on base in the eighth inning of a tie game. Batting righthanded, he twice swung and missed badly at pitches by Wilcy Moore. Then he turned around to bat lefthanded and swatted a game-winning single.

His achievements were recognized by the White Sox on a special Red Faber Day on August 20, 1929, prior to a game against the Yankees. A special train carried fans from Dubuque and Cascade to Chicago for the game and Faber was presented with $2,750 in gold, a large radio, a diamond ring and bunches of flowers.[25]

He was used almost exclusively as a relief pitcher in the early 1930s and he enjoyed a renaissance of sorts in 1933. His earned run average of 3.44 that season was an improvement on recent seasons, giving hope that perhaps he still had something left in his aging right arm.

In that era, before interleague play became the norm in baseball, the Cubs and White Sox played a City Series against one another after every season. In Game 2 of the 1933 series, Faber got a surprise start and blanked the crosstown rivals with a five-hit shutout.

He didn't realize at the time that it would be the last game he would ever pitch.

He had earned $10,000 a year for much of his career but had taken a pay cut to $7,000 in 1933. When he received his contract offer for 1934, it was for only $5,000. Faber was understandably offended and after quietly simmering for a few weeks, he told the White Sox he was through, got in the car and drove home to Cascade. He asked for and was granted his release.

He had a chance to catch on with the Oakland team in the Pacific Coast League, a popular refuge for aging major leaguers in that era, and there were rumblings that the Cubs might be interested. Nothing ever came of it. At the age of 45, he was done as an active player.

The Yankees and Babe Ruth (right) were on hand for Red Faber Day at Comiskey Park in 1929. Ruth once described Faber (left) as "the nicest man in the world" (courtesy Cascade, Iowa, Tri-County Historical Society).

Faber later took a stab at coaching, serving as the White Sox' pitching coach under manager Ted Lyons in 1946, 1947 and 1948. He did a variety of other things in his post-playing days, selling real estate, selling cars and owning a bowling alley for about 10 years. He finally found his niche working on a survey crew for the Cook County highway department. He continued to do that until the age of 79.

He also finally found a modicum of happiness in his private life in his later years. In 1920, he had married a Chicagoan named Irene Walsh, who was 10 years younger than he was. She had numerous health issues through the years and there were rumors that she perhaps had an alcohol problem and was addicted to painkillers.[26] It also was reported that she had an affair with White Sox outfielder Johnny Mostil, who attempted suicide in 1927 after allegedly being confronted by Faber.[27] Questions remain as to how much of all that is true. Irene eventually died of a brain hemorrhage at the age of 44 in 1943, about a week after undergoing surgery for the removal of tumors and cysts on her uterus.

Four years later, Faber married a 30-year-old divorcee named Frances Knudtzon and a year after that, at the age of 60, he became a father for the first time when Frances gave birth to Urban C. Faber II, who quickly came to be known as Pepper.

Faber also helped found Baseball Anonymous, an organization that helped retired professional athletes who were facing hardships of some sort.[28]

In 1964, he was elected to the National Baseball Hall of Fame, one of six men inducted by the Veterans Committee that year. One of the others was Burleigh Grimes, the only one of the 17 legal spitballers who outlasted Faber in the majors. Faber clearly was moved by the honor, delivering an emotion-choked acceptance speech in Cooperstown that lasted little more than a minute.[29]

He began to encounter health problems around that time. He had been smoking cigarettes since the age of eight and he had two heart attacks in the 1960s. He died in 1976 at the age of 88.

In the last five years of his life, he was a recluse, seldom leaving his southside home. But friends and acquaintances remembered him as a pleasant, genial man with a subtle sense of humor. Babe Ruth once described Faber as "the nicest man in the world."[30] *Dubuque Telegraph-Herald* sportswriter Bill O'Neill wrote that in a handful of interviews he had with Faber late in his life, "I never once had the impression he was anything but an honest, down-to-earth, humble person."[31]

His humility followed him to the hereafter. The marker on Faber's grave in Chicago's Acacia Park Cemetery makes note of the fact that he was a chief yeoman in the Navy, but makes no mention that he was one of the finest pitchers in the history of baseball.

Outfield
Bing Miller

"Bing Miller was the best curveball hitter of all time. We just couldn't throw him a curveball, he'd wear us out."—Detroit catcher Ray Hayworth[1]

In the early part of the 20th century, it was all the rage for major league baseball players to attempt to catch a ball dropped from a great height. St. Louis Cardinals manager Gabby Street caught a ball dropped from the top of the Washington Monument. Babe Ruth caught a ball thrown from a moving airplane. Brooklyn Dodgers player-manager Wilbert Robinson tried the same thing only to have the female pilot, discovering she did not have a baseball, throw him a grapefruit instead. It exploded on contact, giving Robinson an unexpected citrus shower.

In the middle of the 1929 season, Philadelphia Athletics outfielder Bing Miller took his shot. Standing in the middle of Philadelphia's Shibe Park, three balls were dropped one at a time from the Goodyear blimp *Mayflower*, hovering 600 feet above.

The sure-handed Miller caught the first one. He managed to snag the second one. The third one knocked him to the ground.

It was one more piece of evidence that Miller seemingly could do anything there was to do on a ball field. And if he couldn't do it, he would work at it until he could. Few players in the history of baseball have maximized their natural abilities more than Miller.

On his very first day in the major leagues, Miller was shagging flies in the outfield when he lost one in the sun. It ended up hitting him in the head. Miller made up his mind to work at it and became perhaps the best outfielder in the game at judging fly balls in the sun.

The five-foot, 10-inch, 180-pound Miller was every bit as dedicated to his craft with a bat in his hands. He was the consummate situational hitter. Whether it was a bunt or a sacrifice fly or a ground ball to the right side to move the runner over, Miller could do it. Pitch him inside and he would pull the ball. He did it well enough to hit 116 career home runs. Pitch him outside and he would rifle the ball to the opposite field. He probably hit the curve ball as well as anyone in his era. And although he had only fair speed, Hall of Fame shortstop Joe Cronin said Miller got out of the batter's box faster than any right-handed hitter he ever saw.[2]

Bing Miller.

Miller also considered it an absolute cardinal sin to take a called third strike.[3] He averaged only one strikeout for every 20 at-bats for his entire career.

Over the course of 16 major league seasons, he batted .311 and never was below .280 in any year as a starter. He fell just short of 2,000 hits and 1,000 runs batted in, and earned the nickname "Old Reliable" from adoring Philadelphia Athletics fans.

Edmund John Miller was born on August 30, 1894, on a farm in Polk Township near Urbana, Iowa, just west of Cedar Rapids although his family moved to nearby Vinton when he was very young. He was the second oldest of eight children of Norman and Philomena Miller, who had come to Iowa from New York City.

At a very early age, Edmund became known as "Bing," a nickname given to him by his older brother, Eugene. The *Vinton Eagle* newspaper carried a comic strip that included a character named George Washington Bings and for whatever reason, Eugene began calling his brother Bings.[4] Before very long, the S was dropped. He was Bing from then on.

Norman Miller had played a little bit of baseball in the minor leagues so it was only natural that his sons also would gravitate toward the game. Two of Bing's brothers—Eugene and Ralph—also played organized baseball and Ralph (also known as Lefty) very briefly made it to the major leagues, pitching one inning for the Washington Senators in 1921.

Bing also got his start as a pitcher for the Vinton Cinders at the age of 16 with brother Eugene serving as his catcher. By the time Bing was 18, he became the subject of a bidding war between minor league teams in Cedar Rapids and Clinton. Cedar Rapids, which was near his home, offered $70 a month but Clinton offered $80. In 1914, at the age of 19, Miller began pitching for the Clinton Pilots of the Central Association.[5]

He got off to a promising start as both a pitcher and hitter but in late May came down with typhoid fever. There was speculation that he may miss the remainder of the season and when he did eventually return to the team, he was noticeably weaker. In August, it was reported that he "was not showing any too much stuff since his return" and Miller was sent home for the remainder of the summer.[6] A .336 average in 40 games was reason enough for the Pilots to resign him for 1915, however. The *Herald* noted that "with the experience that he had obtained this season and a winter's rest, [Miller] should prove a winner next year" and the paper's profile of him on the eve of that season noted that "he is the idol of the Clinton fans and is probably the most popular player on the roster."[7]

He apparently was not quite so popular with new manager George Manush. Miller was used sparingly in the first month of the season, playing in just 12 games, only six of those as a pitcher. He batted .325 and had a 3–2 record on the mound but had problems with a chronic sore arm and in mid–June was listed by the Herald as "suspended."[8] He eventually was sold to the rival Mason City Claydiggers and after reinjuring his throwing arm, finished the season back on the farm in Vinton.

Clinton brought him back for the 1916 season, though, this time as an outfielder and backup catcher under another new manager, Tom Drohan, and Miller thrived. He batted .283 with 13 home runs, including a tape-measure shot in Cedar Rapids on May 22 that the *Clinton Advertiser* facetiously said was hit all the way back to Vinton. "When last seen the spheroid had covered the first lap in its journey toward Bingo's burg. It was never recovered," the *Advertiser* reported.[9] A few days later, a Vinton farmer named Si J. Perkins wrote an equally facetious letter to the editor reporting that he found the ball wedged into the fence in his hog pen.[10]

Miller was even better with the Pilots at the outset of the 1917 season and major league scouts finally noticed. On May 30, he signed a contract with the Detroit Tigers, who planned to have him finish the season in Clinton. However, the Pilots withdrew from the Central Association and their players were dispersed to other clubs. Miller was sent to Waterloo, where he was reunited with his brother Ralph, and he finished the season with Peoria in the Three-I League. His next stop might have been Detroit in 1918, but World War I intervened. He was drafted into the Army and saw active duty in France.

After being discharged in 1919, he finished what was left of the season with Atlanta of the Southern League, batting only .253, then picked up some extra money playing for some Iowa town teams following the season. One of those games nearly brought about an end to his career if not his life. Miller played for the Grundy Center team against Wellsburg as part of a special exhibition game at the Grundy County Fair on September 26, 1919. After the game, with bat in hand, he hopped over a fence at the nearby harness racing track and was struck by a passing sulky. According to some newspaper reports, his jugular vein was severed, he lost a great deal of blood and he was feared to be in serious condition.[11]

He apparently recovered quickly and returned stronger than ever in 1920 with the Little Rock Travelers of the Southern League. In fact, it may have been his best season statistically at any level. He batted .322 with 19 home runs, 21 triples and 30 doubles, helped the team win the pennant and finally, at the age of 26, earned his much-awaited shot at the major leagues.

But he had one more hurdle to clear. Little Rock inadvertently sold his rights to two different major league teams—Pittsburgh and Washington—creating a dispute over which team actually held his rights. Judge Kennesaw Mountain Landis had just been named commissioner of baseball, primarily to clean up the infamous Black Sox scandal, but before he did that he ruled that Bing Miller was a Washington Senator.

Miller became a starter almost immediately in Washington and batted a solid but unspectacular .288 in 114 games. He was traded to the Philadelphia Athletics after the season in a three-way deal that also involved the Red Sox and began a long and close association with legendary manager Connie Mack.

The A's, a powerhouse team a decade earlier, had finished last in the American League seven years in a row and Miller became one of the primary building blocks in the franchise's reversal of fortunes. He batted .336 in 1922 with a career-high 21 homers and finished 15th in the league's Most Valuable Player voting. He fell off to .299 in 1923, then hit a career-best .342 in 1924 and .319 in 1925.

The A's were getting close to being a contender and Mack made a desperate move to put his team over the top. Less than two months into the 1926 season, he traded Miller to the St. Louis Browns for star centerfielder Baby Doll Jacobson, then immediately peddled Jacobson to Boston in a five-player deal to obtain pitcher Howard Ehmke.

Ehmke would later become a World Series hero for the A's, but Mack almost immediately regretted parting with his steady right-fielder.

Miller kept banging out hits in St. Louis, batting .331 in the last two thirds of that season and .325 in 1927, and Mack finally brought him back in a December trade for pitcher Sam Gray.

Miller, then 33, teamed with Al Simmons and Mule Haas to form one of the best outfields in baseball over the next half dozen seasons.

The A's finished second to the Yankees in 1928 as Miller took sixth in the AL batting race with a .328 average, and the Philadelphia club finally broke through in 1929. Miller was a big part of it. He put together a 28-game hitting streak in mid-summer and finished at .331 with career highs in stolen bases (24) and triples (16).

The A's defeated the Chicago Cubs in the first two games of the World Series with Miller driving in a pair of runs and Ehmke nearly hurling a shutout in the opener. But the Cubs won Game 3 and opened a seemingly insurmountable 8–0 lead in Game 4. Then the A's strung together several hits in the seventh inning, Cubs center-fielder Hack Wilson lost Haas' routine fly ball in the sun and the A's parlayed that into a 10-run inning to win the game.

The following game produced the moment for which Miller is best remembered. The A's again fell behind and trailed 2–0 going to the ninth inning. They had been unable to do anything against Cubs ace Pat Malone, who had allowed only two hits and retired Philadelphia in order in seven of the eight innings. He struck out pinch-hitter Walt French to start the ninth.

As International News Service sports editor Davis Walsh wrote in his game story, "Hope ... was on its death bed."[12] Connie Mack himself later admitted that he had conceded defeat and was beginning to formulate ideas about what he would do in Game 6.[13]

Bing Miller is tagged out at the plate by Washington catcher Muddy Ruel in a 1925 game.

But then Max

Bishop singled and Haas hit a two-run homer to tie the score. With two outs, Simmons nearly hit the ball out of the park but settled for a double and Malone intentionally walked dangerous Jimmy Foxx to get to Miller. With the count at two balls and two strikes, Malone served up a high fastball on the outside corner and Miller raked it into the right-center field gap to bring in Simmons and give the A's the world championship.

The "As the Sports Editor Sees It" column by Edwin R. Moore, Jr., in the next day's *Waterloo Courier* reflected the pride his home state took in Miller's achievement: "Bing played the role of the 'warhorse.' Not a brilliant player who flashes at every turn, Bing merely followed his steady style and came thru at crucial moments to give the required punch and turn apparent defeat into victory. In the first game he drove in two runs and his drive yesterday to score the winning run already has been recounted with plenty of descriptive color. The point to be made is that Bing was ready for the occasion. He did it yesterday, and, were there a game today, he would remain that same serious threat. Just a small town boy who knows his baseball in big league style, is a description that fits the great Bing."[14]

The same piece, however, indicated that it was likely the last hurrah for the pride of Vinton: "Miller is getting old and his future baseball years, at least in the Big Show, are limited."[15]

Moore was wrong about that. Miller came back even stronger in 1930, playing in every game, batting .303 and recording the only 100-RBI season of his career. The A's repeated as world champions in slightly less dramatic fashion, defeating the St. Louis Cardinals in six games.

The A's won their third straight American League pennant in 1931, but this time they lost to the Cardinals in the World Series. Miller's average dropped to .281, but he had a career-high 43 doubles and struck out only 16 times all season.

Philadelphia finished second to the Yankees in 1932 in what turned out to be Miller's last season as an everyday player. He batted .295 but young Doc Cramer had begun to share playing time with him and the kid batted .336.

Miller became a part-time player thereafter and with the Great Depression gripping the country, Mack forced him to take a pay cut from $10,000 a year to $6,000.

Mack had a history of building winning teams, then abruptly dismantling them after winning a few championships and he followed that pattern again. As the 1932 season ended, he sold Simmons, Haas and third baseman Jimmy Dykes to the White Sox for $150,000. After the 1933 season, star pitcher Lefty Grove and second baseman Bishop were sent to Boston and catcher Mickey Cochrane was dispatched to Detroit for lesser players and more piles of cash.

Miller, who had served Mack so long and so well, was among the last of the stalwarts to go. He finally was released by the A's on January 14, 1935, and signed with the Red Sox the following day. He still was a highly effective player in spots in his final few seasons. He still could be "Old Reliable" on a given day and led the AL in pinch hits in both 1934 and '35.

But after violating his own credo by taking a called third strike in 1936, he decided to call it quits at the age of 41.

He was hired by the Red Sox as a coach in the final weeks of the season and stayed there through 1937.

By 1938, Cochrane had become the manager at Detroit and Miller went there to serve as a coach for a few years, helping the Tigers reach the World Series in 1940. In one game in the middle of that season, he came to the rescue of umpire Joe Rue, who had made a controversial call against New York in Yankee Stadium. The fans began hurling bottles at Rue, who stubbornly refused to take cover. Miller came onto the field and nudged the embattled umpire out toward the middle of the diamond until things calmed down.[16]

In 1942, Miller moved on to Chicago where his old friend and teammate, Jimmy Dykes, was the manager. He and Dykes first got to know one another as teammates in the minor leagues in 1919 and they had a unique relationship. They loved to needle one another for hours on end, sometimes giving outsiders the impression that they were at odds. In truth, Dykes was among Miller's closest and most cherished friends.[17]

By the end of the 1949 season, Dykes had left Chicago and Miller also was let go. He and Cochrane rejoined the A's as coaches with Dykes also there on the staff to help the 87-year-old Mack through his final few seasons as manager. Dykes replaced Mack at the start of the 1951 season and three dismal years later, Miller, Dykes and everyone else was out of a job. The franchise moved to Kansas City.

Miller still continued to work for the team in ensuing years as a scout and minor league instructor but found time to take a few bows for some appreciative supporters back in Iowa. The Urbana team of the Buchanan County League sponsored a Bing Miller Day on September 19, 1954, including a parade, a picnic, a ballgame and appearances by several other former major leaguers from the area, including Hal Trosky, Earl Whitehill, Dutch Levsen and Bill Zuber.[18]

In later years, Miller worked as a pipeline engineer with the Atlantic Coast Construction Company, but he never lost his rapier wit and love of a good wisecrack. Former major league pitcher Frank Gabler loved to tell a story about Miller, who almost who always was unable to attend church on Sundays because of games. One day Miller ran into the minister of his church, who questioned why he hadn't seen him in some time. Miller responded that Sunday normally was a big day for him.

"It's a big day for me, too, only I'm in the right field," the pastor supposedly said.

"Why I am, too," Miller cracked. "And ain't that sun awful?"[19]

In 1966, Miller was living in the Philadelphia suburb of Wynnewood and he and a neighbor named Joseph Greene went to a Phillies game on May 6 at Connie Mack Stadium, the same ballpark in which he had starred four decades earlier. On the drive home, with Greene at the wheel, they were involved in a head-on collision with another car. Greene escaped with minor injuries but Miller was sent diving into the windshield and according to some reports, he suffered severe head injuries. He was taken to Presbyterian Hospital in Philadelphia and died of an apparent heart attack early the next morning.[20]

Cedar Rapids Gazette columnist Gus Schrader eulogized Miller as "a friendly, kindly man and very popular with those who knew him as a baseball player, coach and scout."[21]

New York Times columnist Arthur Daley, recalling Miller's penchant for witty retorts, called him "a delightful guy."[22]

Joe Cronin, who knew Miller as both a rival and a teammate and who was now American League president, said, "Bing was a credit to baseball, on the field and off it."[23]

"He was one of the great ones," Schrader concluded, "from a Golden Era of Sports."[24]

Pitcher
Dazzy Vance

> "Vance was by far the roughest guy I ever hit against. Even worse than Walter Johnson. I mean, he was wicked."—Infielder Rube Bressler[1]

It was September of 1925 and Dazzy Vance was at his fire-balling best. The Brooklyn Robins pitcher had just mowed down the Philadelphia Phillies for nine innings, allowing just one hit, and as he walked off the field he crossed paths with Phillies manager Art Fletcher.

"You lucky stiff," Fletcher growled. "If we don't get more than one hit off you the next time, I'll kiss your foot in Macy's window."[2]

Vance calmly told Fletcher he planned to do even better the next time. Just four days later, he found himself up against Philadelphia again and he again had no problem shutting down the Phillies. Through seven innings he had not allowed a single hit and was well on his way to a complete game no-hitter. He waved to Fletcher standing in the third-base coaching box and called out, "Hey Fletch, which window?"[3]

It's the sort of brash, lighthearted banter that came to be expected from Vance, who usually was able to back up almost anything he said on the playing field.

Vance enjoyed a remarkable and colorful career in which he played for 12 different minor league teams and failed miserably in three attempts to make it at the major league level before landing with Brooklyn at the age of 31. Then he led the National League in strikeouts seven consecutive years, won 197 games and ended up being inducted into baseball's Hall of Fame.

Vance was born in 1891 near Orient, Iowa, in Adair County, about 60 miles southwest of Des Moines. He was the youngest of five children of Albert and Sarah Vance, a farming couple who had migrated from Indiana to Illinois to Iowa. Their youngest was only six years old when the family pulled up stakes again and moved to Pleasant Hill Township near the town of Cowles in southern Nebraska.

His given name was Charles Arthur Vance. At least, that's what his mother wrote in the family bible when he was born, but it became a gleeful point of conjecture through his entire life. He was listed that same way in the 1900 and 1910 censuses but when Vance registered for the draft during World War I, he decided to give his name as Arthur Charles Vance and when he signed autographs, he frequently wrote A.C. Vance. He later told some reporters that his name was Clarence Arthur Vance and he still is listed that way in some sources. When he was inducted into the baseball Hall of Fame many years later, he told Cooperstown officials he wanted his plaque to say Arthur Charles Vance.

Dazzy Vance (Los Angeles Dodgers).

By his late teens, it didn't matter what his given name was. Everyone called him "Dazzy."

However, there even is disagreement over the origin of that name. It often was reported through the years that he got the name because his fastball was so dazzling. It was a good story but in truth, the name had other, less compelling roots. As a youngster in Nebraska, Vance befriended an older neighbor who had wild animal pelts and cowboy paraphernalia stored in a shed. Occasionally the neighbor would hold up one of his treasures and ask, "Ain't it a dazzy?" He meant to say "daisy." An amused Vance mimicked the fractured pronunciation often enough that by the time he was 11 years old it became his name.[4]

Vance claimed he never saw an actual nine-player baseball game until he was in his teens although he and his brother Fred spent plenty of time staging their own two-player games on the family farm in short intervals between helping with chores around the place. They used an old bat held together by nails and tape, and an old ball that continually had to be patched and re-sewn.[5]

As with his given name and his nickname, there is all sorts of contradictory information about Vance's teen years and the start of his baseball career. Throughout his life, he seemed to delight in perpetuating untruths and creating confusion about his past.

Some authoritative sources indicate that he attended high school in Hardy, Nebraska, within a stone's throw of the Kansas border. Others say he went to Hastings High School, which is more than 60 miles away. He does appear to have played for a semi-pro team in Hastings before being signed to a minor league contract.

He struck out 22 batters for a team called the Corn Crackers in 1909 and eventually organized his own town team in Cowles, arranging games with teams from other towns in south central Nebraska.

While baseball-reference.com lists his first minor league stop as being a team called the York Prohibitionists of the Class D Nebraska State League, many other sources say his first season was spent with the Red Cloud club of the same league. Vance made his pro debut at the age of 21 in 1912, beginning a long and undulating 10-year quest to get to the major leagues. He was a sub-.500 pitcher in that first season and with the Superior Brickmakers in the same league in 1913. But at Hastings in 1914, he emerged as a star. He went 17-4 in a half season there and was promoted to Class A St. Joseph's in the Western League, where he recorded a no-hitter against Topeka. He had a combined total of 26 victories for the season.

Because he was so effective, managers had a tendency to use him too much. After reportedly pitching four complete games in one week, Vance came down with a sore right arm. He lost his velocity and his arm began to hurt every time he threw.

His 1914 performance earned him a chance to play in the major leagues with Pittsburgh in April 1915 but he lasted just one game. He gave up three hits, walked five and hit a batter in less than three innings of work and it was back to St. Joseph's, where he managed to win 17 games. He finished the season back in the big leagues with the New York Yankees, where he actually was moderately effective in eight appearances although his record was 0-3.

The Yankees decided he needed more seasoning and over the next several years Vance bounced from one minor league team to another. He was with the Columbus Senators and the Memphis Chickasaws and the Rochester Hustlers before getting another brief shot with the Yankees in 1918. It didn't go well. He pitched in two games and nine of the 15 batters he faced hit safely.

The Yankees sold him to the Sacramento Senators. From there, he went back to Memphis for awhile and finally landed with the New Orleans Pelicans of the Southern Association in 1920.

Legend has it that Vance was involved in a poker game with his New Orleans teammates one night and as he eagerly went to rake in a big pot, he banged his arm on the table and recoiled in pain. The persistent soreness he had felt in his arm for six years was now excruciating and impossible to ignore.[6] Vance went to a doctor and apparently underwent some sort of surgical procedure. Some have speculated that he had bone chips removed from his elbow, but we don't really know. The coy Vance sometimes credited his turnaround to the "salubrious" air of New Orleans.[7] It's another Dazzy mystery.

Whatever the doctor did, Vance was suddenly pain-free and able to throw with the same sort of velocity he had shown in his youth. He went 21–11 with 34 complete games for New Orleans in 1921.

Unfortunately, he was now past the age of 30 and no longer viewed as a viable prospect by most major league clubs. He might not have been heard from again at the big-league level were it not for a catcher named Hank DeBerry.

The Brooklyn Robins were very interested in signing DeBerry and bringing him to the major leagues, and they sent scout Larry Sutton to New Orleans to recruit him. Sutton reported back to Brooklyn owner Charles Ebbets with the news that the Pelicans insisted that Brooklyn take Vance along with DeBerry as a package deal. Furthermore, DeBerry also was insisting. He said Vance made him look good all season.[8]

Ebbets finally reluctantly agreed and bought the duo for $10,000. Vance often joked that it was $9,000 for DeBerry and $1,000 for him.[9]

DeBerry spent nine unspectacular seasons as a journeyman catcher with Brooklyn. Vance became one of the greatest and most beloved players in the history of the franchise.

In Brooklyn, he came under the tutelage of Wilbert Robinson, who had been the catcher on the raucous and super successful Baltimore Orioles teams of the 1890s as well as a close friend and business partner of Giants manager John McGraw. The two men had had a falling-out and Robinson became a fixture as manager of the Brooklyn team, so much so that the team generally was known as the Robins instead of the Dodgers during his regime.

Robinson had a reputation for getting mileage out of pitchers others had given up on, but he wasn't entirely sure what he had in Vance at first. He could see the astonishing velocity. Vance referred to his fastball as his "blue darter" and the name fit. Teammate Johnny Frederick said he "could throw a cream puff through a battleship."[10]

But then in a spring training game, Robinson watched him strike out St. Louis Browns star George Sisler—who was destined to hit .420 that season—with a devastating curve ball. "Ol' Daz threw him a curve," Robinson marveled. "Didn't know he had one."[11]

Robinson was convinced. Vance was given a spot in the Brooklyn rotation.

Vance finally got first major league win on April 26, 1922, in part because of his own offensive contributions. He got three hits while pitching a 10–1 victory over the Boston Braves. He went on to win 18 games that season and led the National League in shutouts (5) and strikeouts (134).

It was the first of seven straight seasons in which he whiffed more batters than anyone else in the league, a mark that's never been equaled.

Vance won 18 games again in 1923, including 10 in a row in one stretch, then really hit his stride in 1924. He put together a 15-game winning streak that stretched from July 11 to September 20, went 28–6, led the league with a 2.16 earned run average, hurled 30 complete games and chalked up 262 strikeouts.

On August 23, he set a National League record by striking out 15 Chicago Cubs in a game. In the second inning of a September 24 game, also against the Cubs, he struck out the side on nine pitches. It would be another 38 years before another pitcher—the Dodgers' Sandy Koufax—would accomplish that feat.

To get an idea of how dominant Vance was that season, his 262 strikeouts were nearly double the total of teammate Burleigh Grimes, who was second in the league with 135. No other pitcher in the league topped 100. Vance accounted for one of every 13 strikeouts recorded in the National League that season.

The Robins finished just a game-and-a-half behind McGraw's Giants in the standings and Vance edged Rogers Hornsby for the league's Most Valuable Player award. All the Cardinals' second baseman had done that season was set a modern-era record by batting .424. Vance's reward for winning the MVP award was $1,000 in gold coins.[12]

Perhaps that whetted his appetite for monetary gain because as the 1925 season approached, both he and Grimes held out for more money. Vance finally relented a few weeks before the season began and signed a three-year contract that paid him just under $16,000 a season. A few years later he would become the highest paid pitcher in the National League at $25,000.

His victory total dropped to 22 in 1925 and his ERA went up by more than a run, but Vance continued to pile up huge numbers of strikeouts and do things other pitchers only dreamed of doing. He struck out 17 Cardinals in a 10-inning game on July 25.

Then there was that week in September in which he one-hit the Phillies one day, then no-hit them five days later, putting together 16 consecutive hitless innings and nearly pulling off the one-of-a-kind feat of back-to-back no-hitters achieved by Cincinnati's Johnny VanderMeer 13 years later.

Vance actually allowed a run in his no-hitter as the Phillies scored on an error by left-fielder Jimmy Johnston in the second inning. But when Johnston caught a fly ball for the final out in the ninth inning, Ebbets Field went crazy.

"The noise before had been but a whisper in comparison," *New York Times* sportswriter Richards Vidmer wrote. "Players rushed up to Vance and slapped him on the back, hats sailed on the field and were kicked into weird shapes by the rejoicing Robins, and while this demonstration was going on Dazzy walked serenely toward the dugout, his uniform wet and his brow dripping with perspiration. His face was calm, but in his heart there must have been a great glow of happiness."[13]

Art Fletcher never did follow through on his Macy's vow, by the way.

The no-hitter probably was the pinnacle of Vance's pitching career.

A large, powerful man, normally listed as six feet, two inches, and 200 pounds, Vance sometimes claimed he lost as much as 10 pounds pitching on a hot summer day because he refused to drink water during games. He said he started out drinking water but found he had better results when he didn't. He added that he usually managed to regain the weight prior to his next start.[14]

He used an extremely high leg kick before exploding toward the batter. He probably threw harder than any other pitcher in the 1920s and complemented his velocity with a diabolical curve ball and an occasional knuckleball.

Rube Bressler, who played for Cincinnati before being traded to Brooklyn where he was Vance's roommate for four years, described the Vance curve as "an apple rolling off a crooked table."[15]

Vance also tried to get every edge he could by wearing a tattered white long sleeve shirt under his jersey. He went so far as to take a razor blade to the lower part of the arms on the shirt so that the sleeves were slashed to ribbons and flapped wildly when he fired the ball to the plate. He felt his fastball was much more effective when it came flying out of those strips of cloth.

Many opponents, including McGraw, accused Vance of slashing the shirt on purpose but he claimed it was his lucky shirt that he had used since his New Orleans days and that it was just naturally tattered. Bressler, who was Vance's roommate for four years, remembered that Dazzy was especially effective on Monday because so many Flatbush residents did their laundry and hung it out to dry that day.

"You couldn't hit him on a Monday," Bressler recalled. "He cut the sleeve of his undershirt to the elbow and on that part of it he used lye to make it white, and the rest he didn't care how dirty it was. Then he'd pitch overhand out of the apartment houses in the background at Ebbets Field. Between the bleached sleeve of his undershirt waving and the Monday wash hanging out to dry—the diapers and undies and sheets flapping on the clothesline—you lost the ball entirely. He threw balls by me I never even saw."[16]

Casey Stengel remembered that the flapping sleeves were disconcerting, but not the only thing that made Vance great.

"It used to bother the opposing hitters, but it wasn't the undershirt that made them swing and miss like they claimed, but the stuff he had on the ball," Stengel said.[17]

About the only thing Vance did not do well on the mound was hold runners on base. Because of the leg kick, he was one of the easiest pitchers in baseball to run on.

"It don't matter none," Robinson once said. "When Daz is pitching, a steal is really only a loan."[18]

Vance was just as well known for his personality as for his pitching. Bressler described him as "one of the great storytellers of all time."[19] *New York Times* columnist Arthur Daley described him as "a whimsical, homespun philosopher with the dry wit of a Will Rogers."[20]

Although he had grown up in the Midwest, Vance somehow spoke with a southern drawl. And, of course, there was the matter of his actual given name, which seemed to change about every time Vance was asked about it.

The Robins seemingly cornered the market on eccentric personalities in that era and the team came to be known as the Daffiness Boys. It was a ballclub full of unpredictable flakes. It included players such as Babe Herman, whose fielding and baserunning lapses were so frequent and glaring that Vance nicknamed him "the headless horseman of Ebbets Field."[21]

The Robins players had what they called the "4 for 0 Club," so named because so many of them so often went 0 for 4 at the plate in games. Vance, who loved moonshine whiskey and a good cigar, was the president. He even drew up a set of bylaws for the club, including one that read, "Raise all the hell you want but don't get caught."[22]

10. Pitcher: Dazzy Vance

On one occasion, the Robins caught a midnight train out of New York to go to Boston for a series with the Braves and found that the Boston players, who had just finished a series in Philadelphia, were passengers on the same train. Vance and a few teammates took a scissors to some pillowcases and fashioned homemade hoods. Then they went to where the Braves players were sleeping in Pullman cars, dragged some of them from their berths, told them they were with the Ku Klux Klan and demanded that catcher Mickey O'Neill tell them what his signs were. A terrified O'Neill told them everything they wanted to know.[23]

The carefree, devil-may-care personality of the team occasionally came out on the playing field.

Vance and Herman both were involved in a 1926 play that epitomized the personality of the Robins and ranks as perhaps the most famous baserunning gaffe in the annals of the game. DeBerry was on third base with Vance on second and teammate Chick Fewster on first when Herman bashed a long drive off the right-field fence.

DeBerry scored easily and Vance, after waiting to make sure the ball was not caught, was rounding third and headed for the plate. Fewster was well on his way to third when third base coach Otto Miller shouted instructions for Herman to stop at second. Herman either didn't hear or completely disregarded the instructions because he barreled around second with no intentions of stopping. Vance heard Miller shouting, "Back, back" and thought he was talking to him. He stopped in his tracks and retreated to third. He slid back into third base at about the same instant Herman slid into the bag from another direction. Fewster already was standing there between them.

The third baseman got the ball and tagged everyone he could find. Vance while still lying on the ground politely addressed umpire Beans Reardon and told him that he thought under the rules, he should be ruled safe at third. He was right. Fewster and Herman both were called out.[24] It's believed to be the only time in major league history that someone doubled into a double play.

In his later seasons, Vance seldom matched the glorious, sustained success he had in 1924 and 1925. In 1926, his record dropped to just 9–10 and other than an excellent 1928 season in which he went 22–10, had a career-low 2.06 ERA and won the last of his seven straight strikeout titles, he was pretty much a .500 pitcher for the remainder of his years in Brooklyn.

It didn't help that in 1929, the Cubs lodged a complaint about his ragged shirt sleeves and a rule finally was passed outlawing the practice.[25]

After going 12–11 with a 4.20 ERA in 1932, Vance was traded by the Robins to St. Louis along with Gordon Slade for Owen Carroll and Jake Flowers. A year later, the Cardinals put him on waivers and the Reds picked him up prior to the 1934 season. After being released in June, he went back to the Cardinals.

His return to a team known affectionately as the Gashouse Gang afforded Vance his only opportunity to be part of a World Series. After the Cardinals clinched the pennant, Vance gleefully chortled to reporters, "Yes boys, in the general confusion it looks as though the old master finally did sneak into a World Series."[26]

Although he warmed up in the bullpen a few times early in the series, the old master made his one and only post-season appearance in Game 4. Starting pitcher Tex Carleton ran into early problems and was yanked by manager Frankie Frisch with the Cardinals trailing 2–1 in the third inning.

Dazzy Vance pitched for the Cincinnati Reds in the latter stages of his career.

In came the 43-year-old Vance, who induced slugger Hank Greenberg to hit a routine ground ball that found its way through the infield for a run-scoring single. Marv Owen reached base on an infield hit but Vance struck out Pete Fox to end the inning.

In the fourth inning, Vance walked leadoff man Jo-Jo White with one out and White immediately stole second. Catcher Bill DeLancey threw the ball into center field but the Cardinals appeared to have White thrown out at third base only to have Pepper Martin drop the ball. White scored on a Vance wild pitch, but the old master bore down and retired a pair of future Hall of Famers—Mickey Cochrane and Charlie Gehringer—to end the inning.

That was it. He was lifted for a pinch-hitter in the next inning and Detroit went on to win the game 10–4 although St. Louis won the series in seven games. It was Dazzy's last big moment as a player in the national spotlight.

In 1935, he was a free agent again and spent one final nondescript season with Brooklyn, pitching 20 games in relief.

After that, he retired to Homosassa Springs on Florida's Gulf Coast. He and his wife Edythe, who he married in 1917 back in Nebraska, had moved there about 10 years earlier after falling in love with the area. Always a lover of outdoors sports, Vance opened a hunting and fishing camp there, worked as a guide for visitors (including a lot of ballplayers) and even designed his own fishing lures. Sportswriter Bill McCullough paid a visit to Vance in Florida in 1937 and wrote, "Vance seldom talks baseball but will spend half the night telling you how to hook a big grouper or a kingfish."[27]

Vance owned the Homosassa Springs Hotel for 18 years and helped found the local chamber of commerce, serving as the chairman of its board of directors for many years.[28]

He was hospitalized for several months with a severe case of pneumonia during the winter of 1938–39 and lost 70 pounds, but he remained in good health otherwise, playing in numerous old-timers games.

He was elected to the Hall of Fame in 1955, becoming the first Brooklyn player to be so honored. Vance was touched and gratified by the honor. He admitted it felt as though he had now achieved everything he ever dreamed of achieving in life. "Now there's nothing left for me but to let nature take its course," he said.[29]

One day in February 1961, he went out and cleared some brush from his land, did an interview with Hall of Fame historian Ken Smith and seemed to be in perfect health for someone only weeks away from their 70th birthday.[30]

The next morning he was dead of a heart attack.

Of all those who eulogized him, New York sportswriter Frank Graham probably came closest to capturing what Vance was all about: "All he ever wanted to do was play baseball, go fishing or sit in the sun. Everywhere he went, and he went about everywhere in this country, he made friends and had laughs."[31]

Pitcher
Earl Whitehill

"Earl Whitehill was the toughest big-league pitcher I ever faced."—Hall of Fame outfielder Cool Papa Bell[1]

In addition to being one of the steadiest and most consistent pitchers of the 1920s and '30s, Earl Whitehill also was an avid golfer. He consistently scored in the 80s and loved to play as frequently as possible.

One day he and some teammates were playing a course in Arizona during spring training and they were far down the fairway, waiting for a group in front of them, when a ball came flying from behind them and bounded between Whitehill's legs. There had been no warning. No one had shouted, "Fore!"

Whitehill was enraged. He spun on his heels and was determined to charge back to the tee area to confront the offender. "I'm going to go back there right now and punch his lights out!" he told his playing partners. They finally were able to restrain him, calm him down and avert an altercation, which probably was a good thing. The offending golfer was heavyweight boxing champion Jack Dempsey.[2]

The story, told frequently through the years by Whitehill's Detroit teammate, Eldon Auker, was indicative of his competitive fire. The diminutive pitcher from Cedar Rapids was ready and willing to take on anyone at any time in any situation.

Cedar Rapids Gazette columnist Gus Schrader called him "one of the toughest competitors baseball ever knew. He was a defiant man who could never turn down a challenge."[3]

Whitehill pitched 17 seasons in the major leagues with the Tigers,

Senators, Indians and Cubs, winning 218 games. Hall of Famers Bob Feller and Red Faber are the only Iowans ever to win more.

At five feet, nine inches, Whitehill never weighed more than 175 pounds during his career. He was a lefthander with a good curve ball, which he mingled with an assortment of other pitches, none of which moved very fast. He employed a smooth, graceful delivery in which he spun and turned his back almost completely to the hitter. He learned to throw that way during his first professional stop at Birmingham, Alabama. Whitehill only weighed about 140 pounds then and manager Carl Molesworth thought it might help him get a little more velocity on his pitches.[4] Whitehill also found it was a great way to deceive the hitter and keep him from knowing what pitch was coming.

Earl Whitehill.

The hitter, in his mind, was the ultimate enemy and he infuriated more than a few of them by turning his back to them while on the mound, staring at the center-field fence and making them wait for him to throw his next pitch. He once told *Washington Post* sportswriter Shirley Povich, "Any fellow who walks up there with a bat in his hand is trying to take bread and butter out of my mouth."[5]

Born and raised in Cedar Rapids, he was the son of Noah Whitehill, who had a barber shop on the south side of town. Young Earl learned the game on the city's sandlots and played for a variety of amateur and semi-pro teams.

He got his first shot in professional ball in 1919 when Cedar Rapids attorney Harry Johnson convinced an old friend, Tom Fearweather, who owned the Des Moines Boosters of the Western League, to give the local kid a shot.[6] It didn't last long. The 20-year-old Whitehill pitched in only two games and was thoroughly ineffective, allowing nine runs on 13 hits in only 7⅓ innings. The Boosters gave up on him in a hurry and released him.

Cedar Rapids–based scout Cy Slapnicka was there to take advantage of the situation. Slapnicka would become famous for signing Feller and

Cedar Rapids area slugger Hal Trosky, who later became teammates of Whitehill's with the Cleveland Indians, but he worked for Detroit at that time. He signed Whitehill for the Tigers, who sent him to Columbia of the Class C South Atlantic League in 1920.

Whitehill showed what he could do in Columbia, going 20–10 with a 2.22 earned run average. He also pitched one game with Birmingham of the Class A Southern Association that season and was hit very hard, but went back to Birmingham the following year and spent the next three seasons as one of the cornerstones of the Barons' success. The *Atlanta Journal Constitution* noted in 1923 that "when Whitehill is in full command of his repertoire, there is no harder pitcher to beat in the league."[7] He compiled won-loss records of 19–14, 17–14 and 18–13 in those three seasons, working 857 innings, and the Tigers finally were convinced that they could use the little lefty at the major league level. They purchased his contract from Birmingham and brought him to the big leagues for the final three weeks of the 1923 season.

Whitehill pitched in eight games, including two starts, went 2–0 with a 2.73 ERA and must have impressed Detroit manager Ty Cobb. He inserted Whitehill into his starting rotation the following season in place of veteran Hooks Dauss, who remains the winningest pitcher in Detroit history.

Cobb, among the most fiery competitors ever to come across the American sports landscape, was Whitehill's manager in his first four major league seasons and likely had an impact on Whitehill also becoming one of the game's most hard-nosed competitors.

In his first full season, Whitehill went 17–9 with a 3.86 ERA and finished 17th in the American League's Most Valuable Player voting.

He also served notice of what kind of pitcher he was going to be by hitting more batters than any hurler in the league. A few years later, he set a major league record by plunking four hitters in one game. From the very beginning, pitching inside was a big part of Whitehill's philosophy.

"They give me a baseball and that other guy a bat," Whitehill was fond of saying. "He's also got a big box to move around in ... and I'm going to move him."[8]

It wasn't the last time he led the league in a dubious statistic. He gave up more earned runs than any other pitcher in the American League in 1926 and 1935, was the leader in walks in 1927, allowed the most home runs in 1931 and led in hit batsmen again in 1938.

He didn't overpower anyone and walked more batters than he struck out in his career. His single-season high in strikeouts was a paltry 109.

What he did do was take the ball game after game, week after week, year after year and compete as hard as anyone in baseball. Starting with that 1924 season, Whitehill won 11 or more games 13 years in a row and worked more than 200 innings in all but one of those seasons.

He was a leading perpetrator of what latter-day statistician Bill James has labeled a "cheap win"—a victory in which a starting pitcher has sub-par numbers but still wins the game. Modern-day pitcher Jamie Moyer is the all-time leader with 58 cheap wins, according to James, but Whitehill is a close second with 54.[9] While the "cheap win" label implies that a pitcher was lucky and perhaps did not deserve to win, it's more an indication of an ability to pitch out of jams, minimize damage and persevere even when he doesn't have dominating stuff.

No one persevered quite like Earl Whitehill. On September 15, 1933, while pitching for Washington against his old teammates from Detroit, he allowed 15 hits but still managed to win, 4–3. On June 11, 1927, he allowed 20 baserunners—on 13 hits and seven walks—but beat the Philadelphia Athletics 6–5. On April 21, 1929, he allowed 21 St. Louis Browns to reach base—on 14 hits and seven walks—but went all the way to win, 16–9.

Shirley Povich said a manager who took Whitehill out of a game almost always got a cold stare.[10] A fielder who didn't give his fullest effort behind Whitehill often got more than that. Columnist Francis Stann of the *Washington Evening Post* recalled that after third baseman Travis Jackson fumbled a grounder one day when Whitehill was on the mound, the pitcher stared angrily at Jackson, then walked over to manager Joe Cronin at shortstop and said, "I don't care if Travis can hit .400. I want Ossie Bluege playing third base when I pitch. Bluege can't hit any better than I can, maybe but at least he isn't a donkey wearing a glove."[11]

In truth, Whitehill wasn't a bad hitter at all. He batted .204 for his career and in 1929 he hit .256 with three home runs.

Schrader recalled that Whitehill liked to be in charge on the mound, rather than deferring to the judgment of his catcher, as many pitchers did. He and a teammate once had an argument about the value of an experienced catcher. Whitehill insisted that he could win with any catcher and to prove the point he asked his manager to put a fresh, young rookie behind the plate in his next start.

"Before the game Earl told the rookie catcher that all signals would be given from the mound instead of the orthodox way," Schrader wrote. "The catcher would know whether Earl was going to throw a fast ball, curve or change of pace by the way Earl held his glove. Then Whitehill went out, with his usual bulldog determination, and pitched one of his best games."[12]

Some thought that Whitehill may have suffered from overwork at times in Detroit although he insisted that he never had a sore arm. In addition to starting 30 or more games in almost every season, Whitehill also was used frequently out of the bullpen. In both 1927 and 1929, he made 10 relief appearances.

Umpire Billy Evans, in a 1927 column, wrote, "There are some who believe that the weakening of Whitehill in a number of games has been caused by too much relief work. Earl has been used in the rescue role quite often this year with only fair success. Some pitchers insist that relief work for a couple of innings at high pressure takes more out of them than a whole game. Whitehill is listed as such a pitcher."[13]

But it wasn't long after that that Whitehill had perhaps the best stretch of his entire career. He put together an 11-game winning streak in the middle of the 1930 season that ran from early July until the third week of August. He threw nine complete games and 98 innings in the streak, compiling an ERA of 2.20.

Like most players of his era, Whitehill picked up some extra money by playing in games after the regular season was over. He was part of a team of major league players who went up against a squad of Negro League all-stars in October 1929. The black players won six of eight games. The only two games they lost were the ones in which they went up against Whitehill.[14]

Whitehill also occasionally would bring major league players back to his hometown for exhibition games following the season, including such high-profile stars as the Tigers' Harry Heilmann. On one such occasion, Whitehill was almost invincible on the mound. Going to the ninth inning, he had 19 strikeouts and in a display of cocksure showmanship, he called all his outfielders and infielders in to stand behind the mound as he pitched the final inning. He struck out the first batter in the inning, then the second. Heilmann, hoping to get a head start on his departure, began walking toward the first base line as Whitehill pitched to the final hitter. The batter ripped a line drive that Heilmann calmly reached up and snagged for the final out.[15]

Whitehill continued to be a consistent winner throughout 10 years in Detroit. He won 17 games for the Tigers again in 1930 and won 16 in 1926, 1927 and 1932.

But by then Cobb, Slapnicka and Whitehill's other biggest supporters were gone from the organization, and in December of 1932 the little lefty was traded to Washington in exchange for Firpo Marberry and Carl Fischer.

As if to prove that the Tigers made a mistake, Whitehill turned in his best season in 1933. He won 22 games, was ninth in the MVP voting (only two pitchers garnered more votes) and helped push the Senators to a rare American League pennant.

After the sort of season he had, it was expected that Whitehill would be on the mound in the opening game of the World Series against New York Giants legend Carl Hubbell. But Whitehill, who sometimes claimed never to have had any arm trouble, apparently came up with a sore left shoulder after pitching against the Yankees the previous week.[16] As a result, the Senators went with Lefty Stewart on the mound in the first game and General Crowder in the second game, and lost both games.

Whitehill finally got the call in the third game at Washington's Griffith Stadium and made the most of what was to be his only opportunity ever to pitch in the postseason.

It was a gala occasion. President Franklin Roosevelt was there to throw out the first pitch and several other major Washington political figures were in attendance. As Whitehill warmed up before the game, he was surrounded by two dozen uniformed police officers who were keeping a path clear for the car that would carry Roosevelt to his box seat behind the first-base dugout.[17]

Once the game began, Whitehill was in complete control. Cronin described his pitching as "marvelous" and he wasn't exaggerating.[18] After allowing two baserunners in both the second and third innings, Whitehill settled into a dominating groove. He needed only four pitches to retire the side in the fifth inning, only five in the sixth and only six in the seventh. Only one ball was hit out of the infield in those three innings. He gave up another hit in the eighth and walked slugger Mel Ott to open the ninth, but held on for a 4–0 victory. He had allowed just five hits and put the Senators right back in contention.

The folks back in Cedar Rapids rejoiced. Noah Whitehill, who had closed his barber shop at 920 S. Third for the day, fired off a telegram to his son, telling him, "I'm the happiest man in Iowa."[19] Earl Coughlin wrote in his "Red Peppers" column in the *Cedar Rapids Gazette*: "Whitehill can now be recorded in capital letters as a Cedar Rapids boy who made good in the city."[20]

Unfortunately, the Senators lost the next two games to the Giants. Whitehill never got into another game in a World Series.

Early in that 1933 season, Whitehill had beaned Yankees superhero Lou Gehrig, who then was close to breaking Everett Scott's record for consecutive games played. Gehrig was knocked unconscious but recovered enough to play the next day and went on to shatter Scott's record. However, it was the start of some bad blood between Whitehill and the AL's perennial powerhouse team.

On April 25 in Washington, the Yankees' Ben Chapman got into a tussle with second baseman Buddy Myer of the Senators and Whitehill couldn't help but also get involved. It began when Chapman bowled over Myer going into second base, spiking him in the process. Myer responded by kicking Chapman in the ribs, setting off a fight between the two and resulting in their ejections.

In order to leave the field, Chapman had to go through the Washington dugout and as he did so, Whitehill said something to him. Chapman later claimed that Whitehill rushed over to him and "called me a name that the Virginian demanded a smile for when he used it, and I promptly knocked him down. Then other Senators jumped on me and in a second we were all battling."[21] Both benches emptied and an estimated 300 fans even came onto the field and became involved in the brawl. Five fans were arrested and it was 20 minutes before the game could resume.

Whitehill, Chapman and Myer each was fined $100 and suspended five days for their parts in the incident.[22] The *Washington Post* launched a campaign to try to get fans to pay off the fines of the Senators players by chipping in a dime apiece, but Washington owner Clark Griffith put a stop to that, fearing it would undermine the authority of league president Will Harridge.[23]

The Yankees got their revenge. Twice during the following season, Whitehill flirted with no-hitters against the New Yorkers only to have it broken up both times. On May 30, it was Chapman himself who thwarted the no-hitter. On August 16, it was Bob Meusel.

Not all of Whitehill's relations with the Yankees were unfriendly. He became very good friends with Yankees slugger Babe Ruth and not only because Ruth hit 11 of his 714 career home runs off Whitehill. The Senators pitcher was part of a team that Ruth and Connie Mack took on a lengthy barnstorming tour to Japan and the Far East following the 1934 season. Whitehill's wife, Violet, who he married in 1924, hit it off with Ruth's wife, Clare, and the two couples became very close. In fact, Violet and Whitehill's younger brother, Edward, sat with the Ruths in the box seats at Whitehill's World Series win in 1933.[24]

Whitehill wasn't quite as sharp in his ensuing seasons with the Senators but he definitely was consistent. He won 14 games in 1934, 14 in '35 and 14 in '36.

In December 1936, he was traded to Cleveland in a three-way deal that also involved the White Sox. Cy Slapnicka, the scout who had signed Whitehill, was now vice president of the Indians, who also employed fellow Iowans Feller and Trosky.

At the age of 37, Whitehill's career began to decline. He worked fewer innings and went 8–8 with a career-worst 6.49 ERA in 1937 and 9–8 with a 5.56 ERA in 1938.

He was released on February 1, 1939, and signed with the Chicago Cubs about two weeks later. In one final season, he went 4–7 in only 89⅓ innings and was released.

In 1940, Whitehill went back to the Indians to serve as their pitching coach under manager Oscar Vitt, who had been his teammate back in Detroit. But after the season, both Vitt and Slapnicka left Cleveland and that spelled the end for Whitehill, too.

He served as the Phillies' pitching coach in 1943 and in 1944 landed a job as the pitching coach of the Tigers' farm team at Buffalo in the International League. With World War II in progress, quality players were in short supply and at the age of 45, Whitehill was called upon to take the mound a few times for the Bisons. He pitched in 10 games, worked 23 innings and compiled an 0–3 record. In true Whitehill fashion, he had almost as many hit batsmen (7) as strikeouts (9).

After that, he found his niche selling sporting goods for the A.G. Spalding Company and obtained an executive position with the company, moving to New York City in 1954.

In August of that year, his wife of 30 years, Violet, filed for divorce and moved to Los Angeles.[25]

Two months later, Whitehill was in Omaha on business when his car was broadsided by a driver who went through a stop sign. Whitehill refused treatment at the scene of the accident but awoke the next morning with a severe headache. A friend, Omaha Cardinals team president Bob Hall, got him to a hospital and Whitehill was placed under observation for a few days. His only daughter, Earlinda, came up from her home in Kansas City and Whitehill seemed to be doing fine. Then, late on October 21, his condition began to worsen. He underwent surgery the next day to relieve a brain hemorrhage, but did not survive the operation.

Francis Stann, who once had a tooth knocked out by Whitehill because of one of his columns but still counted the veteran pitcher among his friends, wrote, "Whitehill was so strangely competitive that it is difficult to believe he died after a mere accident."[26]

Shirley Povich added, "Whitehill yielded to no man among them in the ferocity of his own play, but off the field he was the complete gentleman with a lively interest in the topics of the day. Against the scoffing of his Detroit teammates on the off-days in Washington, he could be found in immaculate dress in the visitors' galleries in congress."[27]

All of those who eulogized him indicated that the hard-nosed Whitehill that people saw on the playing field masked a jovial gentleman and dedicated professional off the field.

Povich suggested that his epitaph simply read "Earl Whitehill, big leaguer. That he was and in more than the baseball sense."[28]

First Base
Hal Trosky

"He was right there, standing on the cusp of greatness, and it all fell apart."—Author Terry Pluto[1]

The 1930s were the decade of the first baseman. Seemingly half the teams in baseball had a fence-busting slugger for the ages playing the position. Lou Gehrig was swatting his way to immortality with the Yankees. Jimmy Foxx was doing the same with the Athletics and Red Sox. Hank Greenberg did it for the Tigers, Bill Terry for the Giants and Johnny Mize for the Cardinals.

All of those players ended up being inducted into baseball's Hall of Fame. And chances are, Hal Trosky would have joined them were it not for some blinding headaches.

Trosky, the first in a long line of great players to come out of the baseball-mad berg of Norway, Iowa, had his career cut short by migraines that began to impair his productivity when he should have been in his prime and which ultimately brought about a premature end to his career.

From 1934 through 1939, Trosky drove in more than 100 runs every year. He batted .330 or better in four of those seasons. In his first full season in the major leagues he drove in 142 runs. Two years later, he batted .343 with 42 homers and 162 RBI.

But by the latter stages of the 1941 season the headaches had pushed him to the sidelines. After two years away from game, he played two more torturous seasons but never was the same.

Born in 1912, Harold Arthur Trojovsky was the youngest of four children of John and Mary Trojovsky, both of whom had been born to immigrants of mixed European lineage that included strains of French, German and Polish.

John and Mary bought a 420-acre farm outside Norway when Hal was only four and, like most rural Iowa kids, he grew up doing an array of chores. He milked eight cows every morning and eight cows every night until the age of 17, and later credited those duties with giving him tremendous strength in his hands and arms.[2]

Many Norway kids in the 1920s dropped out of high school to work on the farm. There was no time for schoolwork when there were chores to be done. But Hal stayed in school—the only one of the four Trojovsky kids to do so—apparently because Norway High needed a catcher.[3] He later branched out into playing the outfield and pitching, grew to be six feet, two inches, and 207 pounds, and developed into an exceptional prospect. He showed promise as both a right-handed pitcher and hitter although he used a peculiar cross-handed grip at the plate.

Several major league teams showed an interest, but the first to make Trojovsky an offer was the St. Louis Cardinals in 1930. The Cardinals wanted to sign him and send him to play for their Danville team in the Three-I League. Unsure how to proceed, he sought the advice of Bing Miller, who had been raised on a farm in the same part of Iowa and had become an established star with the world champion Philadelphia Athletics. After listening to radio broadcasts of Miller playing in the 1930 World Series, Trosky drove up to Vinton to talk to him. Miller had heard about the Trojovsky kid and told him not to do anything until he had a chance to talk to Athletics manager Connie Mack.[4]

Cy Slapnicka, from nearby Cedar Rapids, was a scout for the Cleveland Indians and he first saw Trosky play in a game at a county fair in 1930. He didn't bother to pursue him then. But when he heard from Hal's cousin, Jack Trosky, that the Cardinals and Athletics were interested, he was determined not to let the best prospect in his home area get away. According to some reports, Slap-

Hal Trosky (courtesy Iowa Baseball Museum of Norway).

nicka was sitting in the Trojovsky family kitchen chatting with John Trojovsky when Hal got home from talking to Miller. He had a contract scribbled out on a piece of paper ready for Hal to sign. The money looked good so he signed.[5]

Connie Mack came through with an even better offer just three days later, but it was too late. By then, Hal Trojovsky was the property of the Indians. He signed that first contract Trojovsky but quickly decided to shorten it to Trosky. His brother Victor and sisters Annette and Esther eventually did the same.

Trosky began his pro career as a member of the hometown Cedar Rapids Bunnies of the Mississippi Valley League in 1931 at a salary of $65 a month, but he wasn't there long, eventually being sent to the Dubuque team in the same league for the remainder of the season.

He had a won-loss record of 2–2 with a 4.75 earned run average in 13 games as a pitcher and he also saw action in the outfield, batting a healthy .302 thanks to a prudent suggestion by Slapnicka. The veteran scout cringed when he watched Trosky swing with that cross-handed grip and recommended that the kid keep the grip but turn around and bat lefthanded.[6] It worked wonders. When Trosky reported to the Toledo Mud Hens, the Indians' top farm club in 1932, he was a left-handed hitting outfielder whose pitching days were over.

It was quickly determined that he wasn't quite ready for the American Association and Trosky was sent to Quincy in the Three-I League. He also saw action with Springfield and Burlington in the Mississippi Valley League that summer, batting over .300 at each stop, before finally ending up back at Toledo at the end of the summer. He got to bat just once for the Mud Hens, banging out a single.

It was with Toledo in 1933 that Trosky became a full-time first baseman and really blossomed into a major offensive force. He batted .323 in 131 games and clubbed 33 home runs. He also worked tirelessly with manager Steve O'Neill to refine his defensive skills at first base. He never became terribly smooth at picking up ground balls, but he became a passable first baseman despite contentions by some that he "played first base with all the grace of a blacksmith strumming a harp."[7]

When the American Association season was over, Trosky joined the Indians for the final few weeks of the American League season and immediately was inserted into the cleanup spot in the Cleveland batting order.

But he was quickly reminded that he was a rookie. As he went to take batting practice with the Indians regulars, second baseman Billy Cissell grabbed him by the shirt, shoved him out of the batting cage and told him,

"Get you butt out of here you cornhusker and hit behind the pitcher where you belong."[8]

In another game during his first week with the Indians, Trosky was at first base when Yankees legend Babe Ruth pulled a vicious line drive in his direction. The force of the drive yanked the glove right off Trosky's hand and it landed in shallow right field. Trosky also recalled in later years that he swung and missed at the first 11 pitches the Yankees' Lefty Gomez threw him that day, then got a foul tip on the 12th pitch for his fourth straight strikeout.[9]

But after not getting a hit in his first week in the major leagues, Trosky hit a home run off Boston's Gordon Rhodes and began to settle in. The potential was obvious. Manager Walter Johnson knew that when the following season began, 21-year-old Hal Trosky was going to be his starting first baseman.

Trosky continued to show great promise in spring training with the Indians in 1934, but he was swinging a 40-ounce bat and sometimes having trouble getting around on the top fastball pitchers. Veteran pitcher Sergeant George Connally recommended that he try a lighter bat. Trosky borrowed one of Connally's 34-ounce bats and began having immediate success. He never went back to the heavier bat.

He played for Cleveland for the modest salary of $3,000 in 1934 and the Indians more than got their money's worth. Trosky played every inning of every game, batted .330, hit 35 home runs, drove in 142 runs and finished seventh in the voting for American League Most Valuable Player.

It was the start of arguably the best six-year run of any hitter in Cleveland history. It was pointed out by many observers that he had a better rookie season than any of the other great sluggers of the day, including Gehrig and Greenberg.

Dan Daniel, who wrote for the *New York World-Telegram* and *Baseball Magazine*, named Trosky his rookie of the year and quoted Yankees executive Ed Barrow as saying Trosky "has the best chance to succeed Lou Gehrig as the power house of the American League, and was far and away the outstanding recruit of 1934." Barrow further predicted that Trosky would develop faster and be better than Greenberg. "I have no doubt that in time he will stand out as the greatest first sacker of the majors and the hitter of his league."[10] Other experts, including American League president Will Harridge, predicted that Trosky was "the future Babe Ruth."[11]

In his outstanding 1934 season, Trosky stood far back in the batter's box with a very open stance, his right foot pointed toward first base. It obviously worked for him but the stance was questioned by many. In 1935, responding to the criticism, he changed to a more even stance.[12]

His stats fell off as a result. His average dropped nearly 60 points although he still drove in 113 runs during the season. Late in the season, he lapsed into a major slump in which he got only one hit in 40 at-bats.

He grew so desperate to snap out of his September doldrums that his old Toledo manager, Steve O'Neill, suggested that Trosky try hitting again from the right side of the plate with that awkward cross-hand grip. He smacked a solid single in his first at-bat that way and later clubbed a long right-handed homer off Washington's Leon Pettit. Over the course of two games, he collected four hits as a right-handed hitter but it was only a temporary fix. He went back to batting left-handed after that.

Trosky said he felt his .271 average in 1935 was not due to the changed stance but because he was trying too hard to hit home runs, listening too much to the lofty comparisons to Ruth.

"To the devil with that Ruth stuff," he said on the eve of the 1936 season. "I don't know where anyone got the idea that someone—above all myself—would come along to take his place. It isn't going to be done. Yet I heard and read so much about it that for a while I tried to knock the ball out of the lot every time I came to bat. I began to press badly. I became jittery."[13]

The jitters disappeared in 1936 and Trosky had his best season, for a variety of reasons. He led the American League in RBI with 162 and total bases with 405, setting Indians team records in both categories as well as in home runs with 42. The RBI record stood for 63 years. The total bases mark still stands.

And in September, his wife Lorraine, a Norway girl he married prior to the 1934 season, gave birth to a son. Lorraine Glenn also grew up in Norway and she and Hal had known each other since kindergarten. They both attended St. Michael's Catholic Church and they had been friends and collaborators in high school. Trosky played the saxophone and he often played duets with Lorraine playing the piano. But they never started dating until they were 18.

Their son, Hal Trosky, Jr., was destined to also make it to the major leagues. He pitched in two games with the White Sox in 1958.

Included in that 1936 season was a 28-game hitting streak by Trosky. Like so many great sluggers, he was capable of getting into hot streaks in which he seemingly could do no wrong. On two different occasions in his career—on May 30, 1934, and July 5, 1937—he hit home runs in three consecutive at-bats. He had an especially torrid stretch in the final weeks of

1936. On September 15, he drove in seven runs in a game and also broke Cleveland's single-season record for RBI in a 13–2 victory over Boston. He continued to produce the next day and finished the two-game binge going 8 for 8 with 12 RBI.

It probably didn't hurt that O'Neill, who had played such a role in Trosky's early development, had become the Cleveland manager in the middle of the 1935 season. The two men had great rapport and O'Neill loved Trosky because he didn't drink or smoke and was always in bed in by 10 p.m. "He's never the slightest trouble to a manager, and he's always in condition," O'Neill said.[14]

Trosky had another great season in 1937—32 homers, 128 RBI—and although he dropped to 19 home runs in 1938, he batted .334 with 110 RBI. Over those first five seasons as a regular, he missed only eight games.

That changed in 1939. Although no one knew it at the time, he was beginning to feel the effects of the headaches. It has been reported in some places that Trosky first experienced migraines at the age of 16, but the severity of them increased in 1939 as he missed 32 games and his hitting statistics dropped off.

The headaches dissipated after the season and Trosky consulted several doctors, none of whom were able to identify the problem. The headaches came back in 1940, impairing Trosky's ability to concentrate on the field.

Other things were happening in 1940 that would have given him headaches had he not already been experiencing them. Trosky had become the Indians' team captain in 1939, a role he gladly accepted as a way to serve as a buffer between some of the team's less experienced players and vitriolic manager Oscar Vitt. Vitt was blunt and often harshly critical of his players and when the Indians began to struggle in June of 1940, a mutinous mood came over the team. Trosky, who had been named the team captain in 1939, tried to defuse the feelings even though he too had been a target of Vitt's diatribes.

Nevertheless, a group of veteran players began circulating a petition asking for Vitt to be fired. Pitcher Mel Harder was appointed their spokesman to go talk to owner Alva Bradley. On June 13, Harder called to set up an appointment with Bradley and 11 players—including Bob Feller—showed up to speak to the owner.[15]

Trosky was not among them. On that same day he had received word that his mother had died back in Iowa and he was on his way back to Norway when the dissidents laid out their grievances for Bradley. It was reported in later years that as the players were stating their case to Bradley, the owner received a phone call from Trosky telling him that he was in

12. First Base: Hal Trosky

Hal Trosky (left) and Bob Feller (right) were among a group of Cleveland Indians players who rebelled against the tactics of manager Oscar Vitt (center) in 1940 (courtesy Iowa Baseball Museum of Norway).

agreement with the other players. Bradley assured the players he would look into the matter but warned them not to make their issues public. Unfortunately, word leaked out and the feud between Vitt and his players made headlines on the front page of the *Cleveland Plain-Dealer* the next day.[16]

Trosky's involvement in the attempted mutiny—if he had any at all—remains a bit of a mystery to this day. The *Plain-Dealer* printed a clarification a few days later stating that Trosky never admitted any connection to the plan or that Vitt ever made any allegations against his captain.[17]

Trosky's headaches intensified in the last two months of the season and the Indians ended up finishing second in the American League, just one game behind Detroit. Trosky had a decent season by almost anyone's standards—he hit .295 with 25 home runs—but for the first time as an everyday player he came up short of 100 RBI.

His decline continued in 1941 as the headaches became even worse and he missed several games. Trosky later said that fastballs sometimes looked like "a bunch of white feathers" when he was standing at the plate.[18] On one occasion a pitcher threw a fastball under his chin and he never moved. The home plate umpire told him that the ball just barely missed him. In one game, facing Detroit's hard-throwing Dizzy Trout, he had to remove himself from the lineup. Another time pitcher Mel Harder threw a pickoff throw to him at first and it hit him in the mid-section. He never saw it.[19] He spoke publicly about the headaches for the first time in July, saying he had no intention of retiring.

"But gosh, a fellow can't go on like this forever," he cautioned. "If I can't find some relief, I'll simply have to give up and spend the rest of my days on my farm in Iowa. It was so bad one day last summer that I walked out to Mel Harder who was pitching and asked him not to try to pick the runner off first base. I knew if Mel threw me a fast ball, I wouldn't even see it."[20]

Feller said he thought Trosky's headaches were the result of stress[21] and Trosky admitted that he was sensitive to criticism and sometimes put too much pressure on himself.

"I know the fellows are counting on me," he once said. "I know that I can't always make good for them. I'm all right until I get on that field. Then my head starts hammering."[22]

Cleveland sportswriter Franklin Lewis called Trosky "a worry wart who can't give his best efforts if he's upset,"[23] and his teammates also took note of his fretful nature. They occasionally jokingly called him "Little Sunshine," a sarcastic commentary on his sober, sometimes downcast disposition.[24]

Indians manager Roger Peckinpaugh, who had replaced the embattled Vitt, admitted he had no idea that Trosky had been having such serious problems.[25] When the Indians left for a seven-game road trip in August, Trosky stayed home. He eventually rejoined the club but a few days later in a game in Chicago, he collided with White Sox pitcher Ted Lyons and broke his thumb.

He missed the last 39 games of the season. Little did he know at the time that he would never play in another game for the Indians.

In February of 1942 Trosky announced that he would not be playing that season. He wrote a letter to Alva Bradley asking to be put on the voluntarily retired list. Bradley wrote back, expressing his regrets but admitting that he thought it was the wise thing to do.[26] At the age of 29, Trosky seemingly was finished as a player.

"I have visited various doctors in the larger cities in the United States and they have not helped me," he told the *Des Moines Register* in a telephone interview. "If, after resting this year, I find that I am better, perhaps I'll try to be reinstated. If I don't get any better, then my major league career is over. I know I can't play regularly and the Indians might just as well start the season with some young fellow at first."[27]

Trosky spent that summer on the farm. The Japanese had attacked Pearl Harbor in December and he expressed an interest in enlisting in the service and becoming part of the war effort. However, he was classified 4F because of the headaches.

There were reports in August 1942 that Trosky's headaches had faded[28] and there were additional reports in December that the Yankees were interested in acquiring him. Trosky admitted he had spoken to new Indians manager Lou Boudreau about possibly returning.[29]

"The club that got me would be taking a chance after all because I've been out of baseball a year and I don't know how the absence will affect me," Trosky said.[30]

It would be more than a year after that before he finally did get back in the game. He missed the entire 1942 and '43 seasons. He finally went through a workout for the White Sox and the Indians sold his rights to Chicago for $45,000.

In 1944, Trosky was back in baseball with the White Sox. He put up modest numbers, batting .241 with a team-leading 10 home runs and 71 RBI, and retired again.

He went to work at the Amana Refrigeration plant in Iowa and the headaches eased up again. Fans sent Trosky hundreds of home remedies—including one that involved regular doses of molasses and vinegar—and he seemingly finally figured out ways to control the headaches. He took shots of vitamin B-1 and cut back on his consumption of milk products. Ironically, a man who had grown up on a dairy farm apparently was lactose intolerant.[31]

He decided to give baseball one more try in 1946. He played 88 games with the White Sox and batted only .254 with just two home runs. The White Sox were willing to bring him back for another season and even raise his salary from $21,000 a year to $25,000, but Trosky had had enough. This time he retired for good.

Nearly 70 years later, he still is in the top five on the Indians' all-time list in RBI (fourth), slugging percentage (fourth), home runs (fifth) and extra base hits (fourth). He finished with a career batting average of .302, but it was .313 before those last two struggle-filled seasons with the White Sox. In 1969, he was voted by fans as the first baseman on the Indian's all-time team.[32] One of the oddities of his career is that he never was named to an American League All-Star team. He always got edged out for the honor by Gehrig, Greenberg or Foxx.

Trosky told the *Des Moines Register* in 1965, "I never really did get rid of those migraines till I got out of baseball."[33]

Hal Trosky, Jr., told the *Cedar Rapids Gazette* in 2007 that his father "had a migraine headache every day until he was 50. Those migraines were bears.... How that man ever did one-fifth of what he did, I can't answer."[34]

Trosky continued to work for the White Sox as a scout for a few years and managed a semipro team bankrolled by Amana—the Freezers—that included former major leaguer Jack Dittmer and former NFL star Emlen Tunnell.

He spent most of the rest of his life farming although he also got into the agricultural real estate business in Cedar Rapids in the 1960s. In 1962, he sold his big farm and bought a smaller piece of land where he raised Angus cattle and hogs. He also did plenty of hunting, mostly for pheasants and rabbits, and bought and sold classic cars.

He suffered four heart attacks during the last five years of his life and one of them finally killed him in the spring of 1979.

Ten years earlier, the Indians had named their all-time team. The first baseman was Hal Trosky.

While it would have been easy to feel bitter about the way his career was abbreviated, Trosky was philosophical about what happened to him.

"My career was short, but I loved it," he said just weeks before his death. "I have nothing against the players today.... I don't think they study the game as much, and they 'guess' hit. I always believed in hitting the first pitch that was over the plate. I don't like the popping off some do now. And some can't seem to stand being bossed by a manager. There has to be a boss. You know, you play the game 50 percent for fun and 50 percent for what you get out of it. I think we had more fun in a day than most players now have in a week. I still get a fan letter now and then. Sometimes people ask, 'Why aren't you in the Hall of Fame?' I say, 'Because I don't deserve to be there.'"[35]

If his health had allowed him to have six more years like those first six, there's not much doubt that he'd be there.

Pitcher
Bob Feller

"I don't think anyone is ever going to throw a ball faster than he does. And his curveball isn't human."—Hall of Fame slugger Joe DiMaggio[1]

We'll never really know for sure exactly how Bob Feller's fastball would have measured up against those of modern-day pitchers.

There was no truly reliable technological device for measuring the speed of a baseball when Feller broke into the major leagues in the 1930s. The concept of using radar to quantify the velocity of moving objects didn't come into use until the 1940s. It wasn't used by law enforcement agencies until 1949 and its use in baseball came long after that.

Still, there was enough fascination with the Feller fastball that several attempts were made through the years to gauge its velocity. In 1940, scientists in Chicago tried to do it by having a speeding motorcycle roar past Feller just as he was unleashing the ball. He was supposed to pitch from the stretch but instead used a windup, the result being that the motorcycle was well past him when the ball left his hand. However, the scientists determined that Feller's fast one gained 13 feet on the motorcycle over the course of 60 feet, six inches, and since the motorcycle was traveling 86 mph, they calculated the speed of the pitch at 104 mph.[2]

Another attempt was made in 1946 when Feller was asked to throw 30 pitches through a three-foot wooden frame containing a photoelectric device. Feller later said he wasn't fully warmed up and he also was afraid of breaking the device—which he eventually did—so he didn't really cut loose. Even at that, his fastball was measured at 98.6 mph.

"I'm sure when I opened up in about the third or fourth inning of a ball game, my fastball would be well over 100 miles an hour," Feller said.³

That same year, an early primitive radar device used by the U.S. Army to measure the speed of artillery shells was applied to the Feller fastball at Griffith Stadium in Washington, D.C. The conclusion that day was that he had thrown 107.9 mph.⁴

None of those tests was reliable or conclusive, but one thing is clear: Bob Feller—aka Rapid Robert, aka Bullet Bob, aka the Heater from Van Meter—threw really, really hard, almost certainly harder than anyone else in his era, possibly harder than any man who ever lived.

After striking out on three straight pitches against Feller, Yankees pitcher Lefty Gomez turned to the umpire and mused, "That last one sounded a little low."⁵

Ted Williams, probably the greatest hitter of Feller's era, said he had to gear himself up for days to get ready to face the

Bob Feller (courtesy *Quad-City Times*).

Cleveland Indians fireballer. "I'd sit in my room thinking about him all the time," Williams said. "Allie Reynolds of the Yankees was tough and I might think about him for 24 hours before a game, but Robert Feller: I'd think about him for three days."⁶

The speed of his pitches and a fiery competitive streak helped Feller become the most dominant and effective pitcher of his time. He easily was elected to the Baseball Hall of Fame on his first time on the ballot in 1962 and in 1969 baseball named him the greatest living right-handed pitcher. He won 266 games and registered 2,581 strikeouts despite missing almost four years in his prime to military service. He played his entire 18-year career with Cleveland, leading the American League in wins and innings pitched five times each and in strikeouts seven times. He threw three no-hitters and 12 one-hitters.

All of it turned out exactly the way his father had planned it.

From the time Robert William Andrew Feller was born in 1918 on a farm near Van Meter, Iowa, just west of Des Moines, Bill Feller groomed his son for a career in the major leagues. Bill had played some semi-pro ball without ever getting close to the big time, but he was determined that his son would make it.

Bill Feller built his life around making his son into a ballplayer. Legend has it that little Bob's training began before he even attended school. Bill Feller would sit on the couch, roll a rubber ball to the little guy, then hold up a pillow as the target for the return throw. He cleared an area on the second floor of the barn where he and Bob could throw during the winter months. While most of his neighbors were planting corn, Bill Feller opted for wheat, which required less time and less work, leaving him able to focus on the task of nurturing the abilities of young Bob. When the priest at the Catholic church they attended chastised Bill for letting his son play baseball on the Sabbath, the Fellers abruptly became Methodists.[7]

It's uncertain how Lena Feller felt about her husband's obsession with making her son into a baseball star. A homemaker who formerly taught at a one-room schoolhouse in Van Meter and also was a registered nurse, she was most concerned with making sure her son got an education, frequently forcing him to walk three miles through the snow to school on days when the busses couldn't get through.[8]

When Bob was nine years old, he reportedly could throw the ball 275 feet and as he got into his teens Bill Feller took the youngster's development a step further. He took a portion of his 360-acre farm, chopped down 20 oak trees and constructed a baseball field he called Oakview.[9] He then formed his own semipro team, comprised mostly of players in their late teens and early 20s except for the 13-year-old prodigy who lived there on the premises.

"My father loved baseball and he cultivated my talent," Feller said in later years. "I don't think he ever had any doubt in his mind that I would play professional baseball someday."[10]

Bob played shortstop as well as pitching in his early days, but Bill Feller finally convinced him to focus strictly on pitching. In addition to playing for the Oakview team, he also starred for the team sponsored by American Legion 464 in the nearby town of Adel. His catcher on that team was Nile Kinnick, who was destined to win the Heisman Trophy while playing football at the University of Iowa in 1939.

As good a she was, Van Meter and Adel were a little off the beaten path for major league scouts, but a local resident named Pat Donovan kept writing letters to the Cleveland Indians telling them how good this Feller kid was.[11] In mid-summer 1935, the Indians finally sent their Iowa scout, Cy Slapnicka, over to check him out. Slapnicka, who lived in Cedar Rapids, had signed Earl Whitehill while working for Detroit and had procured the services of Hal Trosky for Cleveland a few years earlier. Some have reported that Slapnicka was more interested in checking out future major leaguer Claude Passeau, who was then in the midst of a 20-win season with the Des Moines team in the Western League, but after one look at Feller he knew he had stumbled upon something special.

In that era, there was a rule stating that major league teams could not sign high school age players. They could sign college players but high school kids were supposed to sign with minor league teams, who could then sell the rights to those players to the majors. Slapnicka cleverly circumvented the rules. Although he was employed by the Indians, he scrawled out a hand-written contract on the back of some stationery from the Warden Hotel in Ottumwa that bound Feller to the Fargo-Moorhead team of the Northern League. Feller and his parents signed the contract, dated July 22, 1935, which called for him to receive the sum of $1 plus an autographed baseball. That contract, which was on display at the Bob Feller Museum in Van Meter for many years, included a clause permitting Feller to leave the team and "visit his folks at any time during the 1936 season."[12]

Feller, who later received a signing bonus of $10,000, never even went to Fargo. There was one report that it was because he developed a sore arm but chances are, the plan never called for him to play there. Feller told reporters in later years that he wanted to continue playing high school baseball and basketball, and

A copy of Bob Feller's first professional contract was on display for many years in the Bob Feller Museum in Van Meter, Iowa.

as a result, the signing was kept secret. His contract eventually was transferred to the New Orleans club, another Cleveland affiliate, but he never pitched an inning there either. He didn't pitch for any pro team until the following summer.

In the meantime, his talents came to the attention of other major league teams. Feller pitched that summer for the Farmers Union team of Des Moines, compiling a 25–4 record and averaging an astonishing 19.4 strikeouts per game.[13] When he pitched well for the team in the opening round of a national semi-pro tournament, there were dozens of major league scouts in the stands. The Detroit Tigers immediately offered Feller $9,000 to sign and when Feller hedged, their suspicions were aroused. It came to light that Feller already was the property of Cleveland and in the ensuing dispute, commissioner Kennesaw Mountain Landis ordered the Indians to pay $7,500 to the Des Moines team.[14] It also ultimately led to the elimination of the impractical rule forbidding major league teams from signing high school kids.

When Feller finally arrived in Cleveland in the summer of 1936, he probably didn't look like much at first glance. He hadn't even started shaving yet at that point. He was not exceptionally large—only five feet, 11 inches, and 180 pounds—but like Trosky, he had built incredible strength by doing chores on the family farm, milking cows, hauling water, bailing hay, feeding livestock.

"There was nothing about him to suggest that he could, very possibly, throw a round object harder than anybody else who ever strode upon God's green earth," Frank Deford wrote in a 2005 *Sports Illustrated* profile of Feller.[15]

Veteran sportswriter Bob Broeg described Feller as "extremely splay-footed with a plow-jockey gait and leg-hiking delivery he'd never lose. He strutted around the mound as if he knew exactly how good he was. And he wound up fiercely in his pitching delivery and followed through as earnestly as Bill Feller had told him."[16]

In Cleveland in 1936, between his junior and senior years of high school, Feller initially was put to work in the Indians' concessions department while waiting to see what he could do as a pitcher. The Indians finally tossed him into one of those Monday exhibition games that major league teams often played in that era. The opponent was the St. Louis Cardinals, the storied Gashouse Gang, who had won three National League pennants in the previous six years and who were leading the NL again at the time.

Less than two years earlier, Feller's father had taken him to the 1934 World Series in St. Louis and the Cardinals' pitching in Game 4 had been less than impressive. In fact, it was the game in which fellow Iowa native Dazzy Vance made his only post-season appearance. Feller, then not quite 16, turned to his dad and whispered, "I can do better than that."[17]

He was right.

He entered the July 6 exhibition game in the fourth inning and the Cardinals must have recognized what they were up against when they saw him warming up. The first batter, Bruce Ogrodowski, tried to bunt for a hit and was thrown out. Feller then struck out the next three men he faced. Over the course of three innings, he gave up two hits, walked two and allowed a run. But he also struck out eight.

Franklin Lewis of the *Cleveland Press* wrote that some observers seemed to be laughing when they watched Feller's exaggerated high leg kick as he warmed up in the bullpen. But, Lewis noted, when he stepped onto the mound and began throwing gas "the guffaws turned to gasps."[18]

Steve O'Neill, the Indians' manager, caught Feller himself in the first two innings of the exhibition and was amazed by what he saw. So was home plate umpire Red Ormsby, who later called Feller "the best pitcher I have seen come into the American League." He said that included Walter Johnson, who won 414 games with the Washington Senators.[19]

After the game a photographer asked Cardinals superstar Dizzy Dean if he would be willing to pose with Feller. "Ask *him* if he'll pose with *me*," Dean said.[20]

The Indians quietly paid New Orleans $1,500 and the 17-year-old Feller officially became a Cleveland Indian.

He made his American League debut on July 19 in the second game of a doubleheader against the Philadelphia Athletics. He did not allow a run in the one inning he pitched, but he walked two and did not record a strikeout.

His first start came on August 23 and it went considerably better. He struck out 15 St. Louis Browns in a 4–1 victory. Three weeks later, on September 13, he equaled Dizzy Dean's major league record by notching 17 strikeouts against the Athletics. He also walked nine men, but won the game, 5–2.

After working 62 innings and going 5–3 for the Indians, he went back to Iowa for his final year at Van Meter High School, where he was elected senior class president. When he graduated in June, the ceremonies were broadcast on the radio from coast to coast by NBC and film of the proceedings was shown in theaters around the country on newsreels.

The previous month he had appeared on the cover of *Time Magazine*. With the probable exception of actress Shirley Temple, he was the most famous teenager in America.

Although he was only 18, Feller already was showing the tough competitive streak that earmarked his career. He loved a challenge.

As spring training was wrapping up in 1937, the Indians and the New York Giants played a series of exhibition games as they gradually wound their way home from New Orleans, stopping in such places as Vicksburg, Mississippi, and Fort Smith, Arkansas, to play one another. As the trek began, Giants shortstop Dick Bartell openly questioned whether Feller really threw that hard and said he thought there were plenty of pitchers in the National League who threw harder. Feller heard the comment and responded. He struck out Bartell 16 times in 19 at-bats on the trip.[21]

It took some time for Feller to refine his enormous talents, however. He went 9–7 in 1937, then made his first All-Star team as a 19-year-old in 1938, going 17–11 and leading the American League in strikeouts for the first time with 240. He also led the league by issuing 208 walks, which remains the major league record for the modern era. The only other pitcher since 1900 to walk more than 200 batters in a season was another fireballing phenom, Nolan Ryan.

Feller broke his own single-game strikeout record by fanning 18 Detroit Tigers on the final day of the 1938 season and in 1939 he really emerged as a finished product. His earned run average dropped by more than a run, to 2.85, and it was the first of three straight seasons in which he led the league in wins and finished among the top three in the AL MVP voting. And, of course, he also led the league in strikeouts all three years.

He threw the only opening day no-hitter in major league history in 1940, beating the White Sox 1–0 on a cold, blustery day at Comiskey Park. Two years earlier, he had thrown a one-hitter in the second game of the season, but this time he was totally untouchable. After issuing a few walks in the early innings, he retired 20 straight batters.

Des Moines Register sports editor Sec Taylor wrote that when Feller was pitching to future Hall of Famer Luke Appling in the ninth inning, he displayed "all the poise of a Russian grand duke of ye old days and the unconcern of a 4-year-old playing with a toy gun."[22]

Catcher Rollie Hemsley drove in the only run of the game with a fourth-inning triple and afterward said he couldn't recall seeing anyone throw harder than Feller had that day. Hemsley showed reporters a left hand reddened and raw from absorbing so many Feller fastballs. "Boy, he burned the glove right off," he said. "The kid had so much swift today that along in the late innings I hated to call for the hard one."[23]

As he turned 23, Feller had become Cleveland's biggest hero.

"It was the Depression and things were pretty bad here, and then this amazing kid came along," journalist Dan August said many years later. "What a lift it gave us. People today who don't know exactly what he did still seem to sense how special Bob Feller was to Cleveland."[24]

His early success also brought Feller financial rewards. After a few seasons, he was earning close to $30,000 a year and he used some of that money to buy his parents a new home. Life on the farm around Van Meter (population 300) hadn't been easy. The Fellers didn't have electricity until Bill finally bought a generator that would provide power for three days at a time and they didn't have indoor plumbing until Bob built his parents a new home in 1940.[25]

By the end of 1941, Feller already had won 109 games and he seemingly was on his way to breaking every pitching record ever established. Nothing could stop him.

Except maybe a world war.

When the Japanese attacked Pearl Harbor on December 7, 1941, Feller's career took a detour. He was in his car just crossing the Mississippi River in Davenport, Iowa, on his way from Van Meter to Chicago to sign a new contract when he heard the news on the radio. When he got to Chicago, he called former heavyweight boxing champion Gene Tunney, who was a lieutenant commander in the Navy, and told him he wanted to enlist. Two days later, he was sworn in, becoming the first major celebrity to join the service.[26]

Feller could have been exempted from the draft because his father was terminally ill—Bill Feller had been fighting brain cancer for a few years and he eventually died early in 1943—but he wanted to serve.

"I didn't worry about losing my baseball career," he said. "We needed to win the war. I wanted to do my part."[27]

After undergoing basic training at the Norfolk Naval Training Station and being assigned to work as a physical fitness instructor there, he requested active duty. He had learned to fly a plane in 1939 and wanted to be a fighter pilot, but he was rejected because of less-than-perfect hearing. Instead, he became a chief petty officer in the artillery and served aboard the battleship U.S.S. *Alabama* in both the European and Asian phases of the war. He ended up winning eight battle stars and five combat ribbons.

While on leave in January 1943 he got married to Virginia Winther, whom he had met in Florida a few years earlier.

Feller was discharged from the Navy on August 22, 1945, and immediately dove back into baseball, steadfastly rejecting the notion that he was any sort of war hero. "The soldiers that didn't come back were the heroes," he said.[28]

Just two days later, on August 24, he started a game against the first-place Tigers and rolled to a 5–2 victory, striking out 12 in front of a crowd of 46,477 at Cleveland Stadium.

He pitched in nine games at end of the 1945 season but as 1946 rolled around, there were doubts as to how four years away from the game might have affected his pitching. Reporters in places such as New York speculated that he couldn't possibly be the same.

It didn't take him long to show them. On April 30, he tossed another 1–0 no-hitter against the powerful Yankees. It was the first no-hitter ever pitched at Yankee Stadium and Feller often referred to it as "my most satisfying victory."[29]

If anything, his time in the military enhanced Feller's abilities. He always had been a two-pitch pitcher before that, complementing the blazing fastball with a curve ball that was better than average. During down times aboard the Alabama, he taught himself to throw a slider.

It made him better than ever and he reached career highs in almost every statistical category in 1946, leading the AL in wins (26), games pitched (48), starts (42), innings pitched (371.1), complete games (36), shutouts (10) and strikeouts (348). His 2.18 ERA did not lead the league but it was the best of his career.

Feller also was coming into his own as a businessman. He negotiated a contract with new Indians owner Bill Veeck that called for a base salary of $50,000 but with incentive clauses for wins and attendance he probably earned twice that amount. He made plenty of money in other ways, too. He was among the first professional athletes to incorporate, forming Ro-Fel, Inc., with his

Bob Feller had one of his best seasons in 1946 in his first full season after leaving the Navy (courtesy Cleveland Indians).

father-in-law, W.M. Winther, as vice president and his wife, Virginia, as secretary. Feller claimed that with endorsements from such companies as Wheaties and Wilson Sporting Goods, proceeds from a barnstorming tour, money earned from radio shows and columns, appearance fees and royalties from a book called *Strikeout Story*, he earned about $150,000 in 1947.[30]

But on the field, he injured his knee that season and when he continued to pitch with it, he developed a sore shoulder. He still went 20–11 and led the league in strikeouts but his total dipped to 196. His days as a strikeout machine began to decline.

However, he continued to be a highly effective pitcher. Ted Williams, who ranked Feller among the toughest pitchers he ever faced, said it wasn't just because of his fastball. "Even after he lost his best stuff—and he had more than anybody—Feller was able to win on smartness," Williams said.[31]

Feller went 19–15 in 1948 and the Indians won the AL pennant under youthful manager Lou Boudreau. For the first (and only) time in his career he got a chance to pitch in the World Series.

He got the start in Game 1 against the Boston Braves and allowed just two hits, but the Braves' Johnny Sain was even better and Cleveland suffered a 1–0 loss. The defeat included a bit of controversy. Feller appeared to have picked Phil Masi off second base in the eighth inning but he was ruled safe. Masi scored the only run of the game moments later on a single by Tommy Holmes.

Feller pitched again in Game 5, but was knocked out of the game in the seventh inning after allowing seven runs on eight hits, including three home runs. The Indians won the world championship anyway in the next game. Ironically, the only two games they lost were the ones Feller pitched.

He was not quite as dominant in the years that followed although he led the league in wins one more time by going 22–8 in 1951. He pitched his third no-hitter that season, beating Detroit 2–1.

He became a secondary figure on the Indians staff in his last five seasons as pitchers such as Early Wynn, Bob Lemon and Mike Garcia took the spotlight. He went 13–3 as a part-time starter in 1954 as the Indians set an American league record for wins in a season (111), but he did not get into a game in the World Series. While some fans objected to that, Feller shrugged it off.

"I received a lot of mail afterward telling me it was a shame I hadn't pitched, and I appreciated the well-meant sympathy," he said.[32]

Feller also became an activist in those final seasons. He was elected the first president of the Major League Baseball Players Association, and was instrumental in drawing up a pension plan and fighting for other privileges for the players. He retired in 1956, but the following year testified before Congress in opposition to the reserve clause, which bound players to one team indefinitely.

Five years later, he received almost 94 percent of the vote in being elected to the Hall of Fame on his first time on the ballot.

In retirement, Feller became an entrepreneur and an ambassador for the game, but also an outspoken agitator who frequently tiptoed along the edge of controversy.

He expressed criticism of such other major sports figures as Pete Rose and Muhammad Ali, and had an ongoing feud with Jackie Robinson. Many years earlier, after striking out Robinson in an exhibition game in 1945, he announced that he thought Robinson was too muscle-bound to ever make it in the major leagues.[33] He was not a racist—he had been criticized by some for his willingness to play against Negro League teams on his many barnstorming tours in the 1940s—but he also was quoted as saying he didn't think Robinson would have been considered a major league prospect if he had been white.[34]

The two men seemed to be on amicable enough terms when they were inducted into the Hall of Fame together in 1962, but Feller never actually apologized for his remarks or admitted he may have been wrong.

"I'm not PC. My wife is PC, but I am not PC," he told Frank Deford in that 2005 *Sports Illustrated* piece. "I always believe in what Happy Chandler told me once: Make your decision, and then never show doubt."[35]

Feller and Virginia had three sons, but they divorced in 1971 and three years later he was remarried to Anne Thorpe, one of his neighbors in Gates Mills, Ohio.

He often claimed that he was licensed to sell insurance in 39 states, but he apparently was not good at it and in his later years he resorted to other ways of making money. He traveled the world making personal appearances and capitalizing on his fame. He appeared in hundreds of minor league ballparks, throwing pitches to local celebrities until he was well into his 60s.

As late as 2010, he continued to criticize modern players for being paid to sign autographs, noting that he never was compensated for such things during his playing career and telling interviewers, "You will never see a Brinks truck follow a hearse. You can't leave with all the money."[36]

At the same time, he normally sold his own autograph for $10 although he often did it to benefit the Bob Feller Museum, which had been established in Van Meter in 1995.

"I've signed more autographs, traveled more miles, been in more countries, been to more ballparks and done more interviews than anybody in history," he boasted in a 2001 interview at the museum. "I've done double that of anyone you could name. Babe Ruth, Joe DiMaggio. Ted Williams. Anybody."[37]

None of the controversies and contradictions or the occasional political incorrectness kept him from continuing to be an icon in Cleveland. He was revered there not only for his talent but for his patriotism, his candor and his ebullience. A statue of Feller in full windup now stands outside the Indians' Progressive Field.

In August of 2010, Feller was diagnosed with myeloid leukemia, which ultimately led to other health issues, including a heart problem and pneumonia. He died on December 15 at the age of 92.

He did an interview with Dennis Manoloff of the *Cleveland Plain Dealer* during the last year of his life in which he found a modesty and humility that often escaped him in previous interviews.

"I owe baseball everything I am today," Feller said. "Whatever I may be or not be, I owe to baseball.... Living legend? It's a term I respect and appreciate because I started out as a kid with no idea what might happen in the game."[38]

Second Base
Gene Baker

"His determination, his intelligence, and his competitive spirit went way beyond anybody I've ever been around."—Hall of Famer Ernie Banks[1]

By now, everyone is fully aware that major league baseball had an unwritten rule against employing black players until Jackie Robinson made his debut with the Brooklyn Dodgers in 1947. What isn't widely known is that the co-called color line occasionally extended down to lower levels of the sport.

Gene Baker found that out the hard way in 1942.

Baker had grown up playing pretty much every sport there was on the streets and sandlots of Davenport, Iowa, and he was good at all of them, including baseball. By the spring of his junior year at Davenport High School, he already was one of the top players on a basketball team that finished second in the Iowa state tournament that winter. There was no reason in his mind that he wouldn't also find stardom on the baseball diamond.

Except for one thing: He didn't make the team. He was cut from the team. In fact, there were no black players on the Davenport High baseball team that year.

"It made me angry," Baker admitted in an interview about 50 years later. "There wasn't much I could do about it."[2]

Making the Davenport team was no easy feat. The Blue Devils, under coach Midge Makeever, had won state baseball championships the two previous years and the sport was played during the same spring season as track, another sport in which Baker showed great promise. It also has been reported through the years that the school's legendary basketball coach, Paul Moon, did not want his best player risking injury on the diamond.³

Whatever the reason, Baker didn't make the team and he spent the next couple of decades demonstrating what a mistake that was.

He finally got his chance to play baseball when he joined the Navy in 1943. He played with a team at the Ottumwa Naval Air Station and continued on from there to enjoy a long career in the sport, playing eight seasons in the major leagues and continuing to break down barriers after that

Gene Baker.

by becoming the first black man to manage a minor league team in organized baseball and becoming the second black coach at the major league level.

It wasn't quite as long a playing career as it could have been. The Chicago Cubs let Baker languish in the high minors for many years while they summoned the courage to break their own color line. And a severe knee injury shortened Baker's career on the back end.

The pure statistics were fairly modest—a .265 career average and only 39 home runs in 630 games, most of them at second base. But those who played with and against Baker remember a savvy player with uncanny instincts for the game. His friend and teammate, Ernie Banks, who joined the Cubs at the same time, remembered that Baker was one of the few players who could upset the Cardinals' normally unflappable Stan Musial. He always seemed to know exactly where Musial was going to hit the ball.⁴

"Every time Stan would hit his best shot and Gene would be standing right there to catch the ball," Banks said. "Stan kept looking at him like 'How did he know that?' Then Stan would hit the ball up the middle and Gene would be standing right there. I was at shortstop and I'd be all over the place. I didn't know what I was doing. But Gene knew exactly where to play everybody."⁵

Banks also remembered Baker's competitive spirit coming out in a handful of encounters with Dodgers pitcher Don Newcombe, another of the early black players in the National League.

"Newcombe used to brush back Gene and I. He'd knock us down all the time," Banks recalled. "Gene had played against Don back in the Negro Leagues and he knew what was going to happen, but he didn't want to say 'Watch out.' He didn't want to put any fear in me. The thing is, every time Newcombe knocked him down, Gene got up and either got a hit or a home run. Every time. Every time. Gene would dust himself off and the next pitch would be a line drive somewhere or a home run. It was the most amazing thing I've ever seen."[6]

On July 15, 1956, Baker hit one of his three career grand slams off Newcombe. When he came to bat the next time, the first two pitches were aimed right at his head.

Baker was born in Davenport in 1925 and raised in the same neighborhood that later produced such star athletes as San Francisco 49ers running back Roger Craig and world middleweight boxing champion Michael Nunn.

Eugene O. and Mildred Baker had been married about a year and Mildred was only 17 when their son, named Eugene W., was born. The couple was married for 61 years and Mildred actually outlived her son, living to the age of 97. Eugene O., who spent most of his life laboring in iron foundries in a community where most of the world's farm implements were built, died in 1985.

Their son took to sports from the very beginning and was especially good at basketball. He helped Davenport High, a statewide super-power in that era, to a second-place finish in the Iowa state tournament as a junior in 1942. He only started part of the time for a team that also included Jack Spencer, a future All-Big Ten player at Iowa, and several other players who competed in various sports at the college level, but he made his presence felt in some games. After scoring a team-high 12 points in a victory over Muscatine in the sectional championship game, Jack Ogden of the *Davenport Democrat* reported that "Eugene Baker, Davenport's colored forward-guard, gave the Muskie squad a neat exhibition of speed and precision as he climaxed his tight guarding with a brilliant display of offensive finesse."[7]

After not making the baseball team that spring, Baker was a member of the Blue Devils track team although he did not place in the state meet in any event for a squad that breezed to the state title.

The following winter with Spencer graduated, Baker became the star of the basketball team although the Blue Devils finished a disappointing (for them) fourth in the state tournament. Ogden wrote that a state quarterfinal victory over Sioux Center was due largely to "keen passing by Eugene Baker, which bordered on the spectacular side."[8]

Baker, who was listed at that time as six feet, 142 pounds, was named first team all-state by the Iowa Daily Press Association, whose bio on him read as follows: "Most improved player on this year's Davenport cage team. Clean type of player, fouling infrequently. So alert that he caused opposing guards to foul. Best player in Mississippi Valley loop."[9]

Baker had played for a handful of local amateur baseball teams through the years, first as a pitcher and later as an outfielder, and he chose to do that again that spring rather than return to the track team. On the same day that the Davenport High baseball team was eliminated from the state tournament, he clubbed a 10th-inning home run to lift the all-black American Legion Post 482 team to victory in the Hawkeye League at Davenport's Lindsay Park.[10]

World War II was raging when he graduated from high school and like many of his peers, Baker chose to enlist. Even though he did not know how to swim, he joined the Navy and spent much of the rest of the war in his home state, at the Ottumwa Naval Air Station. Ironically, Midge Makeever also enlisted in the Navy at almost the exact same time and was commissioned as a lieutenant.

After being discharged in 1946, Baker came home to find that plenty of local semi-pro teams were eager to have him play for them although he earned his living during that period as a carpenter. He also briefly attended St. Ambrose College in Davenport.

That led to bigger things. Within two years after leaving the Navy, Baker became the starting shortstop for the Kansas City Monarchs of the Negro American League, playing the same position on the same team that had employed Jackie Robinson before he signed with Brooklyn. Baker batted .294 for the Monarchs in 1948 and .285 in 1949.

In the meantime, Robinson had broken baseball's color line with the Dodgers in 1947 and the idea of black players in the major leagues gradually was gaining acceptance. There were four black players in the majors in 1948 and nine in 1949. They were lumped on three teams—the Dodgers, Giants and Indians—but other clubs were beginning to realize the inevitability of integration.

That included the Cubs. They invited three Negro League players for a tryout in the spring of 1950—Baker, Kansas City pitcher Bob Thurman and second baseman Junior Gilliam of the Baltimore Elite Giants. They liked what they saw of Baker and Thurman but rejected Gilliam, who later became a starting infielder with the Dodgers. The Cubs purchased Baker's contract from the Monarchs, who eventually replaced him at shortstop with Banks.

While the Cubs were willing to sign black players, they weren't quite ready to bring them to the major leagues. Baker played three games with the Springfield Cubs of the International League in 1950, then was sent to Des Moines of the Western League, where he batted .321 in 49 games. He played the final 100 games of that season with the Cubs' Los Angeles farm team in the Triple-A Pacific Coast League. His .280 average there gave every indication that he was ready for a shot at the majors.

The Cubs apparently didn't think so. They sent Baker back to L.A. in 1951. And 1952. And 1953. He played in 504 games over those three seasons and batted .260 or better each year. In 1953, he also smacked 20 home runs and drove in 99 runs.

Meanwhile, the Cubs weren't exactly loaded at the shortstop position in those years. Their starter for most of that time period was Roy Smalley, who led the National League in errors three years in a row. And Smalley missed half the 1951 season with a broken ankle. It clearly was a need area for them.

The Cubs did finally invite Baker to spring training with the major league team in 1953 although general manager Wid Mathews was quoted as saying he "may be a year away."[11]

Baker felt he didn't improve significantly as a player between 1950 and 1953. He thought he was ready for the majors when the Cubs first signed him.[12] Bobby Bragan, who managed the rival Hollywood team in the PCL in the years Baker played for Los Angeles, agreed. He was quoted as saying Baker "was as good a shortstop as I've ever seen."[13]

The *Chicago Defender*, a newspaper primarily for the African American community, reported that several Chicago papers were campaigning for the Cubs to bring Baker to the major leagues to remedy their weakness at short.[14]

Finally, in the waning weeks of the 1953 season, the Cubs were ready. On September 14, the 28-year-old Baker was one of two shortstops who became the first two black players ever to wear a Cubs uniform at the major league level. The other one was Banks, a shy and much less experienced 22-year-old who had been signed after playing in a Negro League all-star game across town at Comiskey Park and who had not spent a single day in the minor leagues.

Baker was nursing a pulled muscle in his rib cage when he joined the club and was not able to play for a few days. He made just one pinch-hitting appearance in a game against St. Louis while Banks immediately found his way into the Cubs' lineup.

Gene Baker (left) and Ernie Banks (right) joined the Chicago Cubs and manager Phil Cavaretta (center) late in the 1953 season.

When the team traveled to Cincinnati for a series, Baker was tired of waiting for his opportunity.

"I finally told the trainer to tape me up, and I told the manager [Phil Cavaretta] I was ready to play," Baker recalled. "He said, 'OK, you play tonight.' Before the game, we took infield practice and I ran out to shortstop, and Ernie was standing there. He said, 'I'm the shortstop.' I went back and looked at the lineup card and they had '2B' behind my name. I'd always been a shortstop. I'd never played second base in my life."[15]

But Baker played the position that night in both ends of a doubleheader, collecting only a double in seven at-bats and handling five chances in the field without an error.

He played the last seven games of the season at second base even though he admittedly was learning the position on the fly, especially the art of evading sliding runners on the double play.

"I don't know how many double plays Ernie and I turned the rest of the season, but I didn't see any of them," Baker said. "I was always on the ground."[16]

Buck O'Neil, who had managed both Banks and Baker with the Monarchs, knew Baker could handle anything because he was "a pro." His advice to the two youngsters was simple: "I told them just be a ballplayer, just like anybody else."[17]

Baker and Banks, who was five years younger and destined to become an all-time great, started together in the middle of the Cub infield for the next three years. They became known affectionately as the Bingo and Bango twins.

The six-foot, one-inch, 175-pound Baker—aka Bango—led the league's second basemen in errors all three years, but he also got to balls that few other second basemen reached. He led the league in putouts and assists in 1955 and in double plays in 1956, and tied a National League record with 11 assists in one game in 1955. He also was a productive hitter in the No. 2 slot in the Cubs batting order.

He played every inning of every game in 1955 and was 21st in the National League Most Valuable Player voting although his offensive statistics that season were comparable to what he did in 1954 and 1956. He also was selected to the NL All-Star team in 1955 and got into the game as a pinch-hitter in the seventh inning, flying out to center field against the Yankees' Whitey Ford.

Although many teams in baseball were beginning to blend black players into their rosters, there still were only 20 African American players in the majors at the end of 1953. It still wasn't an easy time for those players. There was plenty of verbal abuse that Baker admitted wasn't that easy to just shrug off.

"There was always somebody who would come down to the railing before the game and yell something at you," he said. "You'd just get a lot of comments, mostly from the fans. You'd get some from the other team's benches sometimes but in most cases you didn't get much of that because there was always the chance they might get on the field and you'd have a chance to get even."[18]

Black players in the 1950s not only faced verbal abuse but also certain restrictions, which were later erased by the civil rights movement. In St. Louis, for example, the black players were not allowed to stay at the same hotel as the rest of the team. The Cubs made the plush Chase Hotel their headquarters but Banks and Baker had to stay at the Olive Hotel in another part of town. They also couldn't frequent the same restaurants and movie theaters as their teammates.

Baker was much more prepared than Banks for what they faced when the two players joined the Cubs. His time in the Navy and his apprenticeship in Los Angeles made him a bit more worldly. He took the younger Banks under his wing and tried to help him find his way through a world that was still adjusting to the concept of African American athletic heroes.

Banks, who grew up in Dallas, said he was "like a child back then. I didn't know things."[19] He recalled that Baker made a point of letting him learn some hard lessons for himself.

"I remember we played an exhibition game at Mobile, Alabama, once, and Gene and I had to wait on the bus while the rest of the team changed clothes," Banks said. "There was a bus station there and I told Gene I was going to go get a little candy. He knew what was going to happen. I went in the front door of this Greyhound bus station and everybody stopped. Finally, a white guy came up to me and said, 'You have to go around back to get in.' When I came back, Gene was laughing like hell. He thought it was the funniest thing in the world."[20]

Bill Bryk, who first got to know Baker while working for the Pirates organization, recalled that things gradually changed and black players eventually were allowed to stay in the same hotels as the white players in most cities. But he said Baker often would still opt to stay at the old hotels where he always had been welcome.[21]

Baker had a profound and lasting effect on Banks, who went on to hit 512 career home runs and land in the Hall of Fame. Banks became known for his happy-go-lucky, upbeat persona but he said he didn't necessarily bring that to the major leagues with him. Some of it came from Gene Baker.[22]

"He had a total awareness of everything around him," Banks said at the time of Baker's death in 1999. "That's what I learned from him. He had so much character. He was so positive about everything. Gene kind of instilled that into me. He didn't tell me to be that way, but I learned it just from being around him and watching him."[23]

The Baker-Banks double-play combination stayed together for only a little more than three years. In 1957, the Cubs shifted Baker to third base and on May 1 they traded him along with first baseman Dee Fondy to Pittsburgh in exchange for Dale Long and Lee Walls.

Baker played 111 games with the Pirates that season, seeing action at second, third and short and batting a solid .265.

Just 29 games into the 1958 season, he severely injured his knee in a game in St. Louis. As he was reaching to field a ground ball hit by Curt Flood, his spikes caught and his knee twisted awkwardly. A ligament in the knee was completely severed and Baker was sent back to Pittsburgh for surgery. Doctors warned him before doing the surgery that they could fix his knee so that he could at least walk and perhaps play a little golf. But they said if they tried to fix it for baseball, he likely would have a stiff knee for the rest of his life.[24]

The injury sidelined Baker for a year and a half. While he was unable to play, the Pirates put him to work in other ways, as a scout and minor league instructor.

When Baker finally returned to the field late in the 1960 season, he wasn't the same player. The quickness and reflexes that had made him a quality infielder were gone. He played in 33 games for Pittsburgh that year, being used primarily as a pinch-hitter. He played just seven games at third base and one inning at second. However, after a career of playing for second-division clubs, Baker was finally with a winner. The Pirates claimed the National League pennant, then won the World Series on Bill Mazeroski's dramatic home run in the ninth inning of Game 7. Baker was 0-for-3 as a pinch-hitter in the Series.

He played in nine more games for the Pirates the following season, but it was apparent that his days as an effective player were over. He was released in June.

It wasn't the end of his baseball career, however. The Pirates sent him to the Class D farm team at Batavia in the New York–Pennsylvania League and named him the player-manager of the team on June 19. His off-the-field work with the organization in 1959 and 1960 had not gone unnoticed.

"He has been most valuable to us in the past as a player, an instructor and a scout," Pirates general manager Joe L. Brown said in announcing Baker's appointment. "Gene is a fine gentleman and has outstanding baseball knowledge and experience.... We know he will do a fine job."[25]

There had been at least two black managers for independently-owned minor league teams prior to that. Nate Moreland managed a team in the Arizona-Mexico League and Sam Bankhead headed up a team in the Canadian Provincial League, both in the 1950s, but no major league team ever had employed one in its farm system. Baker was the first.

By all reports, his hiring was well-received by the players on his new team.

"We know he has a job to do and we believe he'll do it," said pitcher Steve Blass, then a 19-year-old prospect who was headed for a lengthy major league career. "He has a reputation for being one heck of a swell guy, one who really knows baseball."[26]

The Batavia Pirates were in seventh place in an eight-team league with a record of 18–23 when Baker replaced Jim Adlam. They went 47–36 the rest of the way and finished third to make the league playoffs. They defeated second-place Erie in the first round, but lost to Olean in the championship series.

Baker also saw action at third base with Batavia. He had gotten just one hit in 10 at-bats in those nine games with Pittsburgh at the start of the season, but at Batavia he batted .387 in 53 games.

Baker was moved up to a coaching job with Columbus of the International League in 1962. He also played in 22 games there, his last as an active player.

In 1963, he became a coach with the Pirates at the major league level. Buck O'Neil had become the first black coach in the majors when he joined the Cubs in the middle of the previous season.

Pirates manager Danny Murtaugh was kicked out of a game in the seventh inning on September 21, 1963, and he turned the reins over to Baker for the rest of the game. In that way, Baker became the first black to manage a team in the majors, even if it was for only two innings.[27]

Baker spent the following winter managing the Aguilas Cibaenas team in the Dominican Republic and in 1964 found himself back at Batavia. He wasn't given nearly as much talent to work with this time as pitcher Dock Ellis was the only player to make the major leagues off a team that finished 33–97.

Some thought Baker would have been an excellent major league manager. Murtaugh once said that he "knows more baseball than fellows twice his age. He's one of the smartest I've ever met."[28]

Banks, who called Baker "Sharp Top" because of his intelligence, even lobbied for Baker as a managerial candidate in his 1971 autobiography, *Mr. Cub*.

"Gene has great knowledge of baseball, and he is blessed with the kind of attitude and disposition so important to a manager in this new era," Banks wrote. "He is astute, has good balance and good instincts. He can communicate well with players, umpires, fans, management and all branches of the news media.... I've often thought the term 'players' manager' is overworked, but it wouldn't be in Gene Baker's case. He is too well-schooled in leadership."[29]

Bill Bryk compared Baker's managerial style in the minors to that of highly successful major league manager Joe Torre and said he, too, thought Baker would have been a great big league skipper because of his baseball acumen. "He was firm but fair and very approachable," Bryk said. "Players could always come and talk to him, whereas a lot of managers in those days were unapproachable."[30]

Author Jim Brosnan, who pitched for the Cubs in the 1950s, said

Baker was one of those players who just exuded leadership on the field. He likened him to Gene Mauch, a longtime infielder who went on to become a solid manager. "Pitchers would pay more attention to what Mauch would say than the catcher or the manager," Brosnan said. "Baker was the same way. Gene [Baker] always sounded like he knew what he was talking about. He knew the game well."[31]

As it is, there was not a black manager in the majors until 1975 when the Cleveland Indians hired Frank Robinson.

Baker left baseball in 1965, returning to the Quad-Cities to work as production scheduler for John Deere, but in 1968, he began a 23-year stint as the Pirates' chief Midwest scout.

He was named to the Quad-City Sports Hall of Fame in his hometown in 1992 and in 1999 he was named to the Baseball Scouts Hall of Fame.

He was too ill to attend the ceremonies in St. Louis and Bob Oldis, an old friend, former teammate, fellow scout and fellow Iowan, accepted the award on his behalf. Oldis never even got a chance to give his old friend the plaque. On December 1, Baker died of a heart attack at the age of 74.

Baker had been battling diabetes for many years and had been on dialysis for five years. He had been hospitalized a few times for related problems. His wife, Janice, said that wore on him and likely led to the heart issues.[32]

Oldis referred to his friend as "one of the real true gentlemen in the game of baseball" and "one of the all-time great guys…. He had no enemies."[33]

In his later years, Baker was interviewed numerous times about his career but he was extremely modest and hesitated to speak about the racial barriers that held him back. There were enough shrugged shoulders and unfinished sentences to make it clear that there was some bitterness and perhaps some regrets, but he saw no need to verbalize them.

"He was just a tremendous, tremendous human being," Banks said, referring to Baker as "the brightest person" he'd ever known.[34]

"Gene had a great smile and a subtle sense of humor," Banks added. "He was the most interesting person. I would have loved to have spent more time with him. This was a man who had everything going for him. He was in control of everything around him."[35]

Bryk called him not only one of the best baseball men he ever met but one of the best people, period. "Everyone loved Gene," he said. "He was the ultimate professional."[36]

Pitcher
Mike Boddicker

"His pitching ability is commensurate with his character, which means he's something special. He has the wholesome, old-fashioned qualities that were found in heroes of a bygone generation."—Sportswriter John Steadman[1]

As a little kid growing up in Norway, Iowa, Mike Boddicker's dream was always to play in the major leagues.

There's nothing too unusual about that. Norway, population 600, probably ranks among the most baseball-crazy small towns in America. The community began fielding town teams as far back as the 1880s and the sport is woven into the town's identity. The local high school won 20 state baseball championships before being absorbed by the nearby Benton Community school district in 1991. It's probably the dream of almost every young boy in Norway to make it to the big leagues.

Boddicker was one of the few to make it, following in the footsteps of Hal Trosky and Bruce Kimm.

But he didn't just make it. He became a playoff MVP and an All-Star. He pitched his way into the national spotlight in the fall of 1983, captivating the country's baseball fans with a tantalizingly unimposing breaking pitch called the foshball and an awe-shucks demeanor that shone through on the mound as well as in the interview room.

At the height of Boddicker's fame in 1983, *Philadelphia Inquirer* columnist Bill Lyon depicted him as "an Iowa farm boy lacking any affectations."[2]

"The refreshing thing about Boddicker is his quality as an individual, the way he's put together and reacts to people and situations," added John

Steadman of the *Baltimore News American.* "There's none of the prima donna about him or the typical athletic mentality."³

Chances are, there were plenty of Norway kids through the years who possessed more natural ability than Boddicker. He was only five feet, 11 inches, and he never topped 175 pounds during his career. Boddicker himself often has insisted that his older brother, Butch, was a much better player. Although his fastball occasionally may have edged over 90 mph while he was in high school, it seldom topped 85 mph by the time he got to the majors. He survived by changing speeds and locating his pitches.

Hall of Fame hitter Rod Carew once described Boddicker's stuff as "Little League slop" and added, "I feed my dogs better stuff than Boddicker throws."⁴ The always modest Boddicker was not inclined to disagree.

Mike Boddicker (courtesy the Baltimore Orioles).

"I just threw a lot of strikes and got people out," he said. "I was pretty blessed in my career, given the mediocre crap that I threw up there."⁵

His best weapon was the foshball, so named by Baltimore Orioles pitching coach Ray Miller because it was a hybrid of a dead fish—the ballplayers' jargon for a change-up—and a forkball. Boddicker picked up the pitch in college and learned that by applying extra pressure on the ball with his thumb, he could give it added spin. The foshball was similar to a circle change but easier to control. Boddicker often said it really was just a "glorified changeup" and he told Steve Wulf in a *Sports Illustrated* interview in 1983 that "it looks like a fastball but it's slow and it sinks. Even the ones they hit, they don't hit very well."⁶

Statistician Bill James also wrote that Boddicker had the best curveball in the majors in the 1980s,⁷ but Boddicker disputed that. He said Bert Blyleven had a better one although he admitted his wasn't bad.⁸ Boddicker relied more on a slider during his younger days but taught himself to throw a curve in the minor leagues after seeing how much success the Orioles' Steve Stone had with his curve in the majors.

"Guys knew that I was going to throw it, but the reason I was able to get them out was that I changed speeds on it quite a bit," Boddicker said.⁹

Born in 1957, Boddicker was the youngest of five children of Harold and Dolly Boddicker. In fact, he was 10 years younger than any of his siblings. His father, who everyone knew as "Bus," traveled from farm to farm in the area milling grain and when that job became obsolete, he found work as the custodian at Norway's elementary school. He died when Mike was only 10, leaving him to be raised by Dolly with help from all those older siblings.

Two older brothers, Butch and Robert, were exceptional players at Norway High and it became apparent very early that little Mike also was going to be part of the community's baseball legacy. All he ever wanted to do as a kid was play ball. In fact, that desire led him to do something that went against his nature: He lied. Kids in Norway had to be five years old to enter the community's youth baseball program but Boddicker began when he was four by misrepresenting his age.[10]

Norway High School coach Jim Van Scoyoc, who married Boddicker's older sister Sheryl (known to most people as Chick), insisted that he always knew the kid was destined to play in the majors.

"I didn't have to spend much time with him, he was such a quick learner," Van Scoyoc said.[11]

Over the course of four years at Norway High, Boddicker had a won-loss record of 76–13 with an unfathomable 0.64 earned run average. He also set a national high school record by logging 1,122 strikeouts in 617 innings. If that wasn't enough, he also batted .397, stole 72 bases, hit 34 home runs and drove in 221 runs.

Those individual numbers translated into two more state titles for Norway. Unlike most states, Iowa's high school baseball season is in the summer months and until 1984 it also held a brief fall season, primarily for schools too small to field football squads. Kimm and his contemporaries really got the Norway tradition rolling by winning six state championships—four against the other small schools in the fall and two against the big boys in the spring and summer season.

Boddicker recalled that as a kid he watched those championship teams come home to be hailed as heroes with parades through the town. "It became infused in every kid in town," he said. "We wanted to do that and be that."[12]

As a 5-10, 145-pound sophomore in the fall of 1972, he got his chance. Boddicker led Norway into the state championship game against another small-town power, Bancroft St. John's, and held the Johnnies to just two singles while striking out 12 men in seven innings. Norway pushed across a run in the bottom of the seventh inning to claim a 1–0 victory.

Boddicker may have had the best season of his high school career in

15. Pitcher: Mike Boddicker

the summer of his junior year. He went 19–0 and allowed only two earned runs while also batting .468 and handling 300 straight chances at third base and pitcher without committing an error.

Norway got back to the fall championship game in Boddicker's senior season in 1974 and he again struck out 12 and threw a complete game, this time against Granville Spalding. But his biggest heroics came at the plate. He hit a solo home run in the sixth inning to tie the score at 2–2, then homered again in the eighth inning to win the state title.

It brought an end to a grueling trek in which he pitched Norway to the state tournament in the summer season, pitched the Cedar Rapids American Legion team to the national World Series in August (something he did three times), then won the state title in the fall.

"I must have pitched in 60 games or maybe more since the spring," Boddicker said after the state championship game. "But I'm not really glad it's over. I love this game."[13]

The following spring he was selected in the eighth round of the 1975 major league draft by the Montreal Expos, but he opted to delay his pro career to play college baseball. He had offers from USC, Arizona State and many of the other top programs in the country, but he chose to play for the University of Iowa because of its proximity to Norway. His mother, Dolly, suffered from rheumatoid arthritis for much of her adult life and was bedridden in her later years. As Boddicker put it, "I couldn't leave Mom."[14]

In three years with the Hawkeyes, he continued to be very effective as both a pitcher and hitter. As a freshman, he earned All-Big Ten honors as a third baseman although he also had a school-record ERA of 0.79. He won eight games and registered 84 strikeouts in 65 innings while also playing some second base as a sophomore and as a junior he again was named All-Big Ten, batting .350 and leading the nation with an average of 11.5 strikeouts per game.

Baltimore selected him in the sixth round of the 1978 draft and this time Boddicker signed. He moved swiftly up the

Mike Boddicker had an earned run average of 0.79 as a freshman at the University of Iowa in 1976 (courtesy *Quad-City Times*).

organizational ladder, seeing action in the rookie league, Double-A and Triple-A in his first season and recording an ERA under 2.00 at each stop.

He split the 1979 season between Double-A Charlotte and Triple-A Rochester and while his statistics weren't quite as impressive as they had been the year before, the potential was obvious.

However, the Orioles were stocked with a wealth of great starting pitchers at the major-league level, including Jim Palmer, Steve Stone, Mike Flanagan, Scott McGregor and Dennis Martinez. Stone and McGregor each won 20 or more games in 1980. In 1982, Palmer, Flanagan, McGregor and Martinez all had 14 or more wins. As a result, Boddicker pretty much hit a brick wall at the Triple-A level. He spent parts of six seasons in Rochester, going 12–9 there in 1980, 10–10 in 1981 and 10–5 in 1982.

Although he came up to the big leagues for a cup of coffee at the end of each of those seasons—he got his first career victory in relief against the Yankees on September 13, 1982—he always was back in the minors when the following season began. That's where Boddicker found himself again at the outset of the 1983 season. He had spoken to Orioles general manager Hank Peters at the end of the 1982 season about possibly being traded if the franchise didn't ever plan to use him, but he decided to remain patient.

It paid off in 1983. Stone was gone from the Orioles by then, Palmer was in the waning days of a Hall of Fame career and Martinez got off to a rough start. Boddicker won three of his first four starts at Rochester and when Palmer went on the disabled list in early May, the Orioles brought him up.

"The only reason he wasn't up here sooner was because we had four good starters ahead of him," Ray Miller later explained. "Two of them were Cy Young winners, one was a 20-game winner and the other was winning 16 every year. He's been an insurance policy for us until this year."[15]

When Flanagan injured his knee in the first game of a doubleheader against the White Sox on May 17, it opened even more of an opportunity for Boddicker. He started the second game of the twin bill and hurled a five-hit shutout, striking out eight while walking just one.

Orioles manager Joe Altobelli was ecstatic with the effort. "It's not like he's a veteran pitcher, but he's got a few years under his belt in Triple-A ball," he said. "He's not in awe out there, and he showed that. He pitched a bang-up game."[16]

Boddicker not only filled Flanagan's spot in the rotation, but he became one of the aces of the staff. He went 16–8 with a 2.77 ERA and although he spent the first month of the season in the minors, only McGregor won more games for the Orioles. Boddicker said he learned a lot from watching McGregor, who also had a less-than-dominating fastball and a similar style.

The Orioles won the American League East by six games over Detroit. As great as he had been in the regular season, Boddicker was even better in the postseason.

The Orioles lost to the White Sox in the first game of the American League Championship Series and Boddicker took the mound for Game 2. He spent the day of the game installing a new CB radio in his pickup truck, then went out and dispatched the Sox with ease. He struck out 14 batters—the most by any pitcher in the AL that season—and became the first AL rookie ever to pitch a shutout in the playoffs, throwing 143 pitches in a complete-game effort. When the series was over and the Orioles had won, he was named the most valuable player of the ALCS.

Back in Norway, there was a massive celebration.

"I think he's got this whole town boppin,'" Dolly Boddicker told reporters. "Mike always said he was going to pitch in the major leagues, but I could never picture it."[17]

The World Series followed a similar scenario. The Philadelphia Phillies beat McGregor in Game 1 in Baltimore, leaving the Orioles in need of a big effort from Boddicker in Game 2. He was masterful again in a 4–1 victory. He allowed just three hits and one unearned run, and capped it off by retiring three Hall of Fame caliber players in order in the ninth inning. After getting Joe Morgan to fly out and Pete Rose to ground out, he struck out Mike Schmidt on three pitches.

Many years later, Boddicker said he was much more relaxed in the World Series game than he had been in the ALCS despite the star power of the Philadelphia lineup. "The White Sox were really good," he said. "I knew if I could handle them I could handle the Phillies."[18]

Dolly, crippled by arthritis, watched the game back in Norway again but almost all of Boddicker's family members rode through the night in an RV to be there to see the World Series in person.[19] As Boddicker strode toward the dugout following the game, Van Scoyoc remembers him looking up at the family and flashing a triumphant thumbs-up.

Boddicker said his curve ball wasn't as good as it had been against the White Sox but his fastball was better and he made more extensive use of the foshball. "He had a great idea of what he was doing," Rose said.[20]

He suddenly was the darling of the sports media from coast to coast.

"The World Series is all even because the Baltimore Orioles have a pitcher who throws feathers instead of fastballs," Bill Lyon wrote.[21]

Alan Goldstein of the *Baltimore Sun* noted that Boddicker "has made big-game pressure look as matter-of-fact as a walk down Main Street in Norway, Iowa, where there are less people than in Section 34."²²

John Steadman added, "This was a rookie who handled himself with poise and maturity. He went right at the Phillies and never backed away. In the end, his pitching performance was the kind that ought to be put in a frame and savored."²³

Boddicker wrote about the experience himself in a daily diary he authored for the *News American*: "I don't think it has all hit me yet. I have to keep reminding myself that this is the World Series. It doesn't seem like it."²⁴

A few weeks later, after the Orioles had finished off the world title, Boddicker found his way back to Norway, where Mike Boddicker Day was celebrated on November 4. About 300 people crammed into the American Legion hall in Cedar Rapids for a huge celebration. The local fans, knowing Boddicker's love of outdoor pursuits, presented him with a Remington 20-gauge shotgun and a gold-plated trap.²⁵

Among the speakers at the banquet was Jim Leyland, who was still a few years away from beginning a successful two-decade stint as a major league manager. "He's an isolated case of outstanding concentration, plus a raw talent and instinct for the game," Leyland said. "And he knows everything about Mike Boddicker. That's as important as knowing the hitters."²⁶

Boddicker took all the banquets and adulation in stride. He talked about possibly going back to his $4.50-per-hour off-season job at the Pollock Grain Elevator and said that if it hadn't been for all the banquets and questions from the media, he would have put the whole World Series experience behind him. He admitted that perhaps it hadn't all sunk in yet. "Maybe," he confessed, "it never will."²⁷

Needless to say, there were huge expectations for Boddicker as the 1984 season rolled around. He was a postseason hero and *The Sporting News* rookie of the year, and at the age of 26, had a glimmering future.

He didn't disappoint. After getting off to an 0–3 start, he got rolling with a May 1 shutout of Cleveland and continued on to lead the American League with 20 wins and a 2.79 ERA. He was fourth in the AL Cy Young Award voting although the Orioles missed the playoffs.

He dropped off to 12–17 in 1985, though, and suffered a torn ligament in the middle finger on his pitching hand in 1986, which affected his ability to throw a curve. He was still above .500 at 14–12 that season but his ERA ballooned to 4.70. The ensuing seasons weren't much better as he went 10–12 and 13–15 the next two years.

The Orioles got off to an abysmal 0–21 start in 1988 and they began to dismantle what was left of their earlier powerhouse teams. Boddicker was only 6–12 when he was traded to the Boston Red Sox on July 29 in exchange for Brady Anderson and Curt Schilling. Boddicker later described it as the "saddest day of my life" and admitted to reporters that he shed some tears as he left Baltimore's Memorial Stadium after being informed of the trade.[28]

But the change of scenery seemed to revive him. Boddicker remembers walking into the Boston clubhouse, looking at the locker of pitching coach Bill Fischer and seeing that his radar gun had a coat of dust on it. "This is my kind of place," he thought.[29]

He went 7–3 in the remainder of the 1988 season although he did not pitch well in the postseason, giving up three straight home runs after being staked to a 5–0 lead in a Game 3 loss to Oakland in the ALCS.

He went 15–11 in 1989 and 17–8 in 1990, winning a Gold Glove as the best fielding pitcher in the American League that season. He again faced Oakland in Game 3 of the 1990 ALCS and pitched much better than he had in 1988. He threw a complete game but allowed two unearned runs in a 4–1 loss.

Boddicker became a free agent after the season and hoped to sign with the St. Louis Cardinals, the team he

Mike Boddicker won 20 games for Baltimore in 1984 (courtesy the Baltimore Orioles).

grew up cheering for. He also wanted to get back to the Midwest to be closer to Dolly, whose health was failing.

The Red Sox had made a very generous five-year offer to have him stay in Boston. The Toronto Blue Jays and Minnesota Twins also were offering big money, but Boddicker had his heart set on being a Cardinal. His agent placed several phone calls to St. Louis general manager Dal Maxvill, but received no response. Boddicker then instructed his flabbergasted agent to tell the Cardinals he would give them a blank contract and play for the major league minimum.[30]

The Cardinals still did not respond. In the meantime, the Kansas City Royals made a modest offer for less money ($3 million per season) and fewer years than the other teams. Boddicker quickly accepted. He thought the Royals had the makings of a contender and he liked Cedar Rapids native John Wathan, who was then the team's manager.[31]

Boddicker went 12–12 in 1991, but there wasn't much life left in his right arm. Wathan was fired during the 1991 season and replaced by Hal McRae, who didn't hold Boddicker in such high regard and dropped him from the Royals' rotation in 1992. He spent some time on the disabled list with arm problems, pitched mostly in relief, recorded just one victory and was sold to Milwaukee early in the 1993 season.

He only lasted a couple of months there and announced his retirement following the season.

He finished with a career record of 134–116 and recorded 10 consecutive seasons with 200-plus innings. In 2,123 innings at the major league level, he never gave up a grand slam. When an Orioles fan website named the top 40 players in the team's history in 2006, Boddicker came in at No. 35.[32]

"Everything worked out perfectly for me," he said many years after retiring. "God blessed me tremendously."[33]

He and his wife, Lisa, daughter of his old American Legion coach Ken Charipar, now have four children and four grandchildren. They stayed in the Kansas City area, where there is a true Midwest feel and easy access to one of Boddicker's favorite pastimes—hunting. He owns five hunting farms, spanning about 700 acres, in Iowa and Kansas. He dabbled in broadcasting for awhile, pitched batting practice for the Royals for many years and helped coach his son's team at St. Thomas Aquinas High School in Overland Park, Kansas.

Boddicker was diagnosed with cancer in his tonsils in 2011, but made a full recovery.

Even as he approaches his 60s, he still regards himself as a country

15. Pitcher: Mike Boddicker

boy at heart. After he made it in baseball, he still came back and worked at the Pollock Grain Elevator in Norway in the off-season. When he won the ALCS MVP award in 1983, he was to receive a new Camaro Z28 but he asked if he could have a four-wheel drive truck instead.[34]

He never has forgotten or forsaken his roots in Norway. When interviewers occasionally made reference to him being from Cedar Rapids, Boddicker invariably corrected them and pointed out that he was from a small town *outside* of Cedar Rapids.

"It's nice to be reminded that there are still hometowns in this world, places that people can go back to," Steve Wulf wrote in his *Sports Illustrated* tribute to Boddicker following the 1983 season. "Norway is as good a hometown as anybody has ever had, and it has had as much to do with Boddicker's success as his famous foshball."[35]

Third Base
Casey Blake

"He was not particularly fast and not particularly strong, but really, really played the game unselfishly."—Longtime Wichita State baseball coach Gene Stephenson[1]

With a career batting average of .264 and the second highest home run total of any Iowan who ever played major league baseball, it goes without saying that Casey Blake could hit. He also was a good fielder, whether he was playing his natural position of third base or filling in at first base or in right field.

But Blake, above all, was a *great* teammate.

No matter where he went in 13 years in the big leagues, Blake provided a unifying influence. When he joined the Los Angeles Dodgers in 2008, he became part of a team torn by cliques and dissension. Older players on the team had nothing to do with the younger players. Players of different races from different backgrounds and different cultures almost never intermingled.

Blake, then an established veteran in his mid 30s, made it his mission to bridge those gaps and bring together a team filled with talent but lacking in unity and chemistry. He twice helped bring the Dodgers to within a few games of the World Series mainly by being what *Wall Street Journal* writer Hannah Karp described as "one of baseball's least selfish players, quietly hell-bent on smashing conflict, extinguishing outsized egos and making the Dodgers' once deeply divided clubhouse a better place."[2]

Blake's unselfishness also manifested itself after his retirement from baseball in contributions he has made to the community that spawned him—Indianola, Iowa.

16. Third Base: Casey Blake

Born in 1973 in Des Moines, Blake was the third oldest of four brothers who grew up playing every sport there was in Indianola, about 15 miles south of the capital city.

The Blake boys all had a competitive drive and their father, Joe, fueled that. Joe Blake had played baseball in the New York Yankees' farm system and spent more than a quarter century as the pitching coach at Simpson College, just two blocks down the street from the Blake home. He knew how much work it took to achieve success at baseball's highest levels.

The Blakes were the family that would go to the park on the weekend and Dad would hit ground balls to the boys. Joe Blake eventually used much of his life savings to build a batting cage in the backyard to help his sons further develop their skills.[3]

All four boys—Joe Jr., Ben, Casey and Pete—became accomplished players. Ben played in the minor leagues in the Cleveland Indians system and later became the head coach at Simpson. Pete may have been the best prospect of all. A left-handed pitcher and hitter, he played in the Minnesota Twins organization before having his career cut short by a series of arm injuries.

Casey is the one who made it. He played four sports during his time at Indianola High School and said baseball wasn't necessarily his favorite. That probably was football. He played quarterback and earned all-state honors despite being overshadowed by some of other QBs around the state, including future Iowa State

Casey Blake (Dan Mendik/Cleveland Indians).

basketball star and coach Fred Hoiberg (at Ames High School) and Ryan Driscoll, who starred at Linn-Mar before going on to play at the University of Iowa.

Blake also was a three-time letter-winner and two-time state place-winner as a hurdler in track. In basketball, he helped Indianola to a third-place state finish as a sophomore on a team led by future Iowa star Chris Street, then made first-team all-state as a senior while leading the Indians to a second-place state finish. In both his junior and senior years, he ranked among the state's top three-point shooters.

"While in school and since, Casey is one of the most humble athletes we have had in Indianola," said Bert Hanson, his high school basketball coach. "He was a leader in every sense of the word. He always strived to get better but of equal importance, he wanted and helped others to get better. That is a quality he has carried through his life as personified by his career."[4]

Blake's size—he was six feet, two inches, but considerably less than his eventual major league weight of 205—kept him from being considered a top-level college recruit in football and basketball. From the very beginning, it seemed his future would be in baseball.

As a junior shortstop at Indianola, he batted .493 with 10 home runs and 43 RBI and he continued that success as a senior, batting .416 and earning first-team Class 4A all-state honors.

He was selected by the Philadelphia Phillies in the 11th round of the 1992 major league draft, but was committed to playing college baseball and had pretty much chosen to attend Creighton over the University of Iowa. He really liked Creighton's head coach, Jim Hendry, who had led the Blue Jays to the College World Series in 1991. But before Blake could sign with Creighton, Hendry took a job as a special assistant to Florida Marlins general manager Dave Dombrowski.

Hendry was good friends with Wichita State coach Gene Stephenson, who didn't normally do much recruiting in Iowa, but Hendry told him about this hot prospect in Indianola. Blake ended up signing with the Shockers before they ever saw him play.

At Wichita State under Stephenson, Blake came into an environment of high intensity and even higher expectations.

"He was an interesting guy to play for," Blake said. "Coming in there, the standard was already set. It was like 'We're going to Omaha every year, no doubt about it.' He wanted mean, tough, blue-collar guys who would just outwork everyone else."[5]

Blake got playing time in a platoon situation early in his first season

16. Third Base: Casey Blake

but eventually emerged as the everyday third baseman. He batted .366 as a freshman but hit .451 in the Missouri Valley Conference tournament and .500 in the NCAA Atlantic Regional, and eventually made the all-tournament team at the College World Series. He appeared on every freshman All-American team and was on his way.

He was named first team all-MVC in each of the next three seasons and was the league's player of the year as a senior in 1996. He also was a two-time academic All-American, a member of Team USA in 1995 and 1996 and a second-team All-American in 1996. His career average was .354 and he was inducted into Wichita State's athletic hall of fame just seven years after leaving there, in 2003.

At the end of his junior season in 1995, Blake fully expected to be a high draft choice and thought he would turn pro. However, he went undrafted until the Yankees finally chose him, almost as an after-thought, in the 45th round.

After talking to Stephenson, Blake decided to play one more year of college ball and as a highly-motivated senior, he batted .320 with career highs of 22 home runs and 101 runs batted in. The Toronto Blue Jays took notice and chose him in the seventh round of the 1996 amateur draft.

John Sickels, a former research assistant to Bill James who writes scouting reports for various websites, wrote many years later that some scouts were skeptical about Blake's long-range potential. "He was considered to be a fine athlete with good defensive skills at third base, but a questionable bat; scouts were worried that he couldn't hit with wood," Sickels wrote.[6]

Blake had only modest success at the plate in his first two years in the minor leagues and thought he might be on the verge of being released. But in 1998, while splitting time between Class A Dunedin and Double-A Knoxville, he batted .357 with 18 homers, 43 doubles, 103 RBI and 19 stolen bases, and emerged as a top prospect.

His average dropped to .245 the following year at Triple-A Syracuse, but he hit 22 home runs and came up to the Blue Jays at the end of the season, batting .256 in 14 games.

Over the next three years, Blake changed teams four times and bounced frequently between the majors and Triple-A. In May of 2000, he was picked up on waivers by the Minnesota Twins but batted only .188 in seven games with the big-league club. In 2001, after batting .318 in 13 games with Minnesota, he was waived again, claimed by Baltimore, played in six games with the Orioles, was waived again three weeks later and reclaimed by the Twins.

He managed to bat .309 at Triple-A Edmonton in both 2001 and 2002 but after playing in nine more games with Minnesota in 2002, he was released after the season.

In December, he signed as a free agent with Cleveland and finally found a home. He became a starter for the Indians in 2003 and over the next eight years, he averaged 20 homers and 73 RBI per season at the major-league level.

"I thought he was an excellent hitter. He was always a major league hitter," said Tim McClelland, a fellow Iowan who watched Blake as a major league umpire for many years. "He did what he had to do. He didn't always get a lot of glory or stardom, but he was a great team player. He's a good guy to have on your team."[7]

Blake really solidified his standing with the Indians in that first season during a mid-season hot streak that earned him American League player of the week honors. On July 5, he had probably the best game of his life against the Minnesota team that twice discarded him, going 5-for-5 with two homers, two doubles and seven RBI in a 13–2 Cleveland victory.

Blake had perhaps his best year in 2004 when he reached career highs with 28 homers and 88 RBI while batting .271. The improved power numbers probably were attributable to a better grasp of the strike zone although Blake, by his own admission, was a player who tinkered with his style of hitting more than most players. He used a wider, less upright, batting stance during most of his years in Cleveland but often would try to emulate things that he saw working for other players.

"I was awful about altering my stance," he admitted. "It was almost a game-to-game thing."[8]

Blake also got moved around to different positions in the field during his major league career. He was Cleveland's starting third baseman in 2003 and 2004, but spent more time in right field in 2005 and 2006 and began 2007 at first base before going back to third. For his career, he played 923 games at third base, 238 in right field, 116 at first base and was even briefly pressed into service at shortstop, second base and left field.

The Indians weren't an exceptionally strong team in Blake's first few years with the team but in 2007 things finally fell into place under manager Eric Wedge. They went 96–66 and won the American League Central Division title.

Blake had been together with many of those same players for about five years—C.C. Sabathia, Jake Westbrook, Travis Hafner, Victor Martinez, Grady Sizemore, Rafael Bettencourt, Cocoa Crisp, Jhonny Peralta—and it was a tight-knit, cohesive group.

"It was a lot of the same guys I broke in with there in 2003," Blake said. "It was just a team where everybody pulled for each other, everybody cared for each other."⁹

He said many of his fondest memories come from that 2007 season, especially from the final month when the Indians were battling to hold off the competition. On September 14, he hit a game-winning home run off Kansas City's David Riske in the bottom of the ninth inning to give Cleveland an important win. Three days later, he did it again, homering off Detroit's Zach Miner in the bottom of the 11th to finish off the Tigers.

The Indians couldn't quite complete the job in the postseason, though. After beating the Yankees in four games in the AL Division Series, they opened a 3–1 lead over Boston in the ALCS only to have the Red Sox win three straight lopsided games to get to the World Series. It was hardly Blake's fault. He batted .346 in the ALCS and went 4-for-10 in those last three losses.

He continued to be a productive player for Cleveland in 2008, but he was scheduled to become a free agent after the season and with the team going nowhere in late July, he was traded to the Los Angeles Dodgers with cash for Jon Meloan and Carlos Santana. Blake's numbers declined slightly after the trade although he still finished with a .274 average, 21 homers and 81 RBI.

With the Dodgers, he joined a team with a completely different aura than what he experienced in Cleveland.

"It was weird for me," Blake said. "Obviously, just being traded for the first time was weird. I was going into a locker room where I didn't know anybody and it was kind of a divided clubhouse."¹⁰

The older players on the team despised the younger players, didn't talk to them, didn't socialize with them.

"I figured as long as I was there, I might as well try to pull everybody together," Blake said. "I'd like to think I made a difference."¹¹

He befriended brash, younger players such as Matt Kemp, who came to view Blake as a big brother. A 2009 *Wall Street Journal* article quoted Kemp as saying, "I know a great dude when I see one."¹²

Blake also made an effort to engage some of the older players. Veteran infielder Jeff Kent had a reputation for being grumpy and surly, but Blake softened him up and found him to be a good guy.

More than anything, he tried to open lines of communication and cultivate camaraderie.

"It seemed like we would get to a new city and these guys would go their own way and these guys would go that way," Blake said. "I would say,

Casey Blake provided a unifying influence when he joined the Dodgers in 2008 (Juan Ocampo/Los Angeles Dodgers).

'Let's all go out to eat. Let's get a room at a restaurant and go have a team meal and spend time together. Let's grow the family.'"[13]

It worked. When Blake joined the Dodgers, they were two games under .500. They ended up winning the National League's West Division and defeated the Cubs in the NLDS before losing to Philadelphia in the NLCS.

When he became a free agent after the season, the Dodgers signed him to a contract that paid him $18 million over three seasons.

Blake, who came to be known for his trademark beard and a distinct jawline that prompted teammates to call him "The Chin," continued to be a Los Angeles stalwart in 2009. He batted .280 and drove in 79 runs as the Dodgers again won a division title. Manager Joe Torre loved the way he continually put the team's interests above his own, calling Blake "a throwback."[14]

Blake created a bit of controversy along the way. When he hit yet another walk-off home run in the 12th inning on May 10 against the San Francisco Giants' flamboyant closer, Brian Wilson, he mimicked the gesture Wilson made after every save. He later admitted he got caught up in the emotion of the moment and also didn't realize Wilson was honoring his faith and paying tribute to his late father with the move.[15]

16. Third Base: Casey Blake

"Of course I didn't mean anything personal by it," Blake later said. "I didn't intend to mock his father or mean any disrespect by it. All anyone sees is what happened afterward. I was excited. I hit a big homer. I got out of my box a little bit."[16]

The Dodgers again came up short of the World Series. After defeating St. Louis in the NLDS, they again couldn't find a way to beat the Phillies.

Blake's stats dropped off a bit in 2010 although he still hit 17 homers and drove in 64 runs while batting .248.

He said he still hoped to be an everyday player in 2011, but a series of ailments kept him from doing so. Early in the season, he began experiencing pain and swelling in his elbow and it was determined that he had a staph infection. He underwent surgery for that and came back at midseason but encountered more problems.

Blake had experienced chronic neck problems throughout his career, but he always had been able to play through the pain and stiffness. This time it didn't go away and actually grew progressively worse.

"It got to where it hurt just to stand in the batter's box and look at the pitcher," he said.[17]

He finally opted to have season-ending surgery in early September to relieve a pinched nerve in his neck. He ended up getting only 202 at-bats that season and he usually wasn't 100 percent even when he did play. He batted just .252.

He became a free agent again following the season and although there was some interest from the Indians in bringing him back to Cleveland, he signed with Colorado. The Rockies had a vacancy at third base and they gave him a non-guaranteed $2 million contract with several performance clauses.

Blake had another setback with his neck in spring training although he was starting to hit the ball better when the Rockies released him near the end of spring training, on March 27.

He could have continued to play. Even though he was 38, the Texas Rangers were very interested in signing him, especially after starting third baseman Sergio Beltre was injured. Blake needed only 42 more days of service in the majors to become fully vested in the players' pension program, but he just couldn't bring himself to continue. He was weary of the mental and physical grind. He turned down the Rangers, retiring after having played 1,283 games over 13 seasons.

"In my mind, in my heart, I knew I was done playing," he said. "I just didn't want to do it anymore."[18]

In the years since retiring, Blake was named one of the top 10 male high school athletes in the history of Iowa and has reaped many other honors. He was inducted into the Iowa High School Athletic Association Hall of Fame in 2013 and the National High School Hall of Fame in 2014. In 2012, a Cleveland Indians website named him one of the 100 best players ever to play for the franchise.[19]

Blake still lives in Indianola, where he and his wife Abbie are raising family of six kids—five girls and a boy—the oldest of whom is 14. He spends some time coaching his children's sports teams and also does plenty of golfing and duck hunting, but he mostly just enjoys being a father.

Abbie, whose maiden name was Archibald, also was an outstanding athlete at Indianola High School five years after Casey was. She earned 17 varsity letters, more than anyone in the history of the school—four each in basketball, volleyball and track, five in softball. She went on to compete in basketball and softball at the college level at both St. Ambrose University and Simpson.

Both Casey and Abbie are concerned with helping the community in which they were raised and in February 2010 they gave $1 million to initiate a foundation, challenging the Indianola community to match their donation. The result is a new multi-purpose sports facility, attached to the local middle school, that serves the needs of the local community.

"It just feels good to be able to help, to be in a position to do something like that," Blake said.[20]

Needless to say, Indianola will be forever grateful.

"He's a hometown hero and so many people look up to him," Indianola athletic director Bernie Brueck said. "For him to want to provide so many opportunities for local kids, that's tremendous."[21]

The Best of the Rest
Position Players

Catchers

Patsy Gharrity

Edward Gharrity, born in Parnell, Iowa, in 1892, played his entire major league career with the Washington Senators and formed a close bond with Hall of Fame pitcher Walter Johnson.

He reached the major leagues in 1916 after only two minor league seasons and was the Senators' starting catcher for five years, from 1919 through 1923. By far his best season was 1921, when he batted .310 with career-high totals of seven home runs and 55 runs batted in. For his career, he batted .262 in 676 games spread over the course of 10 years.

He had the dubious distinction of being behind the plate three times when Ty Cobb stole home, once each in 1920, 1921 and 1922.[1]

Gharrity, who also saw action at first base and in the outfield, retired after the 1923 season and was out of organized baseball from 1924–28, playing in "outlaw" leagues. He eventually was reinstated and came back to the Senators as a player-coach in 1929 when Johnson, who was his roommate in his earlier years, became manager of the Senators. He played in just three games in 1929 and two in 1930. He also served as a coach under Johnson with the Cleveland Indians from 1933 to 1935.

In his later years, Gharrity managed a minor league team in Eau Claire, Wisconsin, and served on the Beloit, Wisconsin, city council before dying in Beloit at the age of 74 in 1966.

Duane Josephson

Duane Josephson made one American League All-Star team during his major league career but injuries and illnesses kept interrupting that career and ultimately prevented him from becoming one of the elite catchers in all of baseball. He ended up playing in only 470 games over eight seasons.

Josephson was born and raised in New Hampton in north central Iowa to a working class family. His father, Carl, was an auto mechanic and his mother, Lucille, was a waitress. Josephson, known to friends and family members as Josie, won 10 varsity letters in baseball, basketball and track at New Hampton High School, and took his talents off to the college now known as the University of Northern Iowa.

He starred in two sports there. In basketball, he was a sharpshooting guard who averaged 18.3 points per game in the 1962–63 season and 16.8 the following year, helping the Panthers and coach Norm Stewart win a conference title. In baseball, he became the school's first All-American by hitting 10 home runs in 24 games as a senior.

Josephson signed with the Chicago White Sox in 1964 and in his third year in the minor leagues in 1966, he was named the most valuable player of the Pacific Coast League. He made brief appearances with the Sox at the end of the 1965 and 1966 seasons and got to the major leagues to stay in 1967. He shared the starting catching job with J.C. Martin that year, but twice missed about a month because of finger injuries.

In 1968, he played in more than 100 games for the only time in his career, leading the American League in assists, double plays and throwing out would-be base stealers. He only batted .247, but still was named to the AL All-Star team.

His physical problems returned in 1969, when he missed two months with a blood clot, and in 1970, when he broke a finger while batting .316.

The White Sox traded him to Boston before the 1971 season and Josephson opened the season as the starting catcher, but he again was sidelined following a collision at the plate. The Red Sox brought promising youngster Carlton Fisk to the majors late in the season and any chance Josephson had of competing with Fisk, a future Hall of Famer, disappeared prior to the 1972 season when he was hospitalized for two weeks with pericarditis, an inflammation of the membranes surrounding the heart. He lost 18 pounds and when he suffered a recurrence of the ailment in mid-season, he was finished.[2] He retired at the age of 30 prior to the 1973 season.

Josephson returned to Iowa, operating a sporting goods store, selling real estate and dabbling in coaching before dying in 1997 at the age of 54.

Tim Laudner

Tim Laudner was the starting catcher for the Minnesota Twins when they won the world championship in 1987 and he was named to the American League All-Star team the following season.

Born in Mason City, he lived in Rockford, Iowa, until the age of seven, then attended Park Center High School in the Twin-Cities suburb of Brooklyn Center. In addition to starring in baseball, he also was an all-state tight end in football and played hockey.

He was chosen by Cincinnati in the 33rd round of the 1976 major league draft but opted instead to continue his career at the University of Missouri. He played the outfield as a freshman at Missouri, then was a catcher for the next two years.

Laudner was drafted by the Twins in the third round in 1979 and played his entire nine-year major league career with Minnesota. He moved up quickly through the minors, setting a Southern League record with 42 home runs in 1981 and playing 14 games with the Twins at the end of that season.

He batted .318 in the 1987 World Series, including a home run in Game 2, and he doubled in his only at-bat in the 1988 All-Star Game.

Laudner injured his knee in 1989, served as a backup to Brian Harper that season, then abruptly retired near the end of spring training in 1990. He later made a brief comeback but after going hitless in 29 at-bats for the Twins' Triple-A team at Portland, he was released.

"There were times I didn't want to be a ballplayer anymore," Laudner said. "I wanted to move on to something else, not just be received as an athlete or ballplayer."[3]

In 734 games at the major league level, he batted .225 with 77 homers, including 16 in 1987 and 13 in 1988.

John Wathan

As a six-foot, two-inch, 205-pound catcher, John Wathan hardly resembled a record-setting base-stealer. But that's exactly what he became.

During the 1982 season, while playing for the Kansas City Royals, he broke the major league record for stolen bases in a season by a catcher. Despite missing five weeks with a broken foot in the middle of the season, Wathan stole 36 bases in 45 attempts, breaking Ray Schalk's 1916 mark of 30 steals.

In anticipation of Wathan breaking the record, the grounds crew at Texas installed an old, beat-up bag at second base, knowing that when he broke the mark Wathan would be entitled to take the base home as a memento of the occasion. He fooled them. He stole third.[4]

Wathan also stole 28 bases the following season and finished with 105 steals and a .262 average over the course of a 10-year career spent entirely with the Royals. He never made an All-Star team, but he finished 24th in the American League MVP voting in 1980 when he batted .305 with 17 stolen bases.

Wathan, born in Cedar Rapids, grew up in southern California and attended the University of San Diego. He stole 30 bases in both his sophomore and junior years and was the fourth player selected in the 1971 January draft.

John Wathan spent his entire 10-year playing career with the Kansas City Royals.

Early in his major league career, he frequently played first base and put together 92 consecutive errorless games at the position from 1977 to 1979.

Kansas City made the playoffs in seven of his 10 seasons. He batted .286 in the 1980 World Series and finally became part of a world championship team in his final season, 1985.

Wathan, who earned the nickname "Duke" for his uncanny impersonations of John Wayne,[5] served as a coach with the Royals in 1986, managed their Omaha farm team for most of 1987, then became manager of the big league club late in the 1987 season. He was fired early in 1991.

In 1992, he became the third-base coach for the Angels and when manager Buck Rodgers was seriously injured in a bus crash, Wathan took over as interim manager for 89 games. His record as a major league manager was 287–270.

He was a bench coach with the Angels in 1993 and was the bullpen coach for the Red Sox in 1994. He also did some broadcasting and worked for several teams in various capacities before joining the Royals' front office in 2008.

Infielders

Dick Green

Dick Green is the only native Iowan to play for three consecutive world championship teams and he's also the answer to a trivia question: Who is the only position player ever to be named a World Series MVP without getting a hit?

Green did it in 1974. Teammate Rollie Fingers was voted the official most valuable player after the Oakland A's secured their third straight world title by beating the Los Angeles Dodgers in five games, but the New York baseball writers gave their Babe Ruth award as the series MVP to Green. He did not get a hit in 13 at-bats in the series, but he made several spectacular defensive plays at second base, including game-ending double plays in Games 3 and 4. He made a diving stop of a ground ball by Von Joshua to start the double play that ended Game 4.

"This award is named after Babe Ruth," an amused Green said in accepting the honor a few months later. "And Babe Ruth was a pitcher and pitchers aren't supposed to hit. That's me, too!"[6]

Green, born in Sioux City, Iowa, in 1941, spent all 12 of his major league seasons with the Athletics, the first five in Kansas City and the last seven in Oakland.

He grew up in South Dakota and signed with the Athletics in 1960 after just one year at Black Hills State College. He actually showed good power as a hitter in the minor leagues, hitting 51 home runs in four years, including 18 with the Lewiston Broncs of the Northwest League in 1961.

Green came up to the majors at the end of the 1963 season and became the Athletics' regular second baseman the following year. He played more than 100 games in nine seasons and committed only 96 errors in 12 years, but never became a major offensive force. He batted only .240 with 80 home runs in 1,288 games and had two years as a starter (1967 and 1970) in which he hit under .200. His best season came in 1969 when

Dick Green was the defensive hero of the 1974 World Series (courtesy South Dakota Sports Hall of Fame).

he batted .275 with 12 homers and a career-high 64 runs batted in while also leading American League second basemen in fielding.

The A's made the playoffs in his last four seasons and won the world title in the last three. Green, who batted only .155 and scored just one run in 36 career post-season games, actually announced that he was retiring after the 1971 and 1973 seasons, but each time owner Charlie Finley talked him into coming back.[7]

In early March of 1975, little more than a month after accepting the Babe Ruth Award, he was granted his outright release by the team.

Jerry Hairston, Jr.

Jerry Hairston, Jr., a third-generation major leaguer, didn't live in Iowa for very long. But he was born there, in Des Moines, while his father was playing for the Iowa Oaks in the White Sox farm system in 1976.

Hairston ended up spending 16 years in the majors as a reliable utility man, batting .257 with 70 home runs and 147 stolen bases.

His father, Jerry Sr., played 14 years with the White Sox and his grandfather, Sam, played four games with the Sox in 1951.

Jerry Jr., attended Naperville North High School in the suburbs of Chicago and Southern Illinois University before being drafted by Baltimore in the 11th round in 1997.

He got to the majors late in the 1998 season and stayed there through the end of 2013, seeing action with nine different teams. He played every position except pitcher and catcher, seeing the most service at second base. He played 650 of his 1,442 games there.

He saw his most extensive action in 2001 when he played 159 games as the Orioles' starting second baseman. He batted only .233 but stole a career-best 29 bases. He later batted .303 with Baltimore in 2004 and .326 with Cincinnati in 2008.

Hairston was at his best in the playoffs, batting .362 in 17 postseason games. He hit .375 for Milwaukee in the 2011 National League Division Series and .391 in the National League Championship Series. He also was part of the Yankees' world championship team in 2009.

Lee Handley

Few players have had to overcome more adversity during their major league careers than Lee Handley.

The five-foot, seven-inch, 160-pound infielder, who was born in Clarion, Iowa, in 1913, played in 968 games in a 10-year career that was punctuated by a couple of major injuries that nearly cost him his life. He hit only 15 home runs, but was a solid .269 hitter for his career and struck out only 204 times in 3,698 at-bats.

Handley, known to teammates as "Jeep," first emerged as a prospect at Bradley University and was signed by the Cincinnati Reds, who sent him to Toronto of the International League for most of the 1935 and 1936 seasons.

He played in 24 games with the Reds at the end of 1936, but was declared a free agent following the season because of a clerical error and was picked up by the Pittsburgh Pirates.

Handley was the Pirates' starting second baseman in 1937 and was moved to third base in 1938. He emerged as a feisty, scrappy player, batting .268 and reaching career highs in games played (139), hits (153), runs scored (91), runs batted in (51), doubles (25) and home runs (6) in 1938.

His physical problems began the following spring. In an April 9 preseason exhibition game in New Orleans, Handley was struck in the side of the head by a fastball thrown by Cleveland's Johnny Allen. The ball hit him squarely on his left ear—doctors later speculated that the cushioning effect of the ear may have saved his life—and rolled all way to the first base coaching box. Handley was carried from the field unconscious, underwent surgery to remove a blood clot and, although he had no broken bones, he struggled with the after-effects of the incident. He lost 30 pounds, developed whooping cough and missed 52 games.[8]

He still managed to bat .285 and lead the National League in stolen bases that season. He played in 98 games in 1940 and was headed for another good year in 1941 when he was badly spiked in a collision with pitcher Johnny Gee.

Handley encountered more misfortune prior to the 1942 season when he was involved in a serious car accident in Illinois. He was thrown through the canvas roof of the convertible he was driving, suffered serious injuries to his head, right arm and right shoulder, and laid by the side of road for an hour before being found.[9] His throwing ability was greatly impaired and he spent the next two years back in the minors at Toronto, struggling to resurrect his career.

He came back to play three more years with the Pirates, batting .298 in 1945, and spent one final season with the Phillies in 1947. Jackie Robinson later told interviewers that Handley was the first opposing player to wish him well when he broke baseball's color barrier that season.[10]

Handley played three more seasons in the Pacific Coast League before retiring. He died of a heart attack at the age of 56 in 1970.

Bobby Knoop

He never became a highly efficient hitter, but Bobby Knoop was so graceful and acrobatic in the field that he earned the nickname "Nureyev."

Knoop won three consecutive American League Gold Gloves for his skill at second base from 1966 through 1968, and in 2013 he was inducted into the Los Angeles Angels Hall of Fame.

Jim Fregosi, who played shortstop alongside Knoop for his entire Angels career, said, "I've never seen a second baseman who was better on the double-play pivot."[11]

Knoop was born in Sioux City in 1938, but moved to California with his family as a child. He was signed by the Milwaukee Braves out of Montebello, California, High School in 1956 and spent eight years in the minor leagues, forming a double play combination with fellow Iowa native Denis Menke at Cedar Rapids in 1958. His best year in the minors was 1963, when he batted .283 with 20 home runs at Hawaii in the Pacific Coast League.

Bobby Knoop came back to Iowa to manager the Quad-City Angels after his playing career was over (courtesy *Quad-City Times*).

The Angels selected him in the Rule 5 draft after that season and he played in every game as a rookie in 1964.

In addition to the three Gold Gloves, he was presented the Angels' Owners Trophy for "inspirational leadership, sportsmanship and professional ability" on four different occasions.[12] He also was the starting second baseman for the American League in the 1966 All-Star Game.

After five-plus years with the Angels, he was traded to the White Sox in late May of 1969 and was sent to the Royals prior to the 1971 season. He was released after the 1972 campaign.

Knoop never hit for a high average, but he clubbed 17 home runs in 1966 and led the Angels with 72 RBI. They also turned 186 double plays that season, which was then an AL record.

After finishing with a career average of .236 in 1,153 games, Knoop served as a minor league manager in the Angels' farm system—including a stop back in Iowa with the Quad-City Angels—then served as a major league coach for 21 years, most of that with the Angels (1979–96).

Denis Menke

There were few more versatile or consistent infielders in baseball during the 1960s and 1970s than Denis Menke.

The Bancroft, Iowa, native played for three different National League teams and was a starter at some point in his career at all four infield positions. He made two NL All-Stars teams and reached a high point when he hit a home run off Catfish Hunter in the 1972 World Series.

Born in 1940, Menke was raised on a 480-acre farm not far from the Minnesota border. He starred at St. John's High School in Bancroft and in 1958 signed for the then-exorbitant sum of $125,000 with the Milwaukee Braves, who won a bidding war against 12 other teams.[13]

He had good success at Midland and Cedar Rapids in the low minors in his first two years, then justified the big signing bonus with a great year at Yakima in 1960, hitting .336 with 28 home runs.

He came up to the Braves in 1962 and in his first two years saw action at shortstop, third and second. He was installed as the starting shortstop in 1964 and had one of his best seasons, slugging 20 home runs while batting .283.

He missed more than a month after a collision at home plate in 1965 and was traded to Houston at the end of the 1967 season.

He was the starting second baseman for the Astros in 1968 when regular Joe Morgan missed most of the season with an injury. Back at shortstop, he hit .304 in 1970 and had 90 or more RBI in both 1969 and '70, making the NL All-Star team as a reserve both years. He was 15th in the NL MVP voting in 1969.

By 1971, he began to lose some of his range, however, and he played mostly at first base that season.

He was part of a blockbuster trade in November 1971, going to Cincinnati with Morgan in exchange for Lee May and Tommy Helms. He spent two years as the Reds' starting third baseman, becoming part of the famed Big Red Machine. His home run off Hunter in Game 5 of the '72 World Series was one of only two hits he had in 24 at-bats in the series.

Menke went back to the Astros for one last season in 1974. After batting just .103 in 29 at-bats, he retired. During his 13-year career, he played 841 games at shortstop, 420 at third, 233 at second, 162 at first, three in left field and two in right field.

He managed for a couple of teams in the low minors and won a Midwest League championship with the Burlington Bees in 1977, then later served as a coach for four different major league teams.

Johnny Rawlings

As a hitter, fielder and baserunner, he was a fairly average major league player. But few players of his era had more of a knack for getting under the skin of opposing players than Johnny Rawlings.

Rawlings, who was only five feet, eight inches, and 158 pounds, so irritated Babe Ruth with his bench jockeying in the 1922 World Series that Ruth came looking for him after Game 3, barging into the New York Giants locker room.[14]

Born in Bloomfield, Iowa, in 1892, Rawlings attended high school in Los Angeles before entering pro ball. He played six different positions for six different teams in 12 years although he was primarily a second baseman. He batted .250 for his career with 14 home runs with his highlight coming in 1921 when he helped the Giants to the world title by batting .333 against Ruth and the Yankees in the World Series.

Rawlings began his major league career in 1914 with Cincinnati, but in mid-season he jumped to the Kansas City Packers of the Federal League, a third major league that lasted for only two years. He is believed to be the only native Iowan to play in the league.

After the Federal League folded, he spent 1916 back in the minors with Toledo of the American Association, then started for the Boston Braves for three years, splitting time between second base and shortstop. He spent most of the 1920 season with the Phillies, then was traded to the Giants in the middle of the 1921 season.

He was paired with fellow Iowan Dave Bancroft in a double play combination that helped the Giants win the National League pennant. Rawlings batted .278 that year and reached career highs in runs scored, runs batted in and doubles while leading NL second basemen in putouts, assists and double plays.

He played for two more world championship teams before he was done—the 1922 Giants and the 1925 Pirates—but did not play in the World Series either time. He broke his leg sliding into second base late in the 1925 season and was finished after batting just .232 in 61 games in 1926.

Rawlings played in the minors for several years after that and later managed in the All-American Girls Baseball League for eight years, winning a championship with the Grand Rapids Chicks in 1947.

He died in Inglewood, California, in 1972.

Fred Stanley

Fred Stanley was an unimposing figure on the baseball field. He was only five feet, 10 inches, and 165 pounds and had a peculiar gait that prompted teammates to call him "Chicken."

But Stanley somehow managed to stay around the major leagues for 14 years, playing in 816 games and winning a pair of world championships with the New York Yankees in 1977 and 1978.

Stanley was born in 1947 in the small town of Farnhamville, Iowa, in Calhoun County, southwest of Fort Dodge. He attended high school in southern California and was drafted by Houston in the eighth round in 1966. He later went to the Seattle Pilots in the 1969 expansion draft and ultimately spent time with the Brewers, Indians, Padres, Yankees and A's.

He never became a starter, never had more than 260 at-bats in a season and compiled a career average of only .216, but he remained in the majors for a decade and a half by providing steady defense at shortstop.

He is best remembered for his eight-year run with the Yankees from 1973 to 1980, during which time he played in three World Series. He got into 22 post-season games and started every game at shortstop during the 1976 American League Championship Series, batting .333.

He retired after the 1982 season and began a long career as a coach, instructor, minor-league manager and front office executive with several teams, including the Brewers, Mariners, Astros, A's and Giants. He has spent the past 15 years with San Francisco, serving most recently as a special assistant for player personnel.

Outfielders

Larry Biittner

Although he played in 1,217 games at the major league level, Larry Biittner got very few chances to play regularly for any team. But he proved to be a valuable commodity for well over a decade as a fourth outfielder, backup first baseman and lefthanded pinch hitter.

Biittner grew up in Pocahontas, Iowa, and graduated from Pocahontas Catholic High School in 1964. He initially attended Drake University on a basketball scholarship, but transferred after one year to Buena Vista College, where he was able to play both baseball and basketball. He starred in both sports and was voted to the school's athletic hall of fame just four years after graduating.

He was drafted by the Washington Senators in the 10th round of the 1968 draft and within two years was in the major leagues.

After batting .325 in 102 games with Double-A Pittsfield in 1970 and .356 in 25 games with Triple-A Denver in 1971, Biittner earned a promotion to the big leagues. Except for a return to the minors for part of the 1974 season, he stayed in the majors through 1983.

He played for Washington and Cincinnati and had two stints with the Texas Rangers during 14 years in the majors, but he had his biggest moments with the Chicago Cubs from 1976 through 1980.

His best season by far was 1977 when he played in 138 games, split between first base and left field, and batted .298 while reaching career highs in at-bats (493), home runs (12), runs batted in (62), runs scored (74), hits (147) and doubles (28).

Probably his biggest moment came on opening day of the following season, when he hit a walk-off home run against Jim Bibby to give the Cubs a victory over Pittsburgh. Biittner also etched his name in Cubs lore in 1977 when he was pressed into service as a pitcher and in 1979 when he lost his cap while chasing a ball in right field and then momentarily lost the ball under his cap.[15]

Biittner retired in 1983 with a career average of .273. At the time that he quit, he ranked 12th on baseball's all-time list in pinch-hits.

Cliff Carroll

Baseball was a much different game in the 19th century and there's no better evidence of that than a pair of incidents involving Cliff Carroll, who played 991 games in the outfield for six different National League teams.

Carroll, nicknamed "The Farmer," was born in 1859 in Clay Grove, Iowa, a small community in Lee County that no longer even exists. He grew up in Bloomington, Illinois, and was primarily a catcher and first baseman before joining the Providence Grays of the NL in 1882.

He never became a great hitter—his career average was just .251—but had great speed and developed into one of the best defensive outfielders of his era.

He apparently also had a playful streak. Before a workout in Providence in late June 1883, he supposedly doused a man named James Murphy with a hose. Murphy wasn't amused. He went home and returned with a gun, and as the Grays were walking off the practice field, he opened fire. He missed Carroll but hit shortstop Joe Mulvey in the shoulder.[16]

Carroll played with Providence until the team folded following the

1885 season, then spent two seasons with Washington and played five games with Pittsburgh in 1888. He played most of that season with Buffalo of the International Association, then quit the game, going back to Illinois to farm.

He came back to the National League in 1890 and enjoyed the two best offensive seasons of his career while playing under fellow Iowan Cap Anson. He batted a career-best .285 in 1890 and drove in 80 runs in 1891. He played for St. Louis in 1892 and it was there that he was involved in another of those odd incidents.

Playing left field in a game against Baltimore, Carroll tried to scoop up a ground ball only to have the ball become stuck in the pocket of his uniform. By the time he was able to get it out, the batter raced all the way to third base. Volatile St. Louis owner Chris Von der Ahe was enraged. He fined Carroll $50 and suspended him for the remainder of the season.[17]

Carroll played one last season with the Boston Beaneaters in 1893. He went back to the minors after that, playing in 52 games with the Detroit Creams of the Western League before retiring to the farm again. He died in Oregon in 1923.

Ken Henderson

Ken Henderson was a multi-talented, switch-hitting outfielder who was a victim of unrealistic expectations. From the time he first came up to the San Francisco Giants as a 19-year-old in 1965, he was heralded as a future superstar, the heir to Willie Mays as the team's starting centerfielder.

Henderson never quite achieved that sort of success but he had a solid 16-year career as a major league outfielder. He played in 1,444 games, batting .257 with 122 home runs.

Born in Carroll, Iowa, in 1946, Henderson moved with his family to San Diego as a child. He signed with the Giants in 1964 and within a year found himself in the major leagues. He spent most of the next three years at Triple-A Phoenix, however, before finally landing an everyday job in 1969. In 1970, as the Giants' starting left-fielder, he batted .294 with 17 homers and 20 stolen bases.

Despite brief flashes of brilliance—he was the National League's player of the month in August 1972—he never met expectations and was traded to the Chicago White Sox prior to the 1973 season.

He had probably his best season with Chicago in 1974, playing in every game and batting .292 with career highs of 20 home runs and 95 runs batted in.

He never came close to those offensive numbers again, though, and spent the last five seasons of his career bouncing between five different teams—the Braves, Rangers, Mets, Reds and Cubs. After being released by the Cubs in the middle of the 1980 season, he retired.

Ducky Holmes

A capable hitter and daring baserunner, James William "Ducky" Holmes later embarked on a lengthy career as a minor league manager. But he never found a way to get along with people.

The outspoken Holmes was suspended numerous times in his career, including one especially notorious incident stemming from an anti–Semitic remark in an 1898 game.

His abrasive personality probably had a lot to do with the fact that Holmes, who batted .281 and stole 236 bases in 933 games, played for seven different teams during 10 years in the major leagues.

Born in Des Moines in 1869, the stocky, 5-foot-6 outfielder grabbed everyone's attention by batting .519 in 15 games with St. Joseph's in the Western Association in 1893 and began his big-league career with fellow Iowan Fred Clarke on the Louisville Colonels in 1895. He moved on to the New York Giants in 1897 and the St. Louis Browns and Baltimore Orioles in 1898.

A new rule was instituted in the National League that season against the use of vulgar language on the field and after striking out with the bases loaded one day against his former team, the Giants, Holmes walked back to the bench cursing. When heckled by a fan, he shouted, "Well, I'm glad I'm not working for no Sheeny anymore." It was a reference to the Giants' Jewish owner, Andrew Freedman, who came onto the field and insisted that Holmes be kicked out of the game. When Freedman refused to leave, the game was awarded to the Orioles on a forfeit. The NL board of directors voted to suspend Holmes for the season but he eventually was reinstated after 10 games.[18]

Holmes had perhaps his best season with Baltimore in 1899, batting .320, but he continued to bounce from team to team, playing in the American League for Detroit, Washington and Chicago before being released after the 1905 season.

He had one last blast of controversy in that season, getting suspended for three games after verbally abusing umpire Silk O'Loughlin. That incident is often credited with being the start of the longtime feud between Whiter Sox owner Charles Comiskey and AL president Ban Johnson.[19]

Holmes became the manager of Lincoln in the Western League in 1906 and went on to manage eight different minor league clubs over the next 17 years, including two stints at Lincoln and three with Sioux City in the same league.

He died in Truro, Iowa, just south of Des Moines, in 1932.

Danny Moeller

Danny Moeller is the answer to a dubious trivia question: Who was the first major league player ever to strike out 100 times in a season?

Moeller did it in 1912, fanning an American League-leading 112 times while playing for the Washington Senators. But Moeller also was a highly effective leadoff man and solid defensive outfielder during a seven-year major league career.

Born in DeWitt, Iowa, in 1885, Moeller briefly attended Millikin University before beginning his pro baseball career with the Burlington Flint Hills in the Iowa State League in 1905. He played parts of the 1907 and 1908 seasons with the Pittsburgh Pirates, then spent three years in the Eastern League, splitting time between Jersey City and Rochester. It was there that he earned his nickname, "The Rochester Rambler."

He was signed by the Senators in 1912 and was their starting right-fielder for the next four years, hitting 10 triples in each of those seasons and often ranking among the AL's top base-stealers. In 1913, he stole 62 bases to finish second in the league behind teammate Clyde Milan. On July 19, 1915, against Cleveland, Moeller stole second,

Danny Moeller stole 62 bases for the Washington Senators in 1913 (courtesy *Quad-City Times*).

third and home in the first inning as the Senators set a record with eight stolen bases in the inning.

The switch-hitting Moeller batted only .243 in 704 games in the majors, but he was very selective at the plate and frequently ranked among the league leaders in walks. That also led to him taking numerous called third strikes.

He also had a very strong throwing arm, registering 52 outfield assists in his first two seasons as a regular.

Chronic shoulder problems probably shortened his career. In fact, Moeller dislocated his left shoulder so many times during his first year with the Senators that president William Howard Taft, an avid baseball fan, prevailed upon his personal physician to treat Moeller.[20]

He was traded to Cleveland during the 1916 season and after batting just .067 in 25 games with the Indians, he went back to Iowa and the minor leagues. He played for the Des Moines Boosters in 1917, 1920 and 1921, batting .284 with 28 stolen bases at the age of 37 in his final season.

Billy Sunday

He became one of the most famous men in the world in the early part of the 20th century, an evangelist who enthralled audiences and blazed a path for all those who followed that profession. But before he did all that, Billy Sunday was a ballplayer.

Sunday played eight seasons in the early days of the National League, making up for mediocre batting skills by being the fastest and most dynamic player of his era.

Sunday rose from modest beginnings. He was born in a cabin just south of Ames, Iowa, in 1862. He never knew his father, who left to fight in the Civil War before Billy was born and never returned, dying of pneumonia while in the service. When his mother was unable to care for Billy and three siblings, they were shipped off to live in orphanages in Glenwood and Davenport.

In his teens, Sunday gravitated to baseball and became accomplished enough on the sandlots around the middle part of the state that he caught the eye of Cap Anson when the Chicago White Stockings player-manager was home visiting in Iowa. Anson brought Sunday to Chicago to play for his team.

Sunday had an awful beginning, striking out four times in his first game with the White Stockings (now Cubs) in 1883. He never became a great hitter—his career average in 499 games was .248—but he made up for it by being able to run faster than anyone in baseball. He reportedly was able to circle the bases in 14 seconds.[21]

After being sold to the Pittsburgh Alleghenies (now Pirates), he stole 71 bases in 1888 and then stole 84 in 1890, finishing the season with Philadelphia.

Sunday was offered $5,000 to play for Cincinnati in 1891, but he turned it down to take a clerical job with the Philadelphia YMCA, where he launched his career as a religious leader.

Sunday never forgot his baseball days. He often would come onstage by sliding into an imaginary base. Over the next four decades, he attracted huge crowds wherever he went and reportedly made as much as $200,000 a year at one point.[22]

The Best of the Rest
Pitchers

Stan Bahnsen

As a kid growing up in Council Bluffs, Iowa, he spent hours and hours inflicting damage on a garage door while pitching off a makeshift mound in the family driveway.

It all became worth it years later when Stan Bahnsen forged a successful 16-year career in the major leagues.

Bahnsen, born in 1944, grew up to be an exceptional multi-sport athlete at Council Bluffs' Abraham Lincoln High School. He led the school to the state championship game in basketball in 1963, scoring 18 points in a final loss to Newton, and although Lincoln never could measure up to crosstown rival Thomas Jefferson, Bahnsen showed enough to earn a baseball scholarship to the University of Nebraska.

He pitched just one season for the Cornhuskers but set a school record with three shutouts in 1965, earning third-team All-American honors and impressing the New York Yankees enough that they gave him a $30,000 bonus to sign with them. One of the first things he did with the money was to build his father a new garage, replacing the one he had abused for so many years.[1]

At six feet, two inches, and 185 pounds, he threw hard enough to earn the nickname "Bahnsen Burner" and he rose swiftly through the Yankees' farm system. He fired a no-hitter while pitching for Toledo in 1966 and a seven-inning perfect game for Syracuse in 1967, and by 1968 found himself in the Yankees' starting rotation.

He went 17–12 with a 2.05 earned run average for a Yankees team that was only four games above .500, and he might have won more than that were it not for a commitment to the U.S. Army Reserves that limited him to only pitching on weekends for part of the season. As it was, he was voted the American League Rookie of the Year.

His record fell off to 9–16 in 1969 but Bahnsen put together back-to-back 14-win seasons before being traded to the Chicago White Sox prior to the 1972 season. In his debut season in Chicago, he reached a career high with 21 wins but followed that with a season in which he lost 21 times while claiming 18 victories.

The Sox traded him to Oakland in the middle of the 1975 season and Bahnsen finished out his career with 4½ seasons with the Montreal Expos, then split one final season between the Angels and Phillies.

After being a starter for most of his career, he worked primarily out of the bullpen in his last five seasons, finishing with a record of 146–149 with 20 saves and a 3.60 ERA.

He retired to Florida, where he still lives today.

Mace Brown

Although he allowed one of the most famous home runs in major league history during the 1938 National League pennant race, Mace Brown was one of the top relief pitchers in baseball for nearly a decade.

Brown grew up on a farm near North English, Iowa, and competed in basketball, football and track and field at the high school level. His school did not have a baseball team, but Brown played for a town team during the summer months and showed an exceptional throwing arm in other ways, setting a state record in the javelin throw.[2]

He attended the University of Iowa on a track scholarship but found time to play baseball, too, starting out as a catcher for two years before becoming a pitcher and compiling a 9–1 record as a junior in 1929. He played for a semipro team in Marshall, Min-

Mace Brown led the National League in saves in both 1937 and 1940.

nesota, that summer, though, and was declared ineligible to play his final season at Iowa.³

He signed instead with the St. Louis Cardinals and gradually worked his way up through the minor leagues, winning 19 games with Tulsa in 1934. His contract was purchased by Pittsburgh after that season and he made his major league debut with the Pirates the following spring, on his 26th birthday.

In that era, teams were just beginning to use some pitchers as relief specialists and Brown became one of the pioneers of that role. He started only 55 of the 387 games he pitched over the course of his 10-year career and twice led the National League in saves with 7, in 1937 and 1940.

He had perhaps his best season in 1938 when he led the National League in appearances and won 15 games in relief for Pittsburgh. However, with the Pirates battling Chicago for the pennant in the final week of September, Brown was summoned into a crucial game at Wrigley Field. In the ninth inning, with the score tied and dusk beginning to settle over the stadium, Brown served up a hanging curve ball on an 0–2 count to catcher Gabby Hartnett, who hit the ball into the left-field bleachers. The legendary Homer in the Gloamin' put the Cubs in first place and propelled them to the pennant.

Brown was sold to the Brooklyn Dodgers early in 1941 and traded to the Cubs later that summer, pitching temporarily for the Cubs' minor league team in Los Angeles before being returned to Pittsburgh.

In December, he was sold to the Boston Red Sox. He led the American League in games pitched in 1943 and registered a career-high nine saves with a 2.12 earned run average.

The following year Brown was commissioned as a lieutenant in the Navy and served two years. He came back to Boston for one last season in 1946 and registered a career-best 2.05 ERA in an injury-plagued season to help the Red Sox win the pennant. He appeared in just one game against the Cardinals in the World Series, allowing three runs on four hits in the eighth inning of Game 4.

Brown retired following the season but remained with the Red Sox for more than 40 years as a coach, scout and consultant before retiring in 1989.

King Cole

He became a part of one of the most storied pitching rotations in baseball at the age of 24. But by the age of 30, Leonard Leslie Cole was dead.

Cole was born in Toledo, Iowa, in 1886 and spent time living both in Iowa and in the area around Bay City, Michigan. He starred are Leander Clark College in Toledo, a school that merged with Coe College in 1919, and got his start as a professional with Bay City in the Southern Michigan League in 1909.

Displaying a sizzling fastball and an above-average curve, he went 21–17 that season and by the end of the summer found himself with the Chicago Cubs. He made his major league debut in the first game of a doubleheader on the last day of the season and hurled a six-hit shutout against St. Louis.

The following season he became part of a rotation that included future Hall of Famer Mordecai "Three-Finger" Brown, Ed Reulbach and Orval Overall. Cole went 20–4 with a league-leading 1.80 earned run average to help the Cubs win their fourth pennant in five years. He started Game 4 of the World Series against the Philadelphia Athletics and engaged in a pitcher's duel with Chief Bender, being replaced by Brown after eight innings. The Cubs won in the 10th inning, but it turned out to be their only victory of the series.

Cole went 18–7 in 1911 but in 1912 he was suddenly thoroughly ineffective. His ERA was 10.89 when the Cubs traded him to Pittsburgh at the end of May and he won just three games all season. He went back to the minors, rediscovered his touch and went 23–11 with Columbus, throwing a no-hitter and leading the American Association with 341 innings pitched.

That got him back to the major leagues, with the New York Highlanders of the American League. He went 10–9 in 1914 but underwent surgery in April 1915 for the removal of a tumor from his groin and was told by doctors that his career probably was over.[4] Disdaining their orders to rest, Cole returned to the field in May but suffered dizzy spells on the field and was sent home to Bay City to rest.

He eventually pitched in 10 games for the Highlanders that season and showed occasional flashes of the old brilliance. In the final weeks of the season, he outdueled the White Sox' Eddie Cicotte in a head-to-head battle but after the season he was diagnosed with tuberculosis. He died just a few months later, on January 6, 1916, at the age of 29.[5]

Jesse Duryea

Seldom has any pitcher gotten off to a more auspicious start in the major leagues than Jesse Duryea. And were it not for an eye injury suffered in only his second season, the pitcher known as "Cyclone Jim" might have become one of the outstanding hurlers of the last decade of the 19th century.

Duryea was born in Osage, Iowa, in 1859 and lived in Goodell, Iowa, before being discovered by Ted Sullivan, owner of the St. Paul team of the Northwestern League, in 1886. After watching the five-foot, ten-inch, 175-pound Iowan fire a fastball through a six-foot plank of wood, Sullivan gave him his memorable nickname.[6] Duryea compiled a 14–11 record in 1887 and went 23–11 in 1888, prompting the Cincinnati Red Stockings of the American Association (then considered a major league) to pay the then-extravagant sum of $2,500 to procure his services.

Duryea appeared to be worth every penny as he went 32–19 with a 2.56 earned run average in 1889. His 401 innings pitched are the most ever recorded in one season by a native Iowan. He was the subject of a prolonged bidding war between Cincinnati and the Brooklyn Gladiators of the Players League prior to the following season. It was reported at one point that he would sign with Brooklyn,[7] but he ultimately re-signed with the Red Stockings for $4,000.

He went 16–12 in 1890 before being struck in the left eye by a pitch. His vision in the eye was permanently impaired and Duryea never was the same after that. He went 2–10 while splitting the 1891 season between Cincinnati and St. Louis and had similarly sub-par results while pitching for Cincinnati and Washington in the National League in the next two seasons.

He returned to the minor leagues with Binghamton, Allentown, Minneapolis and Rochester, but after going 7–18 in 1895, he called it quits. His final major league record was 59–66.

Duryea operated hotels in Britt and Algona for many years and also worked at Barry's Recreation Hall in Algona before dying in 1942.

Cal Eldred

We can only imagine how glorious a career Cal Eldred might have had were it not for a nightmarish string of injuries to his right elbow. At the outset of his major league career, he gave every indication of becoming one of the game's brightest stars.

As it is, he went 86–74 over the course of 14 years in the major leagues.

Born in Cedar Rapids in 1967, Eldred grew up in the small town of

18. The Best of the Rest: Pitchers

Urbana but still attracted enough attention from major league scouts to be selected by the New York Mets in the 26th round of the 1986 draft.

He opted instead to attend the University of Iowa and after three years of pitching for the Hawkeyes, he was taken in the first round by Milwaukee in 1989. This time he signed and moved up quickly through the minor leagues, being called up to Milwaukee after going 13–9 at Triple-A Denver in 1991. He won two games in the final weeks of that season and after going 10–6 at Denver in the first half of 1992, the Brewers brought him up again.

The six-foot, four-inch, 215-pound Eldred, skillfully mixing three pitches, was one of the best pitchers in baseball over the second half of the season, winning 10 straight games in one stretch and going 11–2 with a 1.79 earned run average. He was the American League's pitcher of the month for September and was fourth in the Rookie of the Year voting despite only spending half the season in the majors.

Cal Eldred had a 10-game winning streak in the second half of the 1992 season (courtesy *Quad-City Times*).

He went 16–16 in 1993, leading the AL in games started and innings pitched, and he again led the league in starts while going 11–11 in the strike-shortened 1994 season.

Then the injuries began piling up. Elbow problems early in 1995 led to Tommy John surgery and Eldred didn't pitch again until the middle of the 1996 season. When he did return, he wasn't the same. He was 13–15 with a 4.99 ERA in 1997, then endured more elbow injuries the next two years.

After being traded to the White Sox prior to the 2000 season, he got off to a 10–2 start but the elbow problems returned. Eldred had a screw surgically inserted into the joint late in the season. He pitched in just two games in 2001, none in 2002.

He revived his career again as a relief pitcher with St. Louis. He started just once in his last three years but pitched in 145 games and was a highly effective reliever in helping the Cardinals to the World Series in 2004 and a playoff berth in 2005.

He retired after that season and worked for awhile in the Cardinals' front office.

Joel Hanrahan

His nickname is "The Hammer" and it fits. Joel Hanrahan throws a fastball that has been clocked in the neighborhood of 100 mph and he doesn't throw much else, mixing in only an occasional slider that moves as rapidly as some pitchers' fastballs. He employed a change-up early in his professional career, but abandoned it when he began being used exclusively as a relief pitcher.

Despite his limited repertoire and the fact that he had worked only a little more than 400 innings going into the 2015 season, the six-foot, five-inch, 255-pound Hanrahan had recorded 100 saves in the majors, more than any other pitcher from the state of Iowa.

Born in Des Moines, Hanrahan spent part of his childhood in Florida but attended high school in Norwalk, Iowa. He chose to turn pro after being selected by the Los Angeles Dodgers in the second round of the 2000 major league draft.

It would be seven years before he made it to the major leagues. Hanrahan was used almost strictly as a starting pitcher for most of that time and showed occasional flashes of brilliance. In 2003, he went 10–4 and had a 2.43 earned run average with the Jacksonville Suns and was named the pitcher of the year in the Double-A Southern League.

He became a free agent in 2006 and signed with the Washington Nationals, finally getting to the majors in the middle of the following season. He made 11 starts for Washington in 2007 and went 5–3 but had a 6.00 ERA.

The Nationals moved him to the bullpen in 2008 and Hanrahan began to prosper in the new role, pitching in 69 games and registering nine saves after becoming the team's closer in the second half of the season. He pitched in 67 games in 2009, getting traded to the Pittsburgh Pirates in mid-season, and appeared in 72 games in 2010.

In 2011, he got his chance to be the Pirates' full-time closer and responded with 40 saves, then added 36 more in 2012. He made the National League All-Star team both years and in each case pitched a third of an inning and recorded a strikeout in the ninth inning.

Hanrahan was traded to the Boston Red Sox prior to the 2013 season and his career began to unravel. He recorded saves in three of his first four games, then had two bad outings and was placed on the disabled list with a hamstring injury. After coming back, he hurt his arm and underwent surgery on both the flexor tendon and the elbow in his throwing arm.

He was released after the season and after going through spring training in 2014 without a contract, he signed with the Detroit Tigers in early May. He never pitched for Detroit and was not offered a contract extension after the season.

Joe Hatten

He wasn't a big man and he never had overpowering stuff, but Joe Hatten epitomized the term "crafty lefthander" during four years as a member of the Brooklyn Dodgers starting rotation in the late 1940s.

In fact, Hatten had the rare distinction of issuing more walks than he had strikeouts in each of his seven seasons in the major leagues. But he managed to go 65–49 and win another 123 games in the minor leagues, most of those after his major league career was over.

Born in Bancroft, Iowa, Hatten played at St. John's High School, played American Legion ball and pitched for a few semi-pro teams in the northern part of the state before beginning his minor league career with Crookston in the Northern League in 1939.

He went 14–14 that season and worked his way up to pitching for the Dodgers' Montreal farm team in 1942. World War II intervened, however, and Hatten enlisted in the Navy early that season. He served for 41 months and spent more than 10 of those months overseas.

He was 29 by the time he finally got to the big leagues in 1946, but he made an immediate impression on Brooklyn manager Leo Durocher, who said, "All you have to do is look at him and you know that if he can control it, he can be the best southpaw the Dodgers have ever had."[8]

Hatten went 14–11 as a rookie, helping the Dodgers tie for the National League pennant with St. Louis. The Cardinals won a three-game playoff with Hatten taking the loss in Game 2 of the series.

The following season, Hatten was the opening-day starter in the game in which Jackie Robinson made his historic major league debut and he went on to have his best season. He went 17–8 and late in the season showed his durability in a double-header against Cincinnati. He hurled a complete-game victory in the first game for his 15th win, then came on in relief to work another 5⅔ innings in the nightcap to collect win No. 16.

This time Brooklyn won the pennant and Hatten was called upon to start Game 3 of the World Series against the Yankees. The Dodgers staked him to a 6–0 lead, but Hatten struggled and was replaced with one out in the fifth inning of a 9–8 victory. He also pitched in relief in Games 5, 6 and 7, but the Yankees finally prevailed.

Hatten compiled a 13–10 record as the Dodgers finished third in 1948, then went 12–8 in 1949 to help edge the Cardinals by one game in another down-to-the-wire pennant race. He pitched twice in relief in the World Series as the Dodgers again lost out to the Yankees, in five games.

In 1950, he lost his spot in the starting rotation and on June 15, 1951, he was traded to the Cubs as part of a massive eight-player deal. The two teams happened to be playing one another at the time so all eight players simply crossed over to the opposing locker room prior to the game.

Hatten pitched for the Cubs until the middle of the 1952 season, when he we was sent to the team's Los Angeles farm team. In August of 1953, he helped touch off one of the most infamous on-field battles in baseball history. One of Hatten's pitches hit Hollywood's Frank Kelleher in the sixth inning of the first game of a double-header, beginning a series of scuffles between the two teams, the last of which was a 30-minute brawl that required the intervention of 50 police officers.[9]

Hatten won 49 games in 3½ seasons with the Angels and continued to pitch in the minors for teams operated by the Reds, Orioles and Phillies before finally retiring in 1960. He never got back to the major leagues.

Hatten lived the rest of his life in Shasta County, California, although he returned to Bancroft every year for an old-timers game. The street in front of the field there was renamed Joe Hatten Drive.

Joe Hoerner

He once placed a live lizard in the soup of one of his best friends. He also was fond of putting dead snakes in the shoes of teammates, tried (successfully) to hit the roof of the Houston Astrodome with a fungo and once commandeered the team bus following a game.[10]

But in addition to being one of baseball's most notorious pranksters, Joe Hoerner also was a highly effective relief pitcher and an inspirational success story.

Hoerner overcame a heart condition that forced him to alter his delivery and went on to record a 2.99 earned run average and 99 saves in a major league career that spanned 14 seasons. He helped the St. Louis Cardinals reach the World Series in 1967 and '68, was named to the National

18. The Best of the Rest: Pitchers

League All-Star team in 1970 and tied a major league record in 1968 by striking out six consecutive batters.

Hoerner grew up on a farm near Key West, Iowa, not far from Dubuque, and he wasn't necessarily the best pitcher on the Dubuque Senior team that won the 1954 summer state championship. Jack Nora, son of head coach Jim Nora, hurled a one-hit shutout in the championship game although Hoerner, who also played center field, threw a one-hitter in the semifinals and was the winning pitcher in relief in the quarterfinals.

Before that season, Hoerner was out on a date with his future wife, Darlene Naumann, and as he was driving home, he apparently fell asleep and crashed his car. He suffered a separated shoulder and broken ribs, and perhaps other damage that didn't manifest itself for a few years.[11]

After high school, he spent two years pitching for semipro teams and working for the Sears Roebuck store in Dubuque before his talents came to the attention of the Chicago White Sox, who signed him in 1957.

Hoerner went 16–5 for the Sox' farm team at Duluth-Superior in the Northern League that year but clues that his accident may have done some hidden damage began to show up. While pitching for Davenport in the Three-I League in 1958, he collapsed on the mound during a game and remained unconscious for several hours. A priest was summoned to give the late rites, but Hoerner recovered quickly and was back pitching within a week.[12]

The blackouts continued, however, always while he was pitching, and doctors finally deduced they were being caused by a weakness in the muscles around Hoerner's heart. They advised him to quit baseball, but he found another solution. He simply altered his delivery, throwing sidearm to lessen the pressure on his heart when he released the ball.

He spent nine years in the minor leagues, defying doubters but making only brief appearances in the majors in 1963 and '64 with the expansion Houston Colt 45s, who had obtained his rights. He finally was acquired by the Cardinals during the winter before the 1966 season and landed in the majors to stay.

He registered a 1.54 ERA with 13 saves in 1966, helped the Cardinals win a world championship while collecting 14 saves in 1967 and had his best year in 1968, going 8–2 with 17 saves and a 1.48 ERA.

Although he threw left-handed, Hoerner's sidearm sinkers also baffled right-handed hitters. Hall of Famer Hank Aaron failed to get a hit off him in 22 at-bats.

The Cardinals traded him to Philadelphia in 1970 in a deal that altered the course of major league history. Hoerner accepted the trade but centerfielder Curt Flood, who was traded with him, filed suit to fight baseball's long-standing reserve clause. The ensuing court battle led to the advent of free agency.

Hoerner was traded to Atlanta in the middle of the 1972 season, beginning a five-year trek in which he pitched for Kansas City, the Phillies again, then Texas and finally Cincinnati.

When he was released after the 1977 season, he went back to St. Louis and started a travel agency with former teammate Dal Maxvill, the victim of his lizard-in-the-soup ploy many years earlier.

Hoerner died in a farming accident outside St. Louis in 1996, about a month before his 60th birthday.

Bill Hoffer

Bill Hoffer—also known as "Chick" and "Wizard"—was among the premier pitchers in the National League in the mid 1890s, but he made history in the final season of his career in a different league. Hoffer was the starting pitcher for the Cleveland Blues in the very first American League game ever played on April 24, 1901. He recorded the first walk and first strikeout in the history of the league, and also was the first losing pitcher.

Hoffer was born in Cedar Rapids, Iowa, in 1870 and lived his entire life in that city. He got his professional start pitching for the hometown Cedar Rapids Canaries of the Illinois-Iowa League in 1891, going 16–12 with a team that included future New York Giants manager John McGraw. Records from that season indicate that Hoffer allowed 164 runs during the season but only 25 of them were earned, giving him an extraordinary earned run average of 0.91.

He spent the next three years pitching for minor league teams in Joliet, Aurora, Toledo, Nashville and Buffalo before landing with the Baltimore Orioles of the National League. Almost immediately the 155-pound right-hander became the ace of a team loaded with future Hall of Famers. The Orioles, who virtually reinvented the game with such innovations as the hit-and-run and the squeeze bunt, featured McGraw at third base, Hughie Jennings at shortstop, Wilbert Robinson behind the plate and Joe Kelley and Wee Willie Keeler in the outfield.

Hoffer went 31–7 for the Orioles in 1895, 25–7 in 1896 and 22–11 in 1897, helping the Orioles to two championships and working more than 300 innings in each of those seasons.

But after inexplicably getting off to an 0–4 start in 1898, Hoffer was released and picked up by Pittsburgh. He went 8–10 with the Pirates in 1899 before also being released by them.

He caught on with Cleveland of the AL, which was a minor league in 1900 but earned major league status the following year. Despite making history by pitching that first game in 1901, Hoffer didn't last the full season with the Blues. He made his final appearance on the Fourth of July.

Hoffer finished the season with Sacramento of the California League, then spent a few years with Des Moines in the Western League, serving as the team's manager in 1904.

He ended up right back where he started with Cedar Rapids, going 3–6 in 1909. He lived out his life in the city, working for the U.S. Postal Service and as a conductor on the Cedar Rapids and Iowa City Railway.[13] He died in 1959 at the age of 88.

Bob Lee

It took him eight years to reach the major leagues and once he got there, he didn't stay long. But for three years in the 1960s, Bob Lee ranked among the premier relief pitchers in all of baseball.

His career earned run average of 2.71 is among the best ever by a pitcher from Iowa and his 63 career saves are the fifth best mark by anyone from the state. The six-foot, three-inch, 225-pound Lee, known to most teammates as either Moose or Horse, threw very hard but struggled with weight problems throughout his career.[14]

Born in Ottumwa, Lee moved to California with his family and played high school ball in Bellflower.

He signed with Pittsburgh out of high school and began a long trek through the minor leagues. In his eighth year, he found himself back in Class A ball with his 11th different minor league team, but he went 20–2 with Batavia of the New York-Pennsylvania League to finally earn his big chance. Late that season, the Pirates traded his rights to the Los Angeles Angels, who brought Lee to the major leagues in 1964.

Lee worked in 234 games over the next three years and finished among the top six in the American League in saves every year. He had 19 saves and a 1.51 earned run average in 1964, 23 saves with 1.92 ERA in '65 and 16 saves with a 2.74 ERA in '67.

He strung together 21 consecutive scoreless innings spanning his first two seasons—a team record that stood until it was broken by Jered Weaver in 2013—and made the AL All-Star team in 1965.

Lee's velocity began to disappear in that last season, though. After averaging about seven strikeouts per nine innings in those first two seasons, the number dropped to only 4.1 in 1966. He was traded to the Dodgers in the off-season and after pitching in only four games, he was sold to Cincinnati. His ERA ballooned to 4.55 in 1967 and 5.15 in 1968 and at the age of 30, he was given his outright release.

In retirement, he opened a barber shop in Anaheim not far from the Angels' ballpark.

Jon Lieber

In 14 years pitching for four different teams in the major leagues, Jon Lieber never had an earned run average under 3.70. He didn't throw with the extreme velocity of some of his peers. What he did have was superb control, one of the best sliders in baseball, an even-tempered approach and a knack for pitching to contact.

All of that helped him compile a 131–124 record while working 2,198 innings at the big-league level.

Lieber was born in Council Bluffs, Iowa, and raised on a wooded four-acre plot just outside town. He was not viewed as a top prospect coming out of Lincoln High School and while pitching for Iowa Western Community College, he began writing letters to major college programs. He finally got a break when a part-time major league scout tipped off the coaching staff at South Alabama about him. South Alabama pitching coach Ronnie Powell came up to watch him pitch in a summer league game in Elk Horn, Iowa, and liked what he saw.[15]

At South Alabama, Lieber put together back-to-back 12–5 seasons and as a senior was named the Sun Belt Conference player of the year and a third-team All-American.

The Chicago Cubs had drafted him in the ninth round following his junior year in 1991, but he chose to stay in Mobile for one more season and was selected in the second round by the Kansas City Royals in 1992.

About a year after signing his first pro contract, he was traded to the Pittsburgh Pirates and after compiling a 15–6 record at three different minor league stops in 1993, Lieber was brought up to the Pirates early in the 1994 season.

He was a part-time starter in his first three years before becoming part of the Pirates' regular rotation in 1997 and 1998. He was only 38–47 for his career when he was traded to the Cubs following the 1998 season.

He went 10–11 and 12–11 in his first two years in Chicago, leading the National League in innings pitched in 2000, then really found himself in 2001, going 20–6, making the NL All-Star team and finishing fourth in the league's Cy Young Award voting.

That level of prosperity didn't last long. Lieber dropped off to 6–8 in 2002, injured his elbow, underwent Tommy John surgery and missed the entire 2003 season.

He signed as a free agent with the Yankees prior to that season and became an important part of the New York rotation in 2004. He went 14–8, walked only 18 men in 176⅔ innings, and got his only chance to pitch in the post-season, throwing seven shutout innings against Boston to win Game 2 of the American League Championship Series.

That was enough to earn him a 3-year, $21 million free agent contract with Philadelphia. Lieber was 17–11 with the Phillies in 2005, but he struggled through two injury-filled seasons after that and was left off the Phillies' postseason roster in 2007.

He played just one more season, going 2–3 while pitching mostly in relief for the Cubs in 2008.

Bob Locker

Bob Locker often told reporters that he derived his strength from "honey—nature's essence."[16] In truth, it was an uncanny sinkerball that helped make him one of the American League's elite relief pitchers of the 1960s and early '70s.

During 10 years in the major leagues, Locker appeared in 576 games, all in relief, and recorded 95 saves with an earned run average of 2.75.

Born in George, Iowa, in the extreme northwest corner of the state, Locker became a pitching star at Iowa State University, where he earned a degree in geology in 1960.

He signed as a free agent with the Chicago White Sox and quickly emerged as a hot prospect as a starting pitcher. With Lincoln in the Three-I League in 1961, he went 15–12 with a 2.57 ERA and led the league with 215 strikeouts.

He was drafted into the army after that, however, and missed two seasons, returning to go 16–9 with a 2.59 ERA at Indianapolis in the Pacific Coast League in 1964.

The White Sox were well-stocked with starting pitchers but Locker became a key reliever for Chicago, appearing in 51 games in 1965 and 56 in 1966.

The six-foot, three-inch, 200-pound right-hander followed that with his best season. Teaming with veteran Don McMahon and knuckleball artists Hoyt Wilhelm and Wilbur Wood, he gave the White Sox a devastating bullpen in 1967. Locker led the American League with 77 appearances and reached career bests with 20 saves and a 2.09 ERA.

He was one of four Iowans on the White Sox roster that season, joining catchers Duane Josephson and Jerry McNertney (a former Iowa State teammate) and backup third baseman Dick Kenworthy.

Locker was traded to the expansion Seattle Pilots in June of 1969 and was sold a year later to Oakland, where he helped the A's to back-to-back post-season appearances, going 13–3 with 16 saves during the 1971 and '72 seasons. He was the losing pitcher in Game 4 of the 1972 ALCS although the A's went on to win the world title anyway.

Locker was traded to the Cubs and had one more solid season, registering 10 wins and 18 saves in 1973. He was traded back to Oakland, missed the entire 1974 season, then was traded back to the Cubs as part of a deal for Hall of Fame outfielder Billy Williams. After getting off to a rough start in 1975, the Cubs released him in late June.

George Pipgras

George Pipgras never spent a full season in the major leagues until he was 28 years old and he won just 102 games in an 11-year career. But the hard-throwing right-hander was an integral part of the pitching staff for one of the great teams in baseball history and he never was beaten in World Series play.

Pipgras was born in Ida Grove, Iowa, in 1899 and lived on a 160-acre farm about five miles outside town. His family later moved and he played baseball at Schleswig-Holstein High School before joining the army at the age of 17 in the early days of World War I.

After leaving the service, Pipgras was playing semi-pro ball in Minnesota, when he was discovered and signed by the Yankees, and sent to the minor leagues.

He pitched a handful of games for the Yankees in 1923 and '24, but struggled to get his blazing fastball under control. He finally got an extended shot during the 1927 season and went 10–3, then won a complete-game victory over the Pirates in Game 2 of the World Series.

The following season, the six-foot, two-inch, 200-pound Pipgras became one of the aces of the Yankees staff. He went 24–13 while leading the American League in games started (38) and innings pitched (300.2). He again pitched Game 2 of the World Series against the Cardinals and this time got off to a rough start. He allowed three runs in the second inning but the Yankees, one of the great offensive juggernauts of all time, scored eight runs in support of him in the first three innings. Pipgras settled down to win, 9–3.

He continued to be part of the Yankees' rotation for most of the next five years although he never again enjoyed the sort of success he had in 1928.

He got one more chance to pitch in the World Series in 1932, working the first eight innings of Game 3 and again coming away as the winning pitcher. Pipgras struck out five times as a hitter in that game, but the contest is best remembered for other reasons. In the fifth inning, with the score tied 4–4, Babe Ruth strode to the plate, pointed at the center-field bleachers and promptly swatted a pitch there. For the last 54 years of his life, Pipgras staunchly insisted that Ruth really did call his shot.[17]

Pipgras got off to a slow start the next season and was traded to the Red Sox in May. He went 9–8 in 22 games with Boston, but in an August 14 contest against Detroit he broke his arm while throwing a pitch. In fact, when doctors performed surgery, they found seven bone fragments.[18]

It was the end of his career. Pipgras pitched in just seven games over the next two seasons, allowing 11 earned runs in 8⅓ innings, and was released in early June 1935. After unsuccessfully trying to revive his career with Nashville, in the Southern Association, he retired.

Pipgras found another way to stay involved with the game, however. He became an umpire in the minor leagues and moved up to the American League in 1938. He did that through 1946 and during one memorable game between the White Sox and Browns in his first season, he ejected 17 players. Pipgras later spent two years as a scout for the Red Sox and worked as an umpire instructor, before retiring to Florida, where he lived until he passed away in 1986.

Pat Ragan

He finished his major league career with a nondescript won-loss record of 77–104, but Don Carlos Patrick Ragan had a stellar earned run average of 2.99 in 11 seasons and in 1914 accomplished something only a few dozen other pitchers ever have achieved when he struck out three men on nine straight pitches.

Ragan was born in 1885 in Blanchard, Iowa, in the southwest part of the state and attended both Simpson and Cornell Colleges before getting his professional start in 1905.

The five-foot, ten-inch, 185-pound right-hander had a breakout season with Omaha in the Western League in 1908, going 29–7, but he pitched in just four games in the big leagues with the Cubs and Reds the following season before going back to the minor leagues. After going 16–11 with Rochester in the Eastern League in 1910, he got another shot with the Brooklyn Robins in 1911.

Ragan gradually worked his way into a major role in Brooklyn, going 7–18 in 1912, 15–18 in 1913 and 10–15 in 1914. It was in the final game of that season, on October 5 against the Boston Braves, that Ragan had his most famous and infamous moment.

With Brooklyn clinging to a 4–1 lead, Ragan blazed three strikes past both Possum Whitted and Butch Schmidt without either of them taking a swing. Ragan, who was a bit of a showboat, began celebrating and bowing to the home crowd after each pitch. When the Braves' Red Smith swung and missed at three straight pitches to end the inning, Ragan again reacted theatrically.[19] He was only the third pitcher ever to accomplish the feat, which has now been done 72 times.

His antics came back to haunt him in the ninth inning. The Braves scored three runs to tie the game, loaded the bases and Whitted slugged a grand slam to give Boston a 9–5 win.

Early in 1915, the Robins put Ragan on waivers and amazingly, it was the Braves who picked him up. He ended up having his best season, compiling a 17–12 record.

However, he went just 23–35 over the next three seasons and in late May of 1919 Boston sent him to the New York Giants as the player to be named later in a trade for native American legend Jim Thorpe. He finished the season pitching one inning in one game with the Chicago White Sox, who became known as the Black Sox when they then threw the World Series.

Ragan pitched in the minor leagues in 1920, went back to Iowa to manage the Waterloo Hawks of the Mississippi Valley League in 1922, pitched one last major league game with the Phillies in 1923 and served as that team's pitching coach in 1924. He spent two more years as a manager in the Blue Ridge League and Middle Atlantic League before retiring from baseball for good in 1927.

Kevin Tapani

Kevin Tapani's father was a professional in a different sport and baseball wasn't necessarily Tapani's best sport in high school. He attended Central Michigan University without a scholarship.

But that didn't keep him from spending 13 years in the major leagues as a solid, steady starting pitcher for five different teams.

Tapani didn't spend much of his childhood in Iowa, but was born in the state while his father, Ray, was a goaltender for the Des Moines Oak Leafs of the International Hockey League.

The Tapani family moved to Milwaukee when Kevin was only a year old and they eventually settled in Escanaba, Michigan, where he quarterbacked his high school football team to a state title in 1981.

Tapani chose to walk on with the baseball team at Central Michigan and developed as a pitcher, helping the Chippewas to three consecutive Mid-American Conference titles.

He was selected by the Chicago Cubs in the ninth round in of the 1985 draft, but chose not to sign. A year later the Oakland A's made him their second-round pick.

He eventually was traded to the New York Mets, who then sent him to the Minnesota Twins in 1989 as part of a multi-player package to obtain Frank Viola.

Tapani blossomed in Minnesota, going 12–8 in his first full season there in 1990 and going 16–9 in 1991. He was named the American League's pitcher of the month for August and carried that success into the postseason, out-dueling Atlanta's Tom Glavine in Game 2 of the World Series to help the Twins become world champions.

Tapani was never an overpowering pitching but he had good control and pitched to contact. He mixed four different pitches for much of his career—a fastball, slider, split-fingered fastball and change-up—but he was unable to throw the splitter after rupturing a ligament in his pitching hand in 1996.[20]

He won 16 games again in 1992 but his career declined after that. He was a sub-.500 pitcher over the next few years and was traded to the Los Angeles Dodgers in the middle of the 1995 season. He signed with the Chicago White Sox for one season, then signed with the Cubs in 1996. He was able to put together one more strong season in 1998, going 19–9 to help the Cubs secure a playoff berth.

He became a free agent again after the 2001 season but at age 37, he didn't feel he had much left. He retired with a career mark of 143–125 and settled in the Twin-Cities.

Eddie Watt

In an era before relief pitchers played heroic roles, Eddie Watt was an integral part of Baltimore Orioles teams that won American League pennants in four of his first six years in the major leagues.

Although small in stature at five feet, ten inches, and 183 pounds, Watt had a 2.91 earned run average and recorded 80 saves while pitching 411 games at the major league level. Watt was a good all-around athlete who excelled in all phases of the game. He batted .304 as a rookie in the major leagues and had a six-year stretch (1967–72) in which he committed only one error.

Born in Lamoni, Iowa, in 1941, Watt moved with his family to West Branch when he was in elementary school and then to Iowa City, where he was a multi-sport athlete at City High.

He attended Iowa State Teachers College (now the University of Northern Iowa) on a basketball scholarship and attracted the attention of pro baseball scouts while pitching in a South Dakota summer league after his sophomore year. He rejected offers from the White Sox and Cardinals and signed with the Orioles, foregoing his last two years of college eligibility.

Watt reached double figures in victories in each of the next four years as a starting pitcher in the minor leagues, going 17–2 while splitting the 1964 season between Aberdeen in the Northern League and Elmira in the Eastern League. He pitched a no-hitter for Elmira on opening day in 1965, then threw another one in his third start of the season. He finished that season with Rochester in Triple-A ball and clearly was headed for the major leagues in 1966.

He got the save in a 13-inning victory over Boston on opening day that year and was on his way. He was pressed into service as a starter 13 times later in the season because of injuries to other pitchers, but for the remainder of his career Watt would be a reliever.

He had 10 or more saves in four straight seasons from 1968 to 1971. In the Orioles' pennant-winning season of 1969, he had 16 saves with a 1.65 ERA.

He pitched in eight post-season games during his career and although he was the losing pitcher in three of those games, his ERA was a solid 2.53.

Watt was plagued by injuries in the later stages of his eight years in Baltimore. He broke his hand in 1971 and missed about a month in the middle of the season although he still had 11 saves and a 1.82 ERA. He underwent knee surgery following the 1973 season and in December the Orioles sold him to Philadelphia.

He spent just one season with the Phillies, who released him at the end of spring training in 1975. Watt signed a minor league contract with the Cubs and after pitching for their Wichita farm team for a few months, he briefly came up to the majors, but was released late in the season.

After pitching in the minors for two years, Watt served as the manager of San Diego's Class A affiliate at Reno in 1978 and '79, and the Padres' Double-A team at Amarillo in 1980 and '81. He won a pennant in each place.

He spent the next couple of decades as a major league pitching coach for the Phillies, Astros and Braves.

Jake Weimer

He spent eight years laboring in the minor leagues before getting his chance in the majors. But once he got there, Jake Weimer proved to be one of the best left-handers in the National League.

Weimer went 97–69 in a brief seven-year career and his earned run average of 2.23 is the best mark of any pitcher from Iowa who spent more than a season or two in the big time.

Weimer, known to most as Tornado Jake, was born in Ottumwa, Iowa, in 1873 and began pitching in the minor leagues in 1895. He spent most of the next six years toiling for teams within the boundaries of his home state, enjoying 20-win seasons with the Burlington Colts in 1895 and the Des Moines Hawkeyes in 1900. He spent 1901 and 1902 with Kansas City in the Western League and finally got his shot at the major leagues at the age of 29.

He went 20–8 as a rookie in with the Chicago Cubs 1903 and followed that with records of 20–14 and 18–12 in the next two years. In 1904, he had a career-best ERA of 1.91 with a career-high 177 strikeouts.

Jake Weimer won 20 games in three of his first four major league seasons.

The Cubs then used him as a bargaining chip to complete one of the game's legendary infields, trading him to Cincinnati for third baseman Harry Steinfeldt, who joined the double-play trio to Joe Tinker, Johnny Evers and Frank Chance.

Weimer went 20–14 with the Reds in 1906 but his career began to decline slightly after that as he went 11–14 in 1907 and 8–7 in the first half of 1908. In July, the Reds traded him to the New York Giants with Dave Brain in exchange for Bob Spade and $5,000.

Weimer demanded that he be given half of the $5,000 in order to report to the Giants or he would go back to Chicago and go into business with father-in-law.[21] He held firm on his demands and spent the rest of the summer playing for semipro teams in Chicago.

He was reinstated early in 1909 after paying a $150 fine[22] and finally pitched in a game for the Giants on May 28. He was shelled in three innings of relief against the Phillies and was done as a major league player. He played the outfield with the minor league New Orleans Pelicans in 1909 and 1910, playing alongside Shoeless Joe Jackson, then went back to Chicago.

He served as the baseball coach at Chicago's Loyola Academy and was instrumental in getting the Giants to sign one of his protégés, Freddie Lindstrom.

Appendix: Iowa Records (Prior to 2015)

Games Played
Season: Bobby Knoop (1964) and Ken Henderson (1974), 162
Career: Cap Anson 2,524

At-Bats
Season: Dave Bancroft (1922), 651
Career: Cap Anson 11,331

Batting Average
Season (minimum 400 ABs): Fred Clarke (1897), .390
Career: Cap Anson .334

Slugging Percentage
Season (minimum 400 ABs): Hal Trosky (1936), .644
Career: Hal Trosky .522

On-Base Percentage
Season (minimum 400 ABs): Fred Clarke (1897), .461
Career: Cap Anson .394

Hits
Season: Hal Trosky (1936), 216
Career: Cap Anson 3,425

Doubles
Season: Hal Trosky (1934 and 1936), 45
Career: Cap Anson 582

Triples
Season: George Stone (1906), 20
Career: Fred Clarke 220

Home Runs
Season: Hal Trosky (1936), 42
Career: Hal Trosky 228

Runs Scored
Season: Hal Trosky (1936), 124
Career: Cap Anson 1,999

Runs Batted In
Season: Hal Trosky (1936), 162
Career: Cap Anson 2,075

Stolen Bases
Season: Billy Sunday (1890), 84
Career: Fred Clarke 509

Bases on Balls
Season: Cap Anson (1890), 113
Career: Cap Anson 984

Games Pitched
Season: Tony Watson (2014), 78
Career: Red Faber 669

Innings Pitched
Season: Jesse Duryea (1889), 401
Career: Red Faber 4,086.2

Wins
Season: Jesse Duryea (1889), 32
Career: Bob Feller 266

Saves
Season: Joel Hanrahan (2011), 40
Career: Joel Hanrahan 100

Shutouts
Season: Jack Coombs (1910), 13
Career: Bob Feller 44

Complete Games
Season: Jesse Duryea (1889), 38
Career: Bob Feller 279

Strikeouts
Season: Bob Feller (1946), 348
Career: Bob Feller 2,581

Earned Run Average
Season (minimum 100 innings): Jack Coombs (1910), 1.30
Career (minimum 300 innings): Jake Weimer 2.23

Chapter Notes

Chapter 1

1. John Liepa, "The Cincinnati Red Stockings and Cal McVey," *Iowa Heritage Illustrated*, Spring 2006, p. 12.
2. nauvoo.net/history.
3. Liepa, "The Cincinnati Red Stockings and Cal McVey," p. 13.
4. *Ibid.*, p. 12.
5. *Ibid.*
6. Gene Elston, *A Stitch in Time: A Baseball Chronology, 1845–2000*, p. 65.
7. William A. Cook, *The Louisville Grays Scandal of 1877: The Taint of Gambling at the Dawn of the National League*, p. 12.
8. outrunchange.com/2012/06/14/typical-wages-in-1860-through-1890.
9. Liepa, "The Cincinnati Red Stockings and Cal McVey," p. 14.
10. *Ibid.*
11. Bill Bryson, *Des Moines Register*, 1968 article on Iowa Sports Hall of Fame.
12. Liepa, "The Cincinnati Red Stockings and Cal McVey," p. 15.
13. Cook, *The Louisville Grays Scandal of 1877*, p. 16.
14. Liepa, "The Cincinnati Red Stockings and Cal McVey," p. 15.
15. *Ibid.*
16. Charles F. Faber, "Cal McVey," Baseball Biography Project, sabr.org.
17. Chris Jaffe, *Evaluating Baseball's Managers: A History and Analysis of Performance in the Major Leagues, 1876–2008*, pp. 74–76.
18. Peter Morris, William J. Ryczek, Jan Finkel, and Leonard Levin, *Base Ball Pioneers, 1850–1870: The Clubs and Players Who Spread the Sport Nationwide*, p. 156.
19. *Sporting Life*, November 4, 1885.
20. *Sporting Life*, May 11, 1895.
21. *Sporting Life*, August 10, 1895.
22. Paul Batesel, *Players and Teams of the National Association*, p. 93.
23. *Sporting Life*, November 3, 1906.
24. Batesel, *Players and Teams of the National Association*, p. 93.
25. *Sporting Life*, November 24, 1906.
26. *Sporting Life*, June 25, 1910.
27. Batesel, *Players and Teams of the National Association*, p. 93.
28. *Sporting Life*, April 10, 1915.
29. Morris, Ryczek, Finkel and Levin, *Base Ball Pioneers, 1850–1870*, p. 156.

Chapter 2

1. Bill James, *The New Bill James Historical Abstract*.
2. Grantland Rice, "Baseball Loses One Of," *New York Herald Tribune*, April 15, 1922.
3. capanson.com, chapter 1.
4. Howard Rosenberg, *Cap Anson 4*, p. 40.
5. "Notre Dame Baseball: Alive and Well in Third Century," 2015 Notre Dame Baseball Media Guide, p. 92.
6. Cap Anson Hall of Fame file.
7. "Cap's pay $66.66 a month," *Chicago Daily News*, April 15, 1922, p. 2.
8. Warren Brown, *The Chicago Cubs*, p. 13.
9. Cap Anson Hall of Fame file.
10. tuffstuff.com/news/baseball/collecting_cap_anson.
11. hardballtimes.com/lessons-from-lakefront-park-1884.

12. Cap Anson Hall of Fame file.
13. Harold Seymour and Dorothy Seymour Mills, *Baseball: The Early Years*, p. 335.
14. Dave Johnson, "Spring training has come a long way since Cap's Anson's day," *Evansville* (IN) *Courier*, March 8, 1988.
15. E.S. Sheridan, *Chicago Tribune*, April 15, 1922.
16. *Ibid.*
17. Fred Stein, "Playing Managers," *The National Pastime* 6, p. 84.
18. Stig Jantz, "Hall of Famer Cap Anson was baseball's best player and most strident racist," *Sport Magazine*, May 1993, p. 70.
19. *Ibid.*
20. *Ibid.*
21. *Ibid.*
22. *Chicago Inter-Ocean*, May 4, 1887.
23. baseballrevisited.wordpress.com/2012/11/04/albert-spaldings-world-tour-18881889.
24. David Fleitz, "Cap Anson," Baseball Biography Project, sabr.org.
25. *Ibid.*
26. "Passing of Capt. Anson," *Chicago Daily News*, January 31, 1898, p. 6.
27. "Fricke's pithing was easy," *Chicago Daily News*, February 3, 1898, p. 10.
28. See note 2 above.
29. John B. Sheridan, "This Was Anson, Great Hero of National Game," *The Sporting News*, April 20, 1922, p. 7.
30. See note 24 above.
31. Cap Anson Hall of Fame file.
32. *Ibid.*
33. *Ibid.*
34. *Ibid.*
35. Edward Prell, "Birthday Recalls Old Cub Hero," *Chicago Tribune*, April 7, 1968, section 3, p. 1.
36. *Ibid.*
37. Rosenberg, *Cap Anson 4*, p. 401.
38. David L. Fleitz, *Cap Anson: The Grand Old Man of Baseball*, p. 268.
39. "Pay Tribute to 'Cap' Anson," *Chicago Daily News*, April 17, 1922, p. 17.
40. Billy Murphy, "'Taking care' of Anson when he's dead and gone is poor stuff," *The Sporting News*, April 27, 1922.
41. Cap Anson Hall of Fame file.
42. Rosenberg, *Cap Anson 4*, p. 406.
43. capanson.com, chapter 5.
44. baseballhall.org, Cap Anson profile.

Chapter 3

1. Fred Lieb, *The Sporting News*, August 24, 1960.
2. Bert McGrane, *Des Moines Register* 1951 article on Iowa Sports Hall of Fame.
3. Angelo Louisa, "Fred Clarke," Baseball Biography Project, sabr.org.
4. Sec Taylor, "Sittin' in with the Athletes," *Des Moines Register*, August 17, 1960.
5. Ronald T. Waldo, *Fred Clarke: A Biography of the Baseball Hall of Fame Player-Manager*, p. 13.
6. *Ibid.*
7. See note 3 above.
8. *Ibid.*
9. Associated Press, August 16, 1960.
10. "The Latest News from All Points of the Compass." *The Sporting News*, July 14, 1894, p. 1.
11. See note 3 above.
12. Waldo, *Fred Clarke*, pp. 31–32.
13. See note 3 above.
14. See note 2 above.
15. thebaseballpage.com, Pirates 1903 season recap.
16. *Ibid.*
17. Joseph Reichler, *The World* Serie, p. 13.s.
18. Waldo, *Fred Clarke*, p. 83.
19. baseballlibrary.com, Fred Clarke chronology.
20. "Will Fight for Heydler," *Washington Post*, December 12, 1909.
21. Ralph S. Davis, "Dreyfuss Plans to Shake Up Pirates," *The Sporting News*, October 14, 1915, p. 6.
22. *Ibid.*
23. Waldo, *Fred Clarke*, p. 198.
24. *Ibid.*, p. 202.
25. Daniel M. Daniel, "How Fred Clarke Taught the Pirates Confidence," *Baseball Magazine*, March 1926.
26. Bill Bryson, "Fred Clarke: Indestructible," *Baseball Digest*, March 1948, p. 45.
27. See note 4 above.
28. See note 26 above.
29. "Spicy Sporting Table Talk," *Syracuse Post Standard*, December 20, 1909, p. 14.
30. Associated Press, August 16, 1960.

Chapter 4

1. George Stone Hall of Fame file.
2. "Stone's Belief," *Sporting Life*, October 6, 1906.

3. Billy Evans, *The Sporting News*, February 27, 1908.
4. "Crouches at Bat," *The Sporting News*, November 3, 1906, p. 7.
5. *Ibid.*
6. "Stone Batting Methods," *Sporting Life*, September 29, 1906.
7. See note 1 above.
8. Bill Bryson, "Iowan's Batting Feat: Beat Cobb," *Des Moines Register*, April 5, 1970.
9. *St. Louis Globe-Democrat* story in Hall of Fame file.
10. *St. Louis Post-Dispatch* story in Hall of Fame file.
11. 1880 federal census for Richland, Sac County, Iowa, p. 236D.
12. See note 8 above.
13. *Kansas City Star* story in Hall of Fame file.
14. Coleridge, Nebraska, story in Hall of Fame file.
15. John McMurray, "George Stone," Baseball Biography Project, sabr.org.
16. "American League notes," *Sporting Life*, February 11, 1905, p. 16.
17. See note 4 above.
18. "Chicago Gleanings," *Sporting Life*, February 10, 1906, p. 2.
19. See note 1 above.
20. See note 10 above.
21. See note 4 above.
22. See note 9 above.
23. See note 1 above.
24. *Ibid.*
25. See note 10 above.
26. See note 1 above.
27. See note 15 above.
28. See note 1 above.
29. "American League notes," *Sporting Life*, December 3, 1910, p. 8.
30. See note 1 above.
31. Coleridge, Nebraska, story in Hall of Fame file.

Chapter 5

1. United Press, April 18, 1957.
2. John P. Tierney, *Jack Coombs: A Life in Baseball*, p. 9.
3. *Ibid.*, pp. 19, 21.
4. William King, "The big leaguer," *Duke University Dialogue*, April 3, 1998.
5. Fred Haney, "Rube Waddell Put on Display for Coombs," *Durham Herald* June 14, 1936.
6. "Colby Jack Coombs Won't Take Credit for 24-inning Tilt," *Durham Sun*, April 22, 1929.
7. William O. Varn, "30 Years Ago Today, Jack Coombs Twirled 24 Innings to Triumph," Associated Press, September 1, 1936.
8. Billy Murphy, "In the Shadow of Baseball Tragedies," *Ogden Standard*, January 10, 1914.
9. Frederick G. Lieb, *Connie Mack: Grand Old Man of Baseball*, p. 126.
10. C. Paul Rogers III, "Jack Coombs," Baseball Biography Project, sabr.org.
11. "Coombs Improves," *Trenton Times*, June 14, 1913.
12. Bert McGrane, *Des Moines Register* 1956 story on Iowa Sports Hall of Fame.
13. "Coombs cured by victory of team," *Anaconda Standard*, October 19, 1913.
14. *Ibid.*
15. "Coombs Will Pitch in July," *Anaconda Standard*, May 10, 1914.
16. See note 10 above.
17. Tierney, *Jack Coombs*, p. 142.
18. "Called Back to the Game," *The Sporting News*, December 19, 1918, p. 1.
19. Tierney, *Jack Coombs*, p. 145.
20. "Finishes Season by Losing to Texas U," *Galveston Daily News*, May 5, 1918, p. 10.
21. Frank Dascenzo, "Shrine honors memory of 'Colby,'" *Durham Sun*, May 6, 1987.
22. See note 10 above.
23. Larry Karl, "Memory of Coombs Lives," *Durham Herald*, April 16, 1957.
24. See note 21 above.
25. See note 23 above.
26. *Ibid.*
27. Jack Coombs, list of coaching points of emphasis in Duke University archives.
28. Jack Coombs, faculty report dated September 1940 in Duke University archives.
29. Jack Coombs, thesis on coaching in Duke University archives.
30. Ken Alexander, "Grand Old Man," *Gastonia Gazette*, April 17, 1957, p. 14.
31. *Ibid.*
32. Jack Coombs, *Baseball: Individual Play and Team Strategy*, pp. 1–2.
33. *Charlotte Observer*, May 19, 1941.
34. Add Penfield, "Colby Jack: A biography with some personal reflections," unpublished manuscript in Duke University archives.

35. *Durham Herald* article in Duke University archives.
36. See note 1 above.
37. See note 30 above.

Chapter 6

1. Norman E. Brown, "Hasn't Drawn Credit Due Him," *Sioux City Journal*, July 19, 1925, p. 19.
2. "Hank to Be Well-Fixed for Talent," *San Antonio Light*, February 16, 1933.
3. "Hats Off to Hank," *Des Moines Register*, June 10, 1936.
4. *Ibid.*
5. Bert McGrane, "Add Severeid to Register's Hall of Fame," *Des Moines Register*, March 25, 1962.
6. Harold Scherwitz, "A Giant Steps Down," *San Antonio Light*, December 18, 1968; pp. 77, 81.
7. "Hank Severeid Tells of Rise from Amateur Ranks to Big Leagues." *Story City Herald* anniversary edition, October 24, 1940.
8. Lou Barbour, "The Hank Severeid Story," unpublished article, April 1965.
9. "Flashback Friday: Catcher Hank Severeid," roarfrom34.blogspot.com, June 5, 2009.
10. See note 8 above.
11. "Severeid Ranks Perkins Below Schalk as Catcher," *Des Moines Tribune*, September 20, 1922.
12. See note 6 above.
13. See note 9 above.
14. *Ibid.*
15. See note 6 above.
16. "Matter Up to Ban," *San Antonio Light*, May 20, 1917, p. 19.
17. *Ibid.*
18. "Browns to Lose Severeid." *Kansas City Star*, January 1, 1918, p. 18.
19. "Hank Severeid a Tanker." *Kansas City Times*, January 11, 1919, p. 8.
20. *Waterloo Courier*, November 18, 1919.
21. Curley Grieve, "Says Yanks Are Powerful Team," *Story City Herald* (reprint from *San Francisco Examiner*), October 6, 1938.
22. See note 8 above.
23. Frederick G. Lieb, "Schang and Snyder Both Great Series Catchers; Severeid Best of Bunch," *Galveston Daily News*, September 23, 1922, p. 7.
24. See note 1 above.
25. "Hank Severeid May Purchase Lincoln Club," *Des Moines Tribune*, January 27, 1927.
26. baseballreference.com, Hank Severeid player page.
27. "Fine Residence Badly Damaged," *Story City Herald*, February 20, 1930.
28. Bill Van Fleet, "Here's the Dope," *Galveston Daily News*, February 15, 1933, p. 6.
29. See note 6 above.
30. "150 Players Enlist in Mission Baseball School," *San Antonio Express*, March 13, 1934, p. 9.
31. See note 6 above.
32. See note 8 above.
33. "Wrestling, Trapping Severeid's Secret of Baseball Durability," *San Antonio Light*, February 21, 1933.
34. Bert McGrane, "Sports Slants," *Des Moines Register*, 1926, exact date unknown (from Baseball Hall of Fame file).
35. See note 6 above.
36. hofdebate.wordpress.com/2009/05/22/introducing-hank-severeid.
37. Sec Taylor, "Hank Severeid," *Story City Herald* (reprint from *Des Moines Register*), April 14, 1932.

Chapter 7

1. "Bancroft, Frisch and Nehf Star with the Giants," *Southeast Missourian*, July 18, 1922, p. 2.
2. *Ibid.*
3. Bert McGrane, *Des Moines Register* 1954 story on Iowa Sports Hall of Fame.
4. *Ibid.*
5. Trey Strecker, "Dave Bancroft," Baseball Biography Project, sabr.org.
6. Billy Evans, "World Series Comparisons of Probable Contenders at Short," *Fort Wayne Journal Gazette*, September 26, 1922, p. 10.
7. *Sioux City Journal*, July 13, 1930, p. 2-B.
8. See note 5 above.
9. "Phillies May Lose Bancroft for Year," *Fort Wayne Journal Gazette*, May 18, 1919, p. 10.
10. "Rebellion Breaks Out in Ranks of Philly Club," *Oakland Tribune*, May 23, 1920, p. 12.
11. Spatz, Lyle and Steinberg, Steve. *1921: The Yankees, the Giants and the Battle for Baseball Supremacy in New York*; p. 44.
12. See note 5 above.
13. *Ibid.*

14. "Philly Fans Are Peeved." *New Castle News*, June 11, 1920; p. 26.
15. *Ibid.*
16. Baseballlibrary.com, Dave Bancroft choronology.
17. "Bancroft Is Best Shortstop in Major Leagues," *Bridgeport Telegram*, August 2, 1922, p. 9.
18. "Bancroft Traded; to Manage Braves," *New York Times*, November 13, 1923.
19. *Ibid.*
20. *Ibid.*
21. *Ibid.*
22. *Ibid.*
23. "Dave Bancroft Takes It Easy" *Sioux City Journal*, December 8, 1923, p. 14.
24. Norman E. Brown, "Dave Bancroft Tells How to Cure a Rookie's Faults," *Sioux City Journal*, March 7, 1926, p. 35.
25. "Baseball Feud Ends in Fight," Associated Press, June 19, 1927.
26. "Dave Bancroft Quits Braves," Associated Press, October 15, 1927.
27. Dan Desmond, "Dave Bancroft, Product of Sioux City's Sandlots," *Sioux City Journal*, December 26, 1928, p. 7.
28. *Ibid.*
29. *Ibid.*
30. Ellsworth Parker, "Dave Bancroft Says He Is Pleased at His Return to New York Giants," *Sioux City Journal*, February 7, 1930, p. 13.
31. Bill James, *Whatever Happened to the Hall of Fame?*, p. 110.
32. David S. Neft, "Is Ozzie Smith Worth $2,000,000 a Season?" *Baseball Research Journal*, 1986, pp. 43–48.

Chapter 8

1. Brian Cooper, "Red Faber," Baseball Biography Project, sabr.org.
2. baseballhall.org, Red Faber profile.
3. "Red Faber dead at 88," *The Sporting News*, October 16, 1976.
4. *Ibid.*
5. See note 2 above.
6. See note 1 above.
7. "'Red' Faber's Wonderful Feat," *Waterloo Courier*, August 20, 1910.
8. *Ibid.*
9. See note 1 above.
10. *Ibid.*
11. See note 3 above.
12. Lee Allen, "Cooperstown Corner," *The Sporting News*, May 30, 1964.

13. *Baseball Magazine*, July 1918.
14. "Where the Breaks Decide," *Baseball Magazine*, December 1917.
15. "The Way Jim Put It," *Cascade Pioneer*, October 18, 1917.
16. Red Faber, told to Hal Totten, *Sports Digest*.
17. *Dubuque Telegraph Herald*, October 18, 1917.
18. *Cascade Pioneer*, October 18, 1917.
19. See note 14 above.
20. Hugh Fullerton, "Chicago White Sox Win World's Championship Baseball Honors," *Winnipeg Free Press*, October 16, 1917, p. 6.
21. "Sox the Goods," *Chicago Herald*, October 16, 1917.
22. See note 3 above.
23. William Farina, *Eliot Asinof and the Truth of the Game: A Critical Study of Baseball*, p. 81.
24. Westbrook Pegler, *Chicago Tribune*, August 25, 1929.
25. Edwards Burns, "20,000 Friends Cheer Veteran in 5–4 Defeat," *Chicago Tribune*, August 21, 1929, p. 17.
26. See note 1 above.
27. *Ibid.*
28. *Ibid.*
29. *Ibid.*
30. *Ibid.*
31. Bill O'Neill, *Dubuque Telegraph-Herald*, October 3, 1976, p. 29.

Chapter 9

1. Bill James, *The New Bill James Historical Abstract*, p. 835.
2. Dick Kelly, "Spotlight on Sports," *Hagerstown Daily Mail*, May 21, 1966.
3. baseballlibrary.com, Bing Miller biography.
4. Bert McGrane, *Des Moines Register* 1961 article of Iowa Sports Hall of Fame.
5. *Ibid.*
6. *Burlington Hawk Eye*, August 13, 1914.
7. *Clinton Herald*, May 8, 1915.
8. *Clinton Herald*, June 22, 1915.
9. *Clinton Advertiser*, May 22, 1916.
10. *Clinton Advertiser*, May 26, 1916.
11. *Muscatine Journal*, October 2, 1919.
12. Davis Walsh, International News Service, October 15, 1929.
13. *Ibid.*
14. "As the Sports Editor Sees It," *Waterloo Courier*, October 15, 1929.

15. *Ibid.*
16. Associated Press, July 22, 1940.
17. Arthur Daley, *New York Times*, May 14, 1966.
18. *Waterloo Courier*, September 3, 1954.
19. Dave Lewis, "Once Over Lightly," *Long Beach Independent Telegram*, February 7, 1965.
20. United Press International, May 7, 1966.
21. Gus Schrader, "Red Peppers," *Cedar Rapids Gazette*, May 8, 1966.
22. See note 17 above.
23. See note 2 above.
24. See note 21 above.

Chapter 10

1. Lawrence S. Ritter, *The Glory of Their Times*, p. 199.
2. Arthur Daley, "Sports of the Times," *New York Times*, February 19, 1961.
3. *Ibid.*
4. John Heidenry, *The Gashouse Gang*, p. 101.
5. John C. Skipper, *Dazzy Vance: A Biography of the Brooklyn Dodger Hall of Famer*, p. 17.
6. Chad Dotson, "The improbable career of Dazzy Vance," hardballtimes.com, January 24, 2014.
7. Skipper, *Dazzy Vance*, p. 111.
8. Charles F. Faber, "Dazzy Vance," Baseball Biography Project, sabr.org.
9. See note 6 above.
10. baseballhall.org, Dazzy Vance profile.
11. See note 2 above.
12. See note 8 above.
13. Richards Vidmer, "Vance Pitches No-Hit Game," *New York Times*, September 14, 1925.
14. Jack Kavanagh and Norman Macht, *Uncle Robbie*, p. 142.
15. Ritter, *The Glory of Their Times*, p. 200.
16. *Ibid.*
17. See note 8 above.
18. See note 2 above.
19. Ritter, *The Glory of Their Times*, p. 198.
20. See note 2 above.
21. baseballlibrary.com, Babe Herman biography.
22. See note 8 above.
23. *Ibid.*
24. Ritter, *The Glory of Their Times*, pp. 198–199.
25. baseballlibrary.com, Dazzy Vance chronology.
26. Heidenry. *The Gashouse Gang*, p. 222.
27. Skipper, *Dazzy Vance*, p. 175.
28. "Dazzy Vance Dead in Florida," *New York Times*, February 17, 1961.
29. Skipper, *Dazzy Vance*, p. 182.
30. *Ibid.*, pp. 183–184.
31. *Ibid.*, p. 184.

Chapter 11

1. John Holway, "How to Score from First on a Sacrifice," *American Heritage*, August 1970.
2. Eldon Auker with Tom Keegan, *Sleeper Cars and Flannel Uniforms*, pp. 191–192.
3. Gus Schrader, "Red Peppers," *Cedar Rapids Gazette*, October 26, 1954, p. 13.
4. "Top Sports Writers Pay Final Tribute to Whitehill," *Cedar Rapids Gazette*, October 31, 1954, p. 5.
5. *Ibid.*
6. Earl Coughlin, "Red Peppers, Hot Sport Chatter," *Cedar Rapids Gazette*, October 7, 1933, p. 10.
7. Cliff Wheatley, "'Babe' Herman Crashes Out His Sixth Circuit Clout," *Atlanta Constitution*, June 10, 1923.
8. See note 4 above.
9. Steve Lombardi, "Most Cheap Wins Since 1920," baseball-reference.com blog, November 14, 2010.
10. See note 4 above.
11. *Ibid.*
12. See note 3 above.
13. Billy Evans, "Billy Evans Says," *Miami News Record*, July 18, 1927.
14. See note 1 above.
15. Jack Ogden, "Fritz Balks, He Was There," *Cedar Rapids Gazette*, April 15, 1951.
16. See note 6 above.
17. "Roosevelt Enjoys Contest in Capital," *New York Times*, October 6, 1933.
18. "Cronin Confident, Lauds New Spirit," *New York Times*, October 6, 1933.
19. "Whitehill's Dad Wires Congratulations," *Cedar Rapids Gazette*, October 7, 1933, p. 10.
20. Earl Coughlin, "Red Peppers, Hot Sport Chatter," *Cedar Rapids Gazette*, October 6, 1933.
21. "Chapman Blames Myer for Trouble," *Chester Times*, April 26, 1933, p. 12.
22. Edward J. Neil, "Three Players Are

Given Fines," Associated Press, April 29, 1933.
23. "Puts Foot Down on Paper's Plan," Associated Press, May 3, 1933.
24. See note 6 above.
25. William Johnson, "Earl Whitehill," Baseball Biography Project, sabr.org.
26. See note 4 above.
27. *Ibid.*
28. *Ibid.*

Chapter 12

1. Terry Pluto, *Our Tribe: A Baseball Memoir*, p. 88.
2. Jim Odenkirk, "Not Tolstoy, Not Trotsky, but Harold 'Hal' Trosky," *Nine: A Journal of Baseball History and Culture*, Fall 2002, pp. 69–81.
3. Leighton Housh, "Iowa Hall of Fame Adds Power Hitter Hal Trosky," *Des Moines Register*, April 4, 1965.
4. Bill Johnson, "Hal Trosky." Baseball Biography Project, sabr.org.
5. *Ibid.*
6. Maury White, "Farm to Fame for Hal Trosky," *Des Moines Register*, April 1, 1979.
7. Pluto, *Our Tribe*, p. 87.
8. See note 6 above.
9. *Ibid.*
10. Dan Daniel, *New York World-Telegram*, January 9, 1935.
11. "Trosky Coming Babe Ruth, Say Baseball Sages," *Salt Lake Tribune*, March 25, 1934, p. 6B.
12. Joe Williams, July 1935 column in Trosky Hall of Fame file.
13. Paul Mickelson, "Trosky Forgets Babe Ruth's Record," Associated Press, March 21, 1936.
14. John J. Ward, *Baseball Magazine*, June 1937, p. 315.
15. See note 4 above.
16. *Ibid.*
17. *Ibid.*
18. *Ibid.*
19. See note 6 above.
20. "Hal Trosky Tells of Old Recurring Severe Headaches," Associated Press, July 13, 1941.
21. Pluto, *Our Tribe*, p. 87.
22. *Ibid.*
23. *Ibid.*
24. See note 2 above.
25. See note 20 above.
26. "Les Fleming to Get Shot at Trosky's Job," Associated Press, February 20, 1942.
27. Gayle Hayes, "Hal Trosky Quits Baseball," *Des Moines Register*, February 18, 1942.
28. "Headaches Cease to Bother Trosky; May Return to Baseball," Newspaper Enterprise Association, August 13, 1942.
29. "Hal Trosky May Return to Action," *Coshocton Tribune*, December 6, 1942.
30. *Ibid.*
31. Jim Ecker, "Hal Trosky Sr.," *Cedar Rapids Gazette*, December 29, 2007, p. 6C.
32. Gus Schrader, "Red Peppers," *Cedar Rapids Gazette*, June 29, 1969, p. D1.
33. See note 3 above.
34. See note 31 above.
35. See note 6 above.

Chapter 13

1. Richard Goldstein, "Bob Feller, Whose Fastball Dazzled, Dies at 92," *New York Times*, December 15, 2010.
2. Zack Hample, *The Baseball: Stunts, Scandals and Secrets Beneath the Stitches*, p. 62.
3. Bob Broeg, *Super Stars of Baseball*, p. 74.
4. See note 2 above.
5. See note 1 above.
6. Frank Deford, "Rapid Robert Can Still Bring It," *Sports Illustrated*, August 8, 2005.
7. *Ibid.*
8. Bob Feller with Bill Gilbert, *Now Pitching Bob Feller*, p. 37.
9. See note 6 above.
10. Donald Honig, *Baseball When the Grass Was Real*.
11. Broeg, *Super Stars of Baseball*, p. 74.
12. Bob Feller contract with Fargo-Moorhead of Northern League, July 22, 1935.
13. Feller, *Now Pitching Bob Feller*, p. 33.
14. Broeg, *Super Stars of Baseball*, p. 75.
15. See note 6 above.
16. Broeg, *Super Stars of Baseball*, p. 75.
17. Broeg, *Super Stars of Baseball*, p. 74.
18. Franklin Lewis, "Farm Boys Turns Laughs into Gasps," *Cleveland Press*, July 6, 1936.
19. Broeg, *Super Stars of Baseball*, p. 75.
20. See note 18 above.
21. Feller, *Now Pitching Bob Feller*, pp. 46–47.
22. Sec Taylor, "Bob Feller Pitches No-

hit Game," *Des Moines Register*, April 17, 1940, p. 7.
23. "Iowa Admits Wind Helped His Fastball," *Des Moines Register*, April 17, 1940, p. 7.
24. See note 6 above.
25. Feller, *Now Pitching Bob Feller*, p. 33.
26. See note 6 above.
27. Mel Antonen, "Hall of Fame pitcher, Indians great Bob Feller dies at age 92," *USA Today*, December 17, 2010.
28. *Ibid.*
29. Broeg, *Super Stars of Baseball*, p. 80.
30. Feller, *Now Pitching Bob Feller*, p. 142.
31. Ted Williams with John Underwood, *My Turn at Bat*, p. 212.
32. Broeg, *Super Stars of Baseball*, p. 79.
33. See note 1 above.
34. *Ibid.*
35. See note 6 above.
36. baseballintheattic.com, August 1, 2010.
37. Don Doxsie, "Feller goes extra mile for his museum," *Quad-City Times*, April 21, 2001, p. D3.
38. Dennis Manoloff, *Cleveland Plain Dealer*, posted online December 9, 2010.

Chapter 14

1. Don Doxsie, "Banks has fond memories of Baker," *Quad-City Times*, December 4, 1999, p. 3S.
2. Don Doxsie, "Baker beat discrimination to play in major leagues," *Quad-City Times*, April 12, 1992, p. 1E.
3. John Naughton, *Des Moines Register* 2009 story on Iowa Sports Hall of Fame.
4. See note 1 above.
5. *Ibid.*
6. *Ibid.*
7. Jack Ogden, *Davenport Democrat*, March 15, 1942, p. 25.
8. Jack Ogden, *Davenport Democrat*, March 19, 1943, p. 16.
9. "Eugene Baker Wins Berth on IDPA All-State Squad," *Davenport Democrat*, March 26, 1943.
10. *Davenport Democrat*, May 27, 1943, p. 21.
11. "Cubs Appear Far Stronger for '53 Race," Associated Press, January 29, 1953.
12. See note 2 above.
13. Rick Swaine, *The Black Stars Who Made Baseball Whole*, p. 151.
14. "Cubs to Bring Gene Baker Up." *Chicago Defender*, September 3, 1953; p. 17.
15. See note 2 above.
16. *Ibid.*
17. Carrie Muskat, *Banks to Sandberg to Grace*, p. 69.
18. Don Doxsie, "Cubs black second baseman had to endure verbal abuse," *Quad-City Times*, April 12, 1992, p. 4E.
19. See note 1 above.
20. *Ibid.*
21. Lisa Winston, "Baker was a blazer of many trails," minorleaguebaseball.com, February 11, 2008.
22. See note 1 above.
23. *Ibid.*
24. See note 2 above.
25. "Negro to Manage Bucs' Farm Club," United Press International, June 20, 1961.
26. Mark Graczyk, "Hidden history: A black manager for Batavia in 1961," thedailynewsonline.com, December 19, 2010.
27. See note 3 above.
28. Swaine, *The Black Stars Who Made Baseball Whole*.
29. Ernie Banks and Jim Enright, *Mr. Cub*, pp. 182–183.
30. See note 21 above.
31. Peter Golenbock, *Wrigleyville: A Magical History Tour of the Chicago Cubs*, p. 348.
32. Don Doxsie, "Baker blazed baseball trail," *Quad-City Times*, December 3, 1999, p. 1S.
33. Don Doxsie, "Baker helped break racial barrier," *Quad-City Times*, December 3, 1999, p. 6S.
34. See note 1 above.
35. *Ibid.*
36. See note 21 above.

Chapter 15

1. John Steadman, *Baltimore News American*, October 13, 1983.
2. Bill Lyon, *Philadelphia Inquirer*, October 13, 1983.
3. See note 1 above.
4. Mike Klingaman, "Catching Up With," *Baltimore Sun*, April 8, 2010.
5. *Ibid.*
6. Steve Wulf, "He Has Returned to His Roots," *Sports Illustrated*, December 19, 1983.
7. Bill James, *The New Bill James Historical Abstract*, p. 299.
8. David Laurila, Mike Boddicker Q&A, baseballprospectus.com, November 29, 2009.
9. *Ibid.*

10. Mike Boddicker Q&A, Iowa Baseball Symposium, Van Meter, Iowa, October 11, 2014.
11. Bob Denney, "'Typical Norway game' shows Mike's a winner," *Cedar Rapids Gazette*, October 8, 1983, p. 3B.
12. See note 10 above.
13. Even, Dan. "Long Season Is Over, Boddicker, Norway Win," *Cedar Rapids Gazette*, October 2, 1974; p. 2D.
14. See note 10 above.
15. Don Doxsie, "It was like a class reunion in Baltimore," *Cedar Rapids Gazette*, October 12, 1983, p. 1B.
16. "Boddicker blanks ChiSox on 5-hitter," Associated Press, May 18, 1983.
17. "Mike's mom: He's got the whole town boppin'," *Cedar Rapids Gazette*, October 7, 1983, p. 1C.
18. See note 10 above.
19. Don Doxsie, "No question, Boddicker a blessing for Baltimore," *Cedar Rapids Gazette*, October 13, 1983, p. 4C.
20. "Phils 'very impressed,'" *Cedar Rapids Gazette*, October 13, 1983, p. 4C.
21. See note 2 above.
22. Alan Goldstein, *Baltimore Sun*, October 13, 1983.
23. See note 1 above.
24. Mike Boddicker, "World Series Diary," *Baltimore News American*, October 13, 1983.
25. Tom Hansen, "Boddicker, Norway glad to see each other," *Des Moines Register*, November 5, 1983, p. 1S.
26. *Ibid.*
27. *Ibid.*
28. See note 4 above.
29. See note 8 above.
30. See note 10 above.
31. *Ibid.*
32. Scott Christ, "The 40 Greatest Orioles of All-Time," camdenchat.com, March 10, 2006.
33. See note 10 above.
34. Mark Dukes, "Boddicker a little breathless from life in limelight," *Cedar Rapids Gazette*, October 11, 1983, p. 1C.
35. See note 6 above.

Chapter 16

1. Hannah Karp, "Casey Blake: The Dodger Diplomat," *Wall Street Journal*, October 20, 2009.
2. *Ibid.*
3. Casey Blake interview, October 31, 2014.
4. "Casey Blake Featured in 2011," Iowa High School Athletic Association Bulletin, October 2011.
5. Blake interview.
6. John Sickels, "Prospect Retro: Casey Blake," minorleagueball.com.
7. Bryce Miller, "Indianola native Blake to retire after 13 seasons," *Des Moines Register*, May 9, 2012, p. 3C.
8. Blake interview.
9. *Ibid.*
10. *Ibid.*
11. *Ibid.*
12. See note 1 above.
13. Blake interview.
14. T.J. Simers, "Nothing corny about Casey Blake's Dodgers stint," *Los Angeles Times*, June 28, 2009.
15. Joseph Santoliquito, "Blake meant no disrespect by gesture," MLB.com, May 12, 2009.
16. *Ibid.*
17. Blake interview.
18. *Ibid.*
19. "The Top 100 Indians: #85 Casey Blake," letsgotribe.com, August 15, 2012.
20. Blake interview.
21. Steve Dilbeck, "More than a season of giving for Casey Blake," *Los Angeles Times* blog, December 24, 2010.

Chapter 17

1. "Ed 'Patsy' Gharrity," Encyclopedia of Baseball Catchers, members.tripod.com/bb_catchers.
2. Bill Nowlin, "Duane Josephson," Baseball Biography Project, sabr.org.
3. Stew Thornley, "Tim Laudner," Baseball Biography Project, sabr.org.
4. Bill Johnson, "John Wathan," Baseball Biography Project, sabr.org.
5. *Ibid.*
6. Associated Press, February 3, 1975.
7. Associated Press, October 17, 1974.
8. Ronald T. Waldo, *Pennant Hopes Dashed by the Homer in the Gloamin'*, pp. 217–218.
9. thebaseballpage.com, Lee Handley profile.
10. Gerald Astor, *The Baseball Hall of Fame 50th Anniversary Book*, p. 222.
11. Mike DiGiovanna, "Former Angeles Bobby Knoop humbled by Hall of Fame

induction," *Los Angeles Times*, September 5, 2013.
12. baseballlibrary.com, Bobby Knoop biography.
13. David E. Skelton, "Denis Menke." Baseball Biography Project, sabr.org.
14. Robert Weintraub, *The House That Ruth Built: A New Stadium, the First Yankees Championship*, p. 1921.
15. John Snyder, *365 Oddball Days in Chicago Cubs History*, p. 26.
16. "I'll Break your Head if I ever get out Again," baseballhistorydaily.com, December 8, 2014.
17. J. Thomas Hetrick, *Chris Von Der Ahe and the St. Louis Browns*, p. 150.
18. Burton A. Boxerman and Benita W. Boxerman, *Jews and Baseball: Volume 1, Entering the Main Stream, 1871–1948*, p. 22.
19. Tim Hornbaker, *Turning the Black Sox White: The Misunderstood Legacy of Charles A. Comiskey*.
20. Norman C. Willis, *Washington Senators All-Time Greats*, p. 171.
21. Mike Chapman, "The Baseball Evangelist," *Iowa History Journal*, January/February 2001, pp. 4–7.
22. Ibid.

Chapter 18

1. John Gabcik, "Stan Bahnsen," Baseball Biography Project, sabr.org.
2. Bill Johnson, "Mace Brown," Baseball Biography Project, sabr.org.
3. *Ibid.*
4. "American League notes," *Sporting Life*, May 22, 1915, 9.
5. "Known as King Cole," *Sporting Life*, January 15, 1916, p. 6.
6. "Duryea's Jump," *Sporting Life*, February 12, 1890, p. 5.
7. *Ibid.*
8. Joseph Wancho, "Joe Hatten," Baseball Biography Project, sabr.org.
9. "Casualties and Fines Heavy in Free-for-All at Hollywood., *The Sporting News*, August 12, 1953, p. 23.
10. Christopher Nelson, "Hoerner remembered as prankster, determined pitcher," *Dubuque Telegraph Herald*, October 7, 1996.
11. Brian Cooper, "Joe Hoerner." Baseball Biography Project, sabr.org.
12. *Ibid.*
13. Jerry Clark, *Anson to Zuber: Iowa Boys in the Major Leagues*, p. 24.
14. baseball-reference.com, bullpen item on Bob Lee.
15. Bonnie DeSimone, "Lieber's success is simple, really," *Chicago Tribune*, October 3, 2001.
16. baseballlibrary.com, Bob Locker biography.
17. Ron Maly, *Des Moines Register* 1976 story on Iowa Sports Hall of Fame.
18. *Ibid.*
19. "Immaculate Inning: Pat Ragan," immaculateinning.com, August 21, 2008.
20. twinstrivia.com, interview with Kevin Tapani.
21. *New York Times*, July 12, 1908.
22. "On Deck Again," *Sporting Life*, February 13, 1909, p. 5.

Selected Bibliography

Books

Achorn, Edward. *The Summer of Beer and Whiskey: How Brewers, Barkeeps, Rowdies, Immigrants, and a Wild Pennant Fight Made Baseball America's Game.* New York: Public Affairs, 2013.
Alexander, Charles. *John McGraw.* Lincoln: University of Nebraska Press, 1988.
Asinof, Eliot. *Bleeding Between the Lines.* New York: Holt, Rinehart, and Winston, 1979.
_____. *Eight Men Out.* New York: Holt, Rinehart, and Winston, 1963.
Astor, Gerald. *The Baseball Hall of Fame 50th Anniversary Book.* New York: Prentice-Hall, 1988.
Auker, Eldon, with Tom Keegan. *Sleeper Cars and Flannel Uniforms.* Chicago: Triumph, 2001.
Banks, Ernie, and Jim Enright. *Mr. Cub.* Chicago: Follett, 1971.
Batesel, Paul. *Players and Teams of the National Association.* Jefferson, N.C.: McFarland, 2012.
Boxerman, Burton A., and Benita W. Boxerman. *Jews and Baseball: Volume 1, Entering the Main Stream, 1871–1948.* Jefferson, N.C.: McFarland, 2006.
Broeg, Bob. *Super Stars of Baseball.* St. Louis: Sporting News, 1971.
Brown, Warren. *The Chicago Cubs.* New York: Putnam's, 1946.
Chapman, Charles S., and Henry L. Severeid. *Play Ball! Advice to Young Ballplayers.* New York: Harper, 1941.
Clark, Jerry. *Anson to Zuber: Iowa Boys in the Major Leagues.* Omaha: Making History, 1992.
Cook, William A. *The Louisville Grays Scandal of 1877: The Taint of Gambling at the Dawn of the National League.* Jefferson, N.C.: McFarland, 2005.
Coombs, Jack. *Baseball: Individual Play and Team Strategy.* New York: Prentice-Hall, 1949.
Cooper, Brian E. *Ray Schalk.* Jefferson, N.C.: McFarland, 2009.
_____. *Red Faber: A Biography of the Hall of Fame Spitball Pitcher.* Jefferson, N.C.: McFarland, 2007.
DeValeria, Dennis, and Jeanne Burke DeValeria. *Honus Wagner: A Biography.* New York: Henry Holt, 1995.
Durso, Joseph. *The Days of Mr. McGraw.* Englewood Cliffs, N.J.: Prentice-Hall, 1969.
Elston, Gene. *A Stitch in Time: A Baseball Chronology, 1845–2000.* Houston: Halcyon Press, 2006.
Faber, Charles F. *Baseball Prodigies: Best Major League Seasons by Players Under 21.* Jefferson, N.C.: McFarland, 2014.

Farina, William. *Eliot Asinof and the Truth of the Game: A Critical Study of Baseball.* Jefferson, N.C.: McFarland, 2011.
Feller, Bob, with Gilbert, Bill. *Now Pitching Bob Feller.* New York: HarperCollins, 1990.
Fleitz, David L. *Cap Anson: The Grand Old Man of Baseball.* Jefferson, N.C.: McFarland, 2005.
Golenbock, Peter. *Wrigleyville: A Magical History Tour of the Chicago Cubs.* New York: Macmillan, 2007.
Hageman, William. *Honus: The Life and Times of a Baseball Hero.* Champaign, IL: Sagamore, 1996.
Hample, Zack. *The Baseball: Stunts, Scandals and Secrets Beneath the Stitches.* New York: Anchor, 2011.
Heidenry, John. *The Gashouse Gang.* New York: PublicAffairs, 2008.
Hetrick, J. Thomas. *Chris Von Der Ahe and the St. Louis Browns.* Lanham, MD: Scarecrow Press, 1999.
Honig, Donald. *Baseball When the Grass Was Real.* Lincoln: University of Nebraska Press, 1975.
Hornbaker, Tim. *Turning the Black Sox White: The Misunderstood Legacy of Charles A. Comiskey.* New York: Skyhorse, 2013.
Jaffe, Chris. *Evaluating Baseball's Managers: A History and Analysis of Performance in the Major Leagues, 1876–2008.* Jefferson, N.C.: McFarland, 2009.
James, Bill. *The New Bill James Historical Abstract.* New York: Free Press, 2003.
_____. *The New Bill James Historical Abstract.* New York: Simon & Schuster, 2010.
_____. *Whatever Happened to the Hall of Fame?* New York: Simon & Schuster, 1995.
Johnson, William H., and Shona Frese. *Norway Baseball: Gone but Not Forgotten.* Iowa Baseball Museum of Norway, 2012.
Kavanagh, Jack, and Norman Macht. *Uncle Robbie.* Cleveland: Society for American Baseball Research, 1999.
Lewis, Franklin. *The Cleveland Indians.* New York: Putnam's, 1949.
Lieb, Fred. *Baseball as I Have Known It.* New York: Coward, McCann and Geoghagen, 1977.
_____. *Connie Mack: Grand Old Man of Baseball.* New York: G.P. Putnam's Sons, 1945.
Morris, Peter. *A Game of Inches: The Stories Behind the Innovations That Shaped Baseball.* Lanham, MD: Rowman & Littlefield, 2006.
_____, William J. Ryczek, Jan Finkel, and Leonard Levin. *Base Ball Pioneers, 1850–1870: The Clubs and Players Who Spread the Sport Nationwide.* Jefferson, N.C.: McFarland, 2012.
Murdock, Eugene. *Baseball Between the Wars.* Westport, CT: Meckler, 1992.
Muskat, Carrie. *Banks to Sandberg to Grace.* Chicago: Contemporary, 2001.
Pluto, Terry. *Our Tribe: A Baseball Memoir.* New York: Simon & Schuster, 1999.
Reichler, Joseph. *The World Series.* New York: Simon & Schuster, 1979.
Ritter, Lawrence S. *The Glory of Their Times.* New York: Macmillan, 1966.
Robinson, Ray, and Christopher Jennison. *Greats of the Game.* New York: Harry N. Abrams, 2005.
Rosenberg, Howard. *Cap Anson 4.* Arlington: Tile, 2006.
Seymour, Harold, and Dorothy Seymour Mills. *Baseball: The Early Years.* Oxford: Oxford University Press, 1960.
Skipper, John C. *Dazzy Vance: A Biography of the Brooklyn Dodger Hall of Famer.* Jefferson, N.C.: McFarland, 2007.
Smith, Robert. *Baseball's Hall of Fame.* New York: Bantam, 1973.
Snyder, John. *365 Oddball Days in Chicago Cubs History.* Cincinnati: Clerisy Press, 2010.
Spatz, Lyle, and Steve Steinberg. *1921: The Yankees, the Giants and the Battle for Baseball Supremacy in New York.* Lincoln: University of Nebraska Press, 2010.

Selected Bibliography

Stout, Glenn, Richard A. Johnson, and Dick Johnson. *The Cubs: The Complete Story of Chicago Cubs Baseball.* Boston: Houghton Mifflin, 2007.
Swaine, Rick. *The Black Stars Who Made Baseball Whole.* Jefferson, N.C.: McFarland, 2006.
Thomas, Henry. *Walter Johnson: Baseball's Big Train.* Washington, D.C.: Phenom Press, 1995.
Tierney, John P. *Jack Coombs: A Life in Baseball.* Jefferson, N.C.: McFarland, 2008.
Vaught, David. *The Farmers' Game: Baseball in Rural America.* Baltimore: Johns Hopkins University Press, 2013.
Waldo, Ronald T. *Fred Clarke: A Biography of the Baseball Hall of Fame Player-Manager.* Jefferson, N.C.: McFarland, 2011.
_____. *Pennant Hopes Dashed by the Homer in the Gloamin'.* Jefferson, N.C.: McFarland, 2013.
Weintraub, Robert. *The House That Ruth Built: A New Stadium, the First Yankees Championship.* Boston: Little, Brown, 2011.
Williams, Ted, with John Underwood. *My Turn at Bat.* New York: Simon & Schuster, 1969.
Willis, C. Norman. *Washington Senators All-Time Greats.* Xlibris, 2004.

Periodicals

American Heritage
Anaconda Standard
Atlanta Constitution
Baltimore News American
Baltimore Sun
Baseball Digest
Baseball Magazine
Baseball Research Journal
Bridgeport Telegram
Burlington Hawk Eye
Cascade Pioneer
Cedar Rapids Gazette
Charlotte Observer
Chester Times
Chicago Daily News
Chicago Defender
Chicago Herald
Chicago Inter-Ocean
Chicago Tribune
Cleveland Plain Dealer
Cleveland Press
Clinton Advertiser
Clinton Herald
Coshocton Tribune
Davenport Democrat
Des Moines Register
Des Moines Tribune
Dubuque Telegraph Herald
Duke University Dialogue
Durham Herald
Durham Sun
Evansville Courier
Fort Wayne Journal Gazette
Galveston Daily News
Gastonia Gazette
Hagerstown Daily Mail
Iowa Heritage Illustrated
Iowa History Journal
Kansas City Star
Kansas City Times
Long Beach Independent Telegram
Los Angeles Times
Miami News American
Miami News Record
Muscatine Journal
The National Pastime
New Castle News
New York Herald Tribune
New York Times
New York World-Telegram
Nine: A Journal of Baseball History and Culture
Oakland Tribune
Ogden Standard
Philadelphia Inquirer
Quad-City Times
St. Louis Globe-Democrat
St. Louis Post-Dispatch
Salt Lake Tribune
San Antonio Express
San Antonio Light
San Francisco Examiner

Sioux City Journal
Southeast Missourian
Sport
Sporting Life
The Sporting News
Sports Illustrated
Sports Digest
Story City Herald

Syracuse Post Standard
Trenton Times
USA Today
Wall Street Journal
Washington Post
Washington Times
Waterloo Courier
Winnipeg Free Press

Wire Services

Associated Press
International News Service

Newspaper Enterprise Association
United Press International

Websites

baseballhall.org
baseballhistorydaily.com
baseballintheattic.com
baseballlibrary.com
baseballprospectus.com
baseball-reference.com
baseballrevisited.wordpress.com
camdenchat.com
capanson.com
hardballtimes.com
hofdebate.wordpress.com
immaculateinning.com
letsgotribe.com

members.tripod.com
minorleagueball.com
minorleaguebaseball.com
mlb.com
nauvoo.net
outrunchange.com
roarfrom34.blogspot.com
sabr.org (Baseball Biography Project)
thebaseballpage.com
thedailynewsonline.com
tuffstuff.com
twinstrivia.com

Index

Numbers in **_bold italics_** indicate pages with illustrations.

Aaron, Hank 16, 197
Aberdeen, South Dakota 206
Acacia Park Cemetery (Chicago) 91
Adair County, Iowa 100
Adams, Babe 34–35, 37
Adel, Iowa 131
Adlam, Jim 149
Aguilas Cibaenas 150
USS *Alabama* 136–137
Alexander, Grover Cleveland 67, 74
Algona, Iowa 192
Ali, Muhammad 139
All-American Girls Professional Baseball League 79, 180
Allen, Johnny 177
Allentown, Pennsylvania 192
Allison, Doug 9
Altobelli, Joe 156
Amana Refrigeration 127–128
Amarillo, Texas 207
American Association 43, 47, 63, 79, 83, 121, 180, 191, 192
American Bowling Congress 24–25
American League 5, 16, 33, 40–41, 43, 45–47, 52, 64, 65–66, 73, 78, 81, 85, 88, 95, 97, 99, 112, 115–116, 121–123, 125, 127, 130, 134–135, 138, 144, 157–159, 166, 171–174, 176, 178, 181, 184–185, 189–191, 193, 198–199, 201–203, 205–206
American League Championship Series 157, 159, 167, 181, 201–202
American League Division Series 167
American Legion 67, 131, 144, 155, 158, 160, 195
Ames, Iowa 164, 186
Anaheim, California 200
Anderson, Brady 159
Anderson, John E. 55
Anson, Adele 25–26
Anson, Adrian C. "Cap" 2, 5–6, 14, 16–27, **_17_**, **_24_**, 32–33, 183, 186, 209

Anson, Adrian C. (son) 26
Anson, Adrian H. 26
Anson, Dorothy 25–26
Anson, Grace 26
Anson, Henry (grandfather) 17–18, 26
Anson, Henry (grandson) 26
Anson, Jennette 17
Anson, Melville 17
Anson, Sturgis 17–18, 26
Anson, Virginia (daughter) 26
Anson, Virginia "Jennie" (Fiegel) 21, 26
Anson Colts 25
Appling, Luke 80, 135
Arizona 110
Arizona-Mexico League 149
Arizona State University 155
Asinof, Eliot 88
Atlanta Braves 184, 198, 205, 207
Atlanta Crackers 95
Atlanta Journal Constitution 112
Atlantic City, New Jersey 53
Atlantic Coast Construction Company 98
Atlantic League 31
Atlantic Richfield 57
August, Dan 136
Auker, Eldon 110
Aurora, Illinois 198
Australia 22, 85

Bahnsen, Stan 6, 188–189
Baker, Eugene O. 143
Baker, Eugene W. 2–3, 6, 141–151, **_142_**, **_146_**
Baker, Frank "Home Run" 48, 58
Baker, Janice 151
Baker, Dr. Lenox 56
Baker, Mildred 143
Baker, William 75
Baker Bowl 73–74
Baltimore, Maryland 2, 25, 157, 159
Baltimore Canaries (aka Lord Baltimores) 12

Index

Baltimore Elite Giants 144
Baltimore News-American 153
Baltimore Orioles 23, 47, 63, 103, 153, 155, 157, 159, 165, 176, 183–184, 198, 206
Baltimore Sun 157
Bancroft, Dave 2, 5, 71–80, *72*, 180, 209
Bancroft, Edna 73
Bancroft, Ella 72
Bancroft, Frank 72
Bancroft, Iowa 154, 179, 195–196
Bankhead, Sam 149
Banks, Ernie 2, 80, 141–143, 145, *146*, 147–148, 150–151
Barnes, Ross 13
Barney, Billy 30
Barrow, Ed 28–29, 31, 122
Bartell, Dick 135
Base Ball Players Fraternity 14
Baseball Anonymous 91
Baseball Hall of Fame 5, 8, 14, 27–28, 34, 40, 42, 45, 48, 58–59, 65–66, 70–71, 79–81, 88, 91, 93, 100–101, 108–111, 119, 128–130, 135, 139, 141, 148, 153, 156–157, 171–172, 191, 197–198, 202
Baseball: Individual Play and Team Strategy 58
Baseball Magazine 37, 85, 122
Baseball Scouts Hall of Fame 151
Batavia Pirates 149–150, 199
Bay City, Michigan 191
Bell, Cool Papa 110
Bellflower, California 199
Beloit, Wisconsin 171
Beltre, Sergio 169
Bender, Chief 52–54, 191
Benton Community High School 152
Bergmann, Russ 57
Berkeley, California 69
Bettencourt, Rafael 166
Bibby, Jim 182
Big Ten 143, 155
Bigbee, Carson 37
Biittner, Larry 181–182
Binghampton, New York 192
Bings, George Washington 93
Birmingham, Alabama 111–112
Bishop, Max 96–97
Black Hills State College 175
Black Sox 87–88, 95, 204
Blake, Abbie (Archibald) 170
Blake, Ben 163
Blake, Casey 2, 162–170, *163*, *168*
Blake, Joe, Jr. 163
Blake, Joe, Sr. 163
Blake, Pete 163
Blanchard, Iowa 204
Blass, Steve 149
Bloomfield, Iowa 180
Bloomington, Illinois 182
Blue Ridge League 204
Bluege, Ossie 113

Blyleven, Bert 153
Boddicker, Butch 154
Boddicker, Dolly 154–155, 157, 160
Boddicker, Harold "Bus" 153–154
Boddicker, Lisa (Charipar) 160
Boddicker, Mike 2, 152–161, *153*, *155*, *159*
Boddicker, Robert 154
Boston Beaneaters 23, 183
Boston Braves 54, 76–79, 104, 107, 138, 180, 204
Boston Red Sox (aka Americans) 33, 43, 50, 54, 74, 95, 97, 122, 124, 159–160, 167, 172, 190, 194, 201, 203, 206
Boston Red Stockings 12–13, 18–19
Boudreau, Lou 80, 127, 138
Bowdoin College 50
Bowerman, Frank 34
Bradley, Alva 124–126
Bradley University 177
Bragan, Bobby 145
Brain, Dave 208
Brainard, Asa 9–10
Bressler, Rube 100, 105–106
Bridgeport (Connecticut) Telegram 76
Britt, Iowa 192
Broeg, Bob 133
Brooklyn Atlantics 11
Brooklyn Center, Minnesota 173
Brooklyn Dodgers (aka Robins) 21, 30–32, 54–55, 63, 78, 92, 100, 103–108, 109, 141, 143–144, 190, 195–196, 204
Brooklyn Gladiators 192
Brosnan, Jim 150–151
Brotherhood of Professional Ball Players 23
Brown, Joe L. 149
Brown, Mace 6, *189*, 190
Brown, Mordecai "Three-Finger" 191
Brown, Norman E. 60, 66, 77
Brueck, Bernie 170
Bryk, Bill 148, 150–151
Buchanan County League 98
Buckley, Dick 42
Buena Vista College 181
Buffalo, New York 117, 183, 198
Burkett, Jesse 43
Burlington Bees 121, 180
Burlington Colts 207
Burlington Flint Hills 185
Burlington Pathfinders 61–62
Burns, Tom 24

Calhoun County, Iowa 181
California 13–15, 47, 199
California League 199
Canadian Provincial League 149
Carew, Rod 153
Carey, Max 37
Carleton, Tex 108
Carroll, Cliff 182–183
Carroll, Owen 108
Carroll, Iowa 29, 183

Index 227

Cascade, Iowa 82–83, 86–87, 89–90
Cavaretta, Phil *146*
C.C. Loomis Company 28
Cedar County Bankers Association 47
Cedar Rapids, Iowa 93–94, 110–112, 115, 120, 128, 131, 155, 158, 160–161, 174, 179, 192, 198–199
Cedar Rapids and Iowa City Railway 199
Cedar Rapids Bunnies 121
Cedar Rapids Canaries 198
Cedar Rapids Gazette 2, 99, 110, 115, 128
Central Association 61, 94
Central Michigan University 205
Central Park (San Francisco) 14
Ceylon 23
Champion, Aaron B. 9, 11–12
Chance, Frank 14, 34, 208
Chandler, Happy 139
Chapman, Ben 116
Chapman, Charles 69
Charipar, Ken 160
Charlotte, North Carolina 146
Charlotte Observer 58
Chase Hotel 147
Chicago, Illinois 1, 21–22, 24, 27, 74, 86–87, 89, 91, 129, 136, 176, 208
Chicago Board of Trade 14
Chicago Colleens 79
Chicago Cubs 2, 14, 19, 25, 34, 36, 69, 89, 96, 104, 107, 111, 117, 142, 144–148, 150, 168, 182, 184, 190–191, 196, 200–202, 204–205, 207–208; *see also* Chicago White Stockings
Chicago Daily News 23, 26
Chicago Defender 145
Chicago Herald 87
Chicago Leland Giants 25
Chicago Tribune 21, 86
Chicago White Sox 15, 45–46, 52, 63, 65, 81, 84–90, 97–98, 117, 123, 126–128, 135, 156–157, 172, 176, 178, 183–184, 189, 191, 193, 197, 201–205
Chicago White Stockings 12, 19–24, 26, 32, 186; *see also* Chicago Cubs
China 85
Church of Jesus Christ of Latter Day Saints 8
Cicotte, Eddie 65, 191
Cincinnati, Ohio 9–11, 15, 146
Cincinnati Daily Times 7
Cincinnati Red Stockings 7–13, 15, 192
Cincinnati Reds 13, 15, 62–63, 69, 74, 87, 105, 108, 173, 176–177, 179–180, 182, 184, 187, 195–196, 198, 200, 204, 208
Cissell, Billy 121
Civil War 8, 186
Clarion, Iowa 176
Clarke, Annette 36, 38–39
Clarke, Fred 2, 5, 28–39, *29*, *35*, 83, 184, 209
Clarke, Josh 34
Clarke, Lucy 29

Clarke, William 29
Clay Grove, Iowa 182
Cleveland, Ohio 46, 135–136, 140
Cleveland Indians (aka Blues) 34, 73, 111–112, 116–117, 120–128, 130–138, 140, 144, 151, 158, 163–164, 166–167, 169–171, 177, 181, 185–186, 198–199
Cleveland Plain Dealer 125, 140
Cleveland Press 134
Cleveland Spiders 31
Cleveland Stadium 137
Clinton, Iowa 47, 94
Clinton Advertiser 94
Clinton County, Iowa 42
Clinton Herald 94
Clinton Pilots 94
Cobb, Ty 28, 34, 40–41, 46, 64, 82, 112, 114, 171
Cochrane, Mickey 98, 108
Coe College 191
Cohan, George M. 25
Colburn Classical Institute 49
Colby College 49–51, 58
Cole, Leonard L. "King" 190–191
Coleridge, Nebraska 42–43, 46–47
College World Series 55, 58, 164–165
Collins, Eddie 45
Collins, Jimmy 43
Collins, Pat 67
Colorado 38
Colorado Rockies 169
Columbia, South Carolina 112
Columbus Senators 102, 150, 191
Comiskey, Charles 25, 27, 45, 84, 184
Comiskey, Nan 85
Comiskey Park 86, 90, 135, 145
Connally, Sergeant George 122
Cook County, Illinois 25, 90
Coombs, Ellen (Snow) 49
Coombs, Frank 49
Coombs, Jack 2, 5, 48–59, *49*, *57*, 210
Coombs, Mary (Russ) 51, 55–56, 58
Cooperstown, New York 29, 91
Corbett, Jack 25
Corn Crackers 102
Cornell College 204
Coughlin, Earl 115
Council Bluffs, Iowa 188, 200
Cowles, Nebraska 101–102
Cowley County, Kansas 29
Craig, Roger 143
Cramer, Doc 97
Crane, Sam 19
Cravath, Gabby 74–75
Crawford, Sam 46
Creighton University 164
Crisp, Cocoa 166
Cronin, Joe 93, 99, 113, 115
Crookston, Minnesota 195
Crowder, General 115
Crusinberry, James 42, 86

228   Index

Cuba 79
Cunningham, Bill 76
Cuyler, Kiki 37

Daily, Con 30
Daley, Arthur 99, 106
Dallas, Texas 148
Daniel, Dan 37, 122
Danville, Illinois 120
Dauss, Hooks 112
Davenport, Iowa 2, 83, 136, 141, 143–144, 186, 197
Davenport Democrat 143
Davis, Crash 57
Davis Clothing Company (Sioux City) 72
Dean, Dizzy 134
DeBerry, Hank 103, 107
Deford, Frank 133, 139
DeLancey, Bill 108
Delta Upsilon fraternity 50
Dempsey, Jack 110
Denver, Colorado 182, 193
Des Moines, Iowa 28–29, 67–68, 101, 130, 133, 145, 163, 176, 184–185, 194
Des Moines Boosters 84, 111, 132–133, 186, 199
Des Moines Hawkeyes 207
Des Moines Mascots 29
Des Moines Oak Leafs 205
Des Moines Register 28, 32–33, 38, 70, 126, 128, 135
Des Moines Stars 29
Desmond, Dan 78
Detroit, Michigan 35
Detroit Creams 183
Detroit Tigers 34–35, 46, 51, 53, 55, 64, 67, 85, 88, 92, 94, 98, 109–110, 112–115, 117–118, 125–126, 131, 133, 135, 137–138, 157, 167, 184, 195, 203
DeWitt, Iowa 185
DiMaggio, Joe 129, 140
Dinneen, Bill 33
Dittmer, Jack 128
Dixmoor Golf Club 25
Doheny, Ed 33
Dombrowski, Dave 164
Dominican Republic 150
Donlin, Mike *35*
Donovan, Pat 131
Doolin, Mickey 73
Drake University 181
Dreyfuss, Barney 30–31, 33–34, 36–38
Driscoll, Ryan 164
Drohan, Tom 94
Dubuque, Iowa 82–86, 89, 121, 197
Dubuque Miners 83
Dubuque Telegraph-Herald 91
Dubuque Tigers 83
Dugan, Joe 67
Duke University 49, 55–58
Duluth, Minnesota 72, 197

Dundon, Gus 45
Dunedin, Florida 165
Durham, North Carolina 55, 69
Durham Herald 56
Durocher, Leo 195
Duryea, Jesse 191–192, 210
Dykes, Jimmy 97–98

Eastern League 185, 204, 206
Eau Claire, Wisconsin 171
Ebbets, Charles 103
Ebbets Field 105–106
Edmonton, Alberta 166
Egypt 23, 85
Ehmke, Howard 95–96
Eight Men Out 88
Eldred, Cal 192, **193**
Elk Horn, Iowa 200
Ellis, Dock 150
Elmira, New York 206
England 12, 18, 23, 85
Erie, Pennsylvania 150
Escanaba, Michigan 205
Evans, Billy 41, 72, 114
Evers, Johnny 208

Faber, Francis (Knudzton) 91
Faber, Irene (Walsh) 90
Faber, Margaret 82
Faber, Nicholas 82
Faber, Urban "Pepper" 91
Faber, Urban "Red" 2, 5, 81–91, **82**, **90**, 111, 210
Fargo-Moorhead team 132
Farmers Union team 133
Farnhamville, Iowa 181
Fearweather, Tom 111
Federal League 54, 73, 180
Feller, Anne (Thorpe) 139
Feller, Bill 130–131, 133–134, 136
Feller, Bob 2–3, 5, 111, 117, 124, **125**, 126, 129–140, **130**, **137**, 210
Feller, Lena 131
Feller, Virginia (Winther) 138–139
Ferguson, Bob 11–12
Few, William Preston 55
Fewster, Chick 107
Fingers, Rollie 175
Finley, Charlie 176
Fischer, Bill 159
Fischer, Carl 114
Fisk, Carlton 67, 172
Flanagan, Mike 156
Fletcher, Art 75, 100, 105
Flood, Curt 148, 198
Florida 38, 109, 136, 189, 194, 203
Florida Marlins 164
Flowers, Jake 108
Fondy, Dee 148
Forbes Field 77
Ford, Whitey 147

Index

Forest City team 18
Fort Dodge, Iowa 181
Fort Smith, Arkansas 135
Foster Theater 28–29
Fox, Pete 108
Foxx, Jimmy 97, 119, 127
France 23, 65, 85, 95
Fraser, Chick 34, 38
Frederick, Johnny 103
Freedman, Andrew 24, 184
Freeport, Maine 49
Fregosi, Jim 178
French, Walt 96
Fresno, California 14
Fresno Athletic Club 14
Frisch, Frankie 71, 76, 108
Fullerton, Hugh S. 87
Fultz, Dave 15

Gabler, Frank 99
Galveston, Texas 69
Garcia, Mike 138
Gashouse Gang 108, 133
Gates Mills, Ohio 139
Gee, Johnny 177
Gehrig, Lou 115, 119, 122, 127
Gehringer, Charlie 88–89, 108
George, Iowa 201
Gharrity, Edward "Patsy" 171
Gibson, George 37
Gilliam, Junior 144
Glavine, Tom 205
Gleason, Kid 86, 88
Glenwood, Iowa 186
Goldstein, Alan 157
Gomez, Lefty 122, 130
Goodell, Iowa 192
Goodyear Blimp Mayflower 92
Goslin, Goose 81
Gould, Charlie 9, 12
Graham, Frank 71, 109
Grand Rapids, Michigan 54
Grand Rapids Chicks 180
Grant, Ulysses S. 10
Granville Spalding (Iowa) High School 155
Gray, Sam 96
The Great Depression 97, 135
Great Lakes Naval Station 87
Great Pyramids 85
Green, Danny 45
Green, Dick 6, *175*, 176
Greenberg, Hank 108, 119, 122, 127
Greene, Joseph 99
Griffith, Clark 45, 116
Griffith Stadium 115, 130
Grimes, Burleigh 79, 91, 104
Groat, Dick 56
Groom, Bob 65
Grove, Lefty 97
Grundy Center, Iowa 95

Haas, Mule 96–97
Hackenschmidt, George 69
Hafner, Travis 166
Hairston, Jerry, Jr. 176
Hairston, Jerry, Sr. 176
Hairston, Sam 176
Hall, Bob 117
Hall, George 12
Hamilton, California 14
Handley, Lee 176–177
Hanrahan, Joel 194, 210
Hanson, Bert 164
Harder, Mel 124, 126
Hardy, Nebraska 102
Harper, Brian 173
Harridge, Will 116, 122
Harris, Joe 50
Hart, Jim 23
Hartnett, Gabby 190
Hastings, Nebraska 29, 102
Hatten, Joe 195–196
Hawaii 22, 178
Hawkeye League 144
Hayworth, Ray 92
Hedges, Robert 45–46, 83
Heilmann, Harry 88, 114
Heisman Trophy 131
Helms, Tommy 179
Hemsley, Rollie 135
Henderson, Ken 183, 209
Hendry, Jim 164
Herbert, Dick 59
Herman, Babe 106–107
Herzog, Buck 86
History of Colored Baseball 22
Hoerner, Darlene (Naumann) 197
Hoerner, Joe 6, 196–198
Hoffer, Bill 198–199
Hoiberg, Fred 164
Hollywood Stars 67, 145, 196
Holmes, James W. "Ducky" 61, 184–185
Holmes, Tommy 138
Holy Cross College 49
Homewood, Illinois 25
Homosassa Springs, Florida 109
Hong Kong 85
Hornsby, Rogers 104
Hot Springs, Arkansas 21
Houston, Texas 55
Houston Astrodome 196
Houston Astros (aka Colts 45s) 179, 181, 197, 207
Hubbell, Bill 75
Hubbell, Carl 115
Hulbert, William 19
Hunter, Jim "Catfish" 179

Icarians 8
Ida Grove, Iowa 202
Illinois 17, 24, 101, 177, 183
Illinois-Iowa League 198

Index

Indiana 8, 18, 101
Indianapolis, Indiana 8–9, 12, 201
Indianapolis Actives 9
Indianapolis Westerns 9
Indianola, Iowa 162–164, 170
Inglewood, California 180
International Association 183
International Hockey League 205
International League 22, 69, 117, 145, 150, 177
International News Service 96
Interprovincial Pipeline Company 79
Iowa 2, 5, 13, 17–18, 26, 28–29, 40, 42, 47–49, 67, 86, 93, 95, 98, 101, 115, 120, 124, 126–127, 131, 134, 141, 143, 152, 154, 160, 164, 170, 172, 176, 178–179, 186, 194, 199, 204–205, 207
Iowa City, Iowa 206
Iowa Daily Press Association 144
Iowa High School Athletic Association 170
Iowa Oaks 176
Iowa State League 185
Iowa State University 163, 201–202
Iowa Western Community College 200
Ireland 12, 23
Isbell, Frank 84
Italy 23, 85
Izaak Walton League 69

Jack Coombs Field 56
Jackson, Joe 208
Jackson, Travis 76, 113
Jackson Park (Chicago) 25
Jacksonville Suns 194
Jacobson, William "Baby Doll" 95
James, Bill 16, 79, 113, 153, 165
Japan 85
Jasper, Hi 63
Jennings, Hughie 71, 198
Jersey City, New Jersey 185
Jeter, Derek 71
John Deere Co. 151
Johnson, Ban 65, 184
Johnson, Ernie 65
Johnson, Harry 111
Johnson, Jack 14
Johnson, Walter 85, 100, 122, 134, 171
Johnston, Jimmy 105
Joliet, Illinois 198
Jordan, Dr. Charles E. 56
Josephson, Carl 172
Josephson, Duane 171–172, 202
Josephson, Lucille 172
Joshua, Von 175
Joss, Addie 42
Joyce, Col. Johnny 9

Kansas 36, 38, 102
Kansas City 117, 160
Kansas City Athletics 98, 175
Kansas City Blues 207

Kansas City Monarchs 144–145, 147
Kansas City Packers 180
Kansas City Royals 160, 167, 173–174, 178, 198, 200
Kansas City Times 65
Kansas State League 61
Karl, Larry 56
Karp, Hannah 162
Kauff, Benny 86
Keeler, Wee Willie 31, 198
Kelleher, Frank 196
Kelley, Joe 198
Kellogg's cereal 57
Kemp, Matt 167
Kent, Jeff 167
Kenworthy, Dick 202
Keokuk, Iowa 8
Keokuk Westerns 13
Key West, Iowa 197
Killea, Henry 33
Kimm, Bruce 152, 154
Kinnick, Nile 131
Kittridge, Malachi 51–52
Knoop, Bobby 6, *178*, 179, 209
Knoxville, Tennessee 165
Koob, Ernie 65
Kores, Art 73
Koufax, Sandy 104
Ku Klux Klan 107
Kzryzewski, Mike 56

Lajoie, Napoleon 40–41
Lakefront Park (Chicago) 20
Lamoni, Iowa 206
Landis, Kenesaw Mountain 27, 95, 133
Lardner, Ring 25
Latham, Arlie 24
Laudner, Tim 173
Leach, Tommy 31, 36
A League of Their Own 79
Leander Clark College 191
Lee, Bob 199–200
Lee County, Iowa 182
Leever, Sam 33
Legrand, Iowa 49
Lemon, Bob 138
Leonard, Andy 9
Levsen, Dutch 98
Lewis, Franklin 126, 134
Lewiston Broncs 175
Leyland, Jim 158
Lieb, Fred 28, 66
Lieber, Jon 200–201
Liepa, John 7–8, 24
Lincoln, Nebraska 47, 67, 69, 184–185, 201
Lindsay Park (Davenport) 144
Lindstrom, Freddie 79, 208
Linn-Mar High School 164
Little Pirate Ranch 36
Little Rock Travelers 95
Locker, Bob 6, 201–202

Long, Dale 148
Longview, Texas 68
Los Angeles, California 180
Los Angeles Angels 174, 178–179, 189, 196, 199, 200
Los Angeles Dodgers 101, 104, 162, 167–169, 175, 194, 200, 205
Lost Nation, Iowa 42
Louisville, Kentucky 63
Louisville Colonels 30–31, 184
Loyola Academy (Chicago) 208
Luxembourg 82
Lyon, Bill 152, 157
Lyons, Ted 90, 126

Mack, Connie 48–54, 58, 95–99, 116
Macy's 100, 105
Maine 48–50, 53, 56
Major League Baseball Players Association 138
Makeever, Midge 141, 144
Malone, Pat 96–97
Manoloff, Dennis 140
Manush, George 94
Marberry, Firpo 114
Marshall, Minnesota 189
Marshall County, Iowa 17
Marshalltown, Iowa 17–18, 22, 49
Martin, J.C. 172
Martin, Pepper 108
Martinez, Dennis 156
Martinez, Victor 166
Marylebone Cricket Club 19
Masi, Phil 138
Mason City, Iowa 173
Mason City Claydiggers 94
Massachusetts Institute of Technology 49–50
Mathews, Wid 145
Mathewson, Christy 52–53, 76–77, 85
Mauch, Gene 151
Maxvill, Dal 160, 198
May, Lee 179
Mays, Willie 183
Mazeroski, Bill 149
McAleer, Jimmy 43, 45
McClelland, Tim 166
McCloskey, John 30
McCormick, Barry 77
McCullough, Bill 109
McGill, Bill 46
McGillicuddy, Tom 49
McGraw, John 28, 32–34, 37, 74–76, 78–79, 81, 85, 103–105, 198
McGregor, Scott 156–157
McKechnie, Bill 37
McLean, Larry 63
McMahon, Don 202
McNertney, Jerry 202
McRae, Hal 160
McVey, Abbey 14
McVey, Cal 6–15, *8, 10*

McVey, Caroline 8
McVey, William 8
Meloan, Jon 167
Memorial Stadium (Baltimore) 159
Memphis Chickasaws 102–103
Menke, Denis 178–180
Meusel, Bob 116
Michigan 17
Mid-American Conference 205
Middle Atlantic League 204
Midland, Michigan 179
Midwest League 179–180
Milan, Clyde 185
Miller, Edmund "Bing" 2, 5, 92–99, *93, 96,* 120–121
Miller, Eugene 93–94
Miller, Norman 93
Miller, Otto 107
Miller, Philomena 93
Miller, Ralph "Lefty" 93–94
Miller, Ray 153, 156
Millikin University 185
Milwaukee, Wisconsin 205
Milwaukee Braves 178–179
Milwaukee Brewers 43, 47, 160, 176, 193
Milwaukee Railroad 72
Miner, Zach 167
Minneapolis, Minnesota 83–84, 192
Minneapolis Millers 79, 83
Minnesota 38, 79, 202
Minnesota Twins 160, 163, 165–166, 173, 205
Minnesota-Wisconsin League 72
Mississippi River 7–8, 17, 136
Mississippi Valley Conference 144
Mississippi Valley League 121, 204
Missouri Valley Conference 165
Mr. Cub 150
Mize, Johnny 119
Mobile, Alabama 148, 200
Moeller, Danny *185,* 186
Molesworth, Carl 111
Montebello, California 178
Montgomery, Alabama 30
Montreal, Quebec 195
Montreal Expos 155, 189
Montrose, Iowa 7–8
Moon, Paul 142
Moore, Edwin R. 97
Moore, Wilcy 89
Moreland, Nate 149
Morgan, Joe 157, 179
Morris, Illinois 1, 3
Mostil, Johnny 90
Moyer, Jamie 113
Mulvey, Joe 182
Murphy, Billy 26
Murphy, James 182
Murtaugh, Danny 150
Muscatine, Iowa 143
Musial, Stan 142
Myer, Buddy 116

232　Index

Naperville, Illinois 176
Nashville, Tennessee 198, 203
National Association of Leagues 38
National Association of Professional Base Ball Players 12–13, 18
National Baseball Congress 38
National High School Sports Hall of Fame 170
National League 5, 13, 16, 19–20, 23, 26–27, 30–31, 33, 54, 56, 63, 71–73, 75, 79, 100, 104, 133, 135, 143, 145, 147, 149, 168, 176–177, 179–180, 182–184, 186, 189–190, 194–198, 201, 207
National League Championship Series 168, 176
National League Division Series 168–169, 176
Nauvoo, Illinois 8
NBC 134
Nebraska 101–102, 109
Nebraska State League 29–30, 102
Neft, David S. 79–80
Negro American League 144
Negro Leagues 114, 139, 143–144
Nevada, Iowa 67
New Hampton, Iowa 172
New Orleans, Louisiana 103, 106, 135, 177
New Orleans Pelicans 103, 106, 133–134, 208
New York City 9, 74–76, 85–86, 93, 107, 109, 117, 137, 175
New York City Mutuals 10
New York Giants 24, 32–34, 37, 53, 55, 71–76, 78–79, 81, 85–87, 103–104, 115, 119, 135, 144, 180, 184, 198, 204, 208
New York Herald Tribune 16
New York Journal-American 71
New York Knickerbockers 9
New York Mets 184, 193, 205
New York-Pennsylvania League 149, 199
New York Times 76–77, 99, 105–106
New York World-Telegram 122
New York Yankees (aka Highlanders) 29, 38, 45, 52, 66–67, 71, 75–76, 79, 85, 89–90, 96–98, 102, 115–116, 119, 122, 127, 130, 137, 147, 156, 163, 165, 167, 176, 180–181, 188, 191, 196, 201–203
Newark, New Jersey 9
Newark Little Giants 22
Newcombe, Don 143
Newton, Iowa 188
Nora, Jack 197
Nora, Jim 197
Norfolk Naval Training Station 136
North English, Iowa 189
North Western Christian University 9
Northern League 132, 195, 197, 206
Northwestern League 21, 73, 192
Norwalk, Iowa 194
Norway 61
Norway, Iowa 119–120, 123–125, 152–155, 157–158, 161

Norworth, Jack 25
Nunn, Michael 143

Oakland, California 89
Oakland Athletics 159, 175–176, 181, 189, 202, 205
Oakwoods Cemetery (Chicago) 27
O'Connor, Jack 46
Oeschger, Joe 76
Ogden, Jack 143
Ogrodowski, Bruce 134
Ohio 17
Oklahoma 30, 38
Oldis, Bob 151
Oldring, Rube 51
Olean, New York 150
Olive Hotel 147
O'Loughlin, Silk 184
Omaha, Nebraska 11, 43, 84, 117, 164, 174, 204
Omaha Cardinals 117
Omaha Omahogs 43
Omaha Robin Hoods 68–69
Onawa, Iowa 42–43
O'Neil, Buck 147, 150
O'Neill, Bill 91
O'Neill, Mickey 107
O'Neill, Steve 121, 123–124, 134
Orient, Iowa 100
Ormsby, Red 134
Osage, Iowa 192
O'Toole, Marty *35*
Ott, Mel 115
Ottumwa, Iowa 132, 199, 207
Ottumwa Naval Air Station 142, 144
Ottumwa Packers 62
Overall, Orval 191
Overland Park, Kansas 160
Owen, Marv 108

Pacific Coast League 47, 67, 73, 89, 145, 172, 177–178, 201
Palestine, Texas 51, 56, 58
Palmer, Jim 156
Park Center High School 173
Parnell, Iowa 171
Passeau, Claude 132
Paterson, New Jersey 31
Pearl Harbor 127, 136
Peaster, Harry 84
Peckinpaugh, Roger 126
Pegler, Westbrook 89
Pennsylvania 31
Peoria, Illinois 43, 94
Peralta, Jhonny 166
Perkins, Si J. 94
Perritt, Pol 55
Peters, Hank 156
Pettit, Leon 123
Philadelphia, Pennsylvania 21, 26, 56, 75–76, 99, 107, 187

Index

Philadelphia Athletics 18–19, 43, 48, 50–54, 58, 83, 85, 92–93, 95–98, 113, 119–120, 134, 191
Philadelphia Inquirer 152
Philadelphia Phillies 30, 55, 73–75, 99–100, 105, 117, 157–158, 164, 168–169, 177, 189, 196–198, 201, 204, 207, 208
Philippines 85
Phillippe, Deacon 31, 33
Phoenix, Arizona 183
Pipgras, George 202–203
Pittsburgh, Pennsylvania 148
Pittsburgh Pirates 1–2, 31–38, 56, 66, 76–78, 83–84, 95, 102, 148–151, 177, 180, 182–183, 185, 187, 190–191, 194, 199–200, 202
Pittsburgh Press 37
Pittsfield, Massachusetts 182
Plank, Eddie 54
Play Ball! Advice to Young Ballplayers 69
Players League 23–24, 192
Pleasant Hill Township, Nebraska 101
Pluto, Terry 119
Pocahontas, Iowa 181
Polk Township, Iowa 93
Pollock Grain Elevator 158, 161
Polo Grounds 34
Pope Pius X 85
Portland, Oregon 47, 73, 173
Potawatomi tribe 17
Povich, Shirley 111, 113, 117–118
Powell, Jack 46
Powell, Ronnie 200
Powers, Mike 50–51
Prairie du Chien, Wisconsin 82
Princeton University 55
Progressive Field 140
Providence, Rhode Island 182
Providence Grays 13, 182
Pueblo Indians 83–84

Quad-City Angels 178–179
Quad-City Sports Hall of Fame 2, 151
Quad-City Times 2, 41, 130, 155, 178, 185, 193
Quincy, Illinois 121

Ragan, Pat 203–204
Raleigh News & Observer 59
Rawlings, Johnny 180
Reardon, Beans 107
Red Cloud, Nebraska 102
Reese, Pee Wee 80
Reno, Nevada 207
Reulbach, Ed 191
Reynolds, Allie 130
Rhodes, Gordon 122
Rice, Grantland 16, 24, 58
Rice Institute 55
Rickey, Branch 63, 69
Ripley's Believe It or Not 60, 67
Riske, David 167
Rizzuto, Phil 79

Robinson, Frank 151
Robinson, Jackie 21, 63, 139, 141, 144, 177, 195
Robinson, Wilbert 54–55, 92, 103–104, 106, 198
Rochester, New York 156, 185, 192, 204, 206
Rochester Hustlers 102
Rock Island, Illinois 69
Rockford, Illinois 18
Rockford, Iowa 173
Rodgers, Bill 73
Rodgers, Buck 174
Rodriguez, Ivan 67
Ro-Fel Inc. 137
Rogers, Will 106
Rohe, George 45
Roland, Iowa 61
Roller, Doc 69
Roosevelt, Franklin 115
Root, Charlie 64
Rose, Pete 139, 157
Rourke, William "Pa" 43
Rowland, Pants 85–87
Rue, Joe 98
Ruel, Muddy 66, *96*
The Runaway Colt 24
Ruth, Babe 16, 64, 75, *90*, 91–92, 116, 122–123, 140, 175–176, 180, 203
Ruth, Clare 116
Ryan, Nolan 135

Sabathia, C.C. 166
Sac County, Iowa 42
Sacramento Senators 67, 102, 199
Sacred Heart Academy 82
Sain, Johnny 138
St. Ambrose College 83, 144, 170
St. Cloud, Minnesota 79
St. Joseph's, Missouri 30, 102, 184
St. Joseph's Academy (Dubuque) 82
St. Joseph's College (aka Loras) 83, 86
St. Louis, Missouri 11, 133, 147–148, 151, 198
St. Louis Browns 40, 42–43, 45–47, 53, 63–70, 95–96, 104, 113, 134, 184, 203
St. Louis Cardinals 31, 36, 67, 92, 97, 104–105, 108–109, 119–120, 133–134, 142, 145, 159–160, 169, 183, 190–197, 203, 206
St. Louis Globe-Democrat 45
St. Louis Post-Dispatch 42
St. Louis Star 26
St. Mary's Catholic School 82
St. Michael's Catholic Church 123
St. Paul, Minnesota 192
St. Thomas Aquinas High School 160
San Antonio, Texas 68–69
San Antonio Light 60, 68
San Antonio Missions 68
San Diego, California 14, 183, 207
San Diego Padres 181, 207
San Francisco, California 11, 14
San Francisco earthquake 14

San Francisco 49ers 143
San Francisco Giants 168, 181, 183
Santana, Carlos 167
Savannah, Georgia 30
Savery Hotel 28
Schalk, Ray 70, 81, 173
Scherwitz, Harold 60, 64, 68–69
Schilling, Curt 159
Schleswig-Holstein High School 202
Schmidt, Butch 204
Schmidt, Mike 157
Schrader, Gus 99, 110, 113
Scotland 23
Scott, Everett 115–116
Sears Roebuck 197
Seattle Mariners 181
Seattle Pilots 181, 202
Severeid, Adele Bertha (Messmer) 65
Severeid, Charles 61, *62*
Severeid, Chris 61, *62*
Severeid, Elmer 61
Severeid, Hank 2–3, 5, 60–70, *61*, *62*
Severeid, Lars 61
Severeid, Maria 61
Severeid, Oscar 61, *62*
Seybold, Socks 51
Shasta County, California 196
Sheridan, E.S. 21
Sheridan, John B. 24, 65
Shibe Park 56, 92
Shocker, Urban 66
Sickels, John 165
Simmons, Al 96–97
Simpson College 163, 170, 204
Sioux tribe 17
Sioux Center, Iowa 144
Sioux City, Iowa 6, 72, 79, 84, 175, 178, 185
Sioux City Journal 78
Sioux City Packers 61
Sisler, George 66, 104
Sizemore, Grady 166
Skunk River 67
Slade, Gordon 108
Slapnicka, Cy 111, 114, 117, 120–121, 131–132
Slattery, Dr. W.P. 86
Smalley, Roy 145
Smith, Earl 77–78
Smith, Frank 45
Smith, Joseph 8
Smith, Ken 109
Smith, Red 204
Society for American Baseball Research 79
South Alabama, University of 200
South Atlantic League 112
South Bend Blue Sox 79
South Dakota 38, 175, 206
South Dakota Sports Hall of Fame 175
Southern Association 30, 103, 112, 203
Southern Conference 55
Southern Illinois University 176
Southern League 95, 173, 194

Southern Michigan League 191
Southworth, Billy 76
Spade, Bob 208
Spalding, Albert G. 13–14, 18–19, 22–23, 26–27, 117
Spencer, Jack 143
Sporting Life 14, 43, 45, 46
The Sporting News 24, 29, 41, 45, 158
Sports Illustrated 133, 139, 153, 161
Springfield, Illinois 121
Springfield Cubs 145
Stanley, Fred 181
Stann, Francis 113, 117
Start, Joe 11
Steadman, John 152–153, 158
Steinfeldt, Harry 208
Stengel, Casey 76, 106
Stephenson, Gene 162, 164–165
Stewart, Lefty 115
Stewart, Norm 172
Stone, George 2, 40–47, *41*, *44*, 209
Stone, Hannah 42
Stone, Pearl (Moore) 47
Stone, Sam 42
Stone, Steve 153, 156
Stone, Vean 47
Stoneham, Charles 75, 79
Story City, Iowa 60–63, 67–69
Stovey, George 22
Street, Chris 164
Street, Gabby 92
Strikeout Story 138
Sullivan, Ted 192
Sun Belt Conference 200
Sunday, Billy 26, 186–187, 209
Superior, Wisconsin 73, 77, 79, 197
Superior Blues 72
Superior Brickmakers 102
Sutton, Larry 103
Sweasy, Charles 9
Syracuse, New York 54, 69, 165, 188

Taft, William Howard 186
Take Me Out to the Ballgame 26
Tapani, Kevin 205
Taylor, Oak 15
Taylor, Sec 38, 70, 135
Team USA 165
Temple, Shirley 134
Tener, John 26
Terry, Bill 71, 79, 119
Texas 38, 55–56, 58, 69
Texas League 68
Texas Rangers 169, 173, 182, 184, 198
Thomas, Ira 54
Thorpe, Jim 204
Three-I League 83, 94, 120–121, 197, 201
Thurman, Bob 144
Time Magazine 134
Tinker, Joe 208
Toledo, Iowa 191

Toledo Blue Stockings 21
Toledo Mud Hens 43, 121, 123, 180, 188, 198
Tommy John Surgery 193, 201
Topeka, Kansas 102
Toronto, Ontario 177
Toronto Blue Jays 160, 165
Torre, Joe 150, 168
Traynor, Pie 37, 79
Trojovsky, John 119, 121
Trojovsky, Mary 119
Trosky (Trojovsky), Annette 121
Trosky (Trojovsky), Esther 121
Trosky (Trojovsky), Hal 2, 5–6, 98, 112, 117, 119–128, *120*, *125*, 132–133, 152, 209
Trosky, Hal, Jr. 123, 128
Trosky, Jack 120
Trosky, Lorraine (Glenn) 123
Trosky (Trojovsky), Victor 121
Trout, Dizzy 126
Troy (N.Y.) Haymakers 10–11
Truro, Iowa 185
Tunnell, Emlen 128
Tunney, Gene 136

United States Postal Service 199
University of California 69
University of Iowa 18, 131, 143, 155, 164, 189–190, 193
University of Maine 50
University of Missouri 173
University of Nebraska 188
University of Northern Iowa 172, 206
University of Notre Dame 18
University of San Diego 174
University of Southern California 155
Urbana, Iowa 93, 98, 193
Utah 8

Vance, Albert 101
Vance, Arthur C. "Dazzy" 2, 5, 100–109, *101*, *108*, 131
Vance, Edythe 109
Vance, Fred 101
Vance, Sarah 101
VanderMeer, Johnny 105
Van Meter, Iowa 130–132, 134, 136, 139
Van Scoyoc, Jim 154, 157
Van Scoyoc, Sheryl (Boddicker) 154
Vaughan, Arky 80
Veeck, Bill 137
Vicksburg, Mississippi 135
Victoria, British Columbia 85
Vidmer, Richards 105
Vinton, Iowa 93–94, 97, 120
Vinton Cinders 93
Vinton Eagle 93
Viola, Frank 205
Vitt, Oscar 117, 124, *125*, 126
Von der Ahe, Chris 183
Von Tilzer, Albert 25

Waddell, Rube 31–32, 50
Wagner, Honus 31, 33–36, *35*, 71, 80
Walker, Moses Fleetwood 21
Walker, Tillie 63
Wall Street Journal 162, 167
Walls, Lee 148
Walsh, Davis 96
Walsh, Ed 52
Warden Hotel 132
Washington, D.C. 115–116, 118, 130, 183, 192
Washington Monument 92
Washington Nationals 9–10, 194
Washington Post 111, 113
Washington Senators 37, 43, 50–51, 66, 93, 95–96, 111, 113–116, 123, 134, 171, 182, 184–186
Washington Star 41
Washington Times 40
Waterloo, Iowa 94
Waterloo Courier 83, 97
Waterloo Hawks 204
Waterloo Lulus 61
Waterman, Fred 9–10
Waterville, Maine 49
Wathan, John 160, 173, *174*
Watson, Tony 210
Watt, Eddie 206–207
Wayne, John 174
Weaver, Buck 65, 86
Weaver, Jered 199
Webster City, Iowa 67
Wedge, Eric 166
Weimer, Jake *207*, 208, 210
Wellsburg, Iowa 95
Werber, Billy 56
West Branch, Iowa 206
Westbrook, Jake 166
Western Association 30, 184
Western Golf Association 25
Western League 42–43, 47, 61, 67–68, 83–84, 102, 111, 132, 145, 183–184, 199, 204, 207
Wheaties 138
White, Deacon 13
White, George 68
White, Jo-Jo 108
White, Sol 22
White, Will 13
The White House 10
Whitehill, Earl 2, 98, 110–118, *111*, 131
Whitehill, Earlinda 117
Whitehill, Edward 116
Whitehill, Noah 111, 115
Whitehill, Violet 116–117
Whitted, Possum 204
Wichita, Kansas 207
Wichita Falls, Texas 68
Wichita State University 162, 164–165
Wilhelm, Hoyt 202
Williams, Billy 202
Williams, Claude "Lefty" 88
Williams, Ted 130, 138, 140

Williams College 55
Williamson, Ed 21
Wilson, Brian 168
Wilson, Chief 36
Wilson, Hack 96
Wilson Sporting Goods 138
Winfield, Kansas 36, 38
Winterset, Iowa 29
Winther, W.M. 138
Wood, Wilbur 202
Worcester, Massachusetts 49
World Series 2, 5, 15, 33–34, 37–38, 48, 52–54, 59, 63, 66–67, 71, 74, 76, 85–87, 96–98, 108, 115–116, 120, 133, 138, 149, 157–158, 162, 167, 169, 173–175, 179–181, 190–191, 193, 196, 202–205
World War I 64–65, 87, 95, 101
World War II 117, 136, 144, 195
Wright, George 10, 12, 15

Wright, Glenn 37
Wright, Harry 9–12
Wrightstone, Russ 74
Wrigley Field 190
Wulf, Steve 153, 161
Wynn, Early 138
Wynnewood, Pennsylvania 99

Yakima, Washington 179
Yankee Stadium 67, 98, 137
York Prohibitionists 102
Young, Brigham 8
Young, Cy 33, 83, 156, 158, 201
Young, Ross 76

Ziekursch, T.V. 75
Zimmer, Chief 31
Zuber, Bill 98